Henry Stevens

The Bibles in the Caxton exhibition MDCCCLXXVII

A bibliographical description of nearly one thousand representative Bibles in various languages

Henry Stevens

The Bibles in the Caxton exhibition MDCCCLXXVII
A bibliographical description of nearly one thousand representative Bibles in various languages

ISBN/EAN: 9783337111403

Printed in Europe, USA, Canada, Australia, Japan

Cover: Foto ©Lupo / pixelio.de

More available books at **www.hansebooks.com**

THE BIBLES IN
THE CAXTON EXHIBITION
Mdccc Lxxvii

Or a bibliographical defcription of nearly one thoufand reprefentative Bibles in various languages chronologically arranged from the firſt Bible printed by Gutenberg in 1450-1456 to the laſt Bible printed at the Oxford Univerfity Prefs the 30th June 1877   With an Introduction on the Hiſtory of Printing as illuſtrated by the printed Bible from 1450 to 1877 in which is told for the firſt time the true hiſtory and myſtery of the Coverdale Bible of 1535
Together with bibliographical notes and collations of many rare Bibles
in various languages and divers verſions printed
during the laſt four centuries

Special edition reviſed and carefully corrected with additions
Flavoured with a squeeze of the Saturday Review's homily on Bibles

By Henry Stevens Gmb Fsa Ma Etc

Sometimes Student in Yale College in Connecticut in New England   Now refiding in London Bibliographer and Lover of Books   Fellow of the Royal Geogr & Zoological Societies of London   Foreign Member of the Amer Antiq Society Correſp Member of the Hiſtorical Societies of the States of Maſſachuſetts New York Connecticut Maine Vermont New Jerſey Maryland Pennſylvania & Wifconfin and Secretary of State and American Miniſter near Noviomagus Blk Bld Athm Club London
And Patriarch of Skull and Bones at Yale Univerſity

Bibliography   The Tree of Knowledge

LONDON HENRY STEVENS IV TRAFALGAR SQUARE
SCRIBNER WELFORD & ARMSTRONG NEW-YORK
Messrs Simpkin Marshall & Co Stationers Hall Court
Mdccclxxviii

TO
THE ENLIGHTENED & LIBERTY LOVING
BURGOMASTERS AND COUNCIL OF
ANTWERP
OUR ANCESTORS OWED THEIR FIRST
ENGLISH BIBLE
AND THEREFORE
TO
THE BURGOMASTER AND COUNCIL OF THE
SAME ANCIENT AND RENOWNED
CITY WHICH
ENGLISHMEN & AMERICANS
MUST EVER REGARD AS THE
CRADLE OF THEIR
COVERDALE BIBLE
THIS VOLUME IS APPROPRIATELY
INSCRIBED BY
HENRY STEVENS
of Vermont

Extract from Het Leven van Emanuel van Meteren kortelijck beschreven door sijnen ghetrouvven Vriendt SIMEON RVYTINCK, *folio 672 of Emanuel van Meteren's* Nederlandtsche Historie *the edition in folio of* 1614.

EMANUEL van METEREN, die met grooten vlijt ende vernuft desen Boeck by een versamelt heeft, was t'Antwerpen ghebooren den 9. Julij 1535.

Sijn Vader hiet Jacob van Meteren van Breda, Sone van Cornelius van Meteren. Sijn Moeder hiet Ottilia Ortels, dochter van Willem Ortels van Ausborch, die Grootvader was vanden wijdt-beroemden Wereldt-beschrijver, *Abrahamus Ortelius*.

Sijn Vader in sijn Ieucht hadde gheleert die Edele Konste van't Letter setten, hy was begaeft met de kennisse van veelderley Talen, ende andere goede wetenschappen, wist van in die tijden 't licht t'onderscheyden van duysternisse, ende bethoonde sijnen bysonderen yver in 't bekostighen vande oversettinghe ende Druck vanden Enghelschen Bijbel binnen Antwerpen, daer toe ghebruyckende den dienst van een gheleert Student, met namen Miles Couerdal, tot groote bevorderinghe van het Rijcke Jesu Christi in Enghelandt.

Sijn Moeder was een Godvreesende ende troostelijcke Joffrouwe, die insghelijcks de kennisse der Waerheyt outfangen hadde, ende met haren Man veel daer voor geleden heeft.

't Is ghebeurt (haren Man om sijnen handel na Engelandt ghereyst zijnde) soose swangher was van desen Soone, datmen van d'Overheyt weghe, haer Huys is komen besoecken, om Leonard Ortels haren Oom, die daer plach t' huys te liggen, te vangen, om 't punct vande Religie, ende met eenen to sien offer gheen verboden Boecken te vinden waren; de wreetheyt van dese Ondersoeckers, beweeghde de goede Joffrouwe den Heere vyerichlijcken te bidden, op datse de selve niet vonden, 't welck oock alsoo ghebeurt is, al wast datse verscheyden-mael de handen op de Kiste leyden daer de Boecken in waren, Godes genadige hulpe ende bescherminge daer in speurende, heeft belooft (soose een Soone baerde) den selven *Emanuel* te noemen, dat is, *God met ons*, welcke belofte sy oock volbrocht. Hier uyt heeft Emanuel oorsake genomen, tot sijn Manlijck verstandt gekomen zijnde, by 't woordt *Emanuel*, ghemeenlijck te voegen, *Quis contra nos?* dat is, *Is God met ons, wie is tegen ons?* om aen die voorighe weldaet te beter te gedencken, ende in alle gevaer op den Heere te betrouwen.

Sijnen Edelen Vriendt ende Cousijn Daniel Rogersius, heeft daer op dit Latijns vers gedicht.

AD SYMBOLUM

EMANVELIS DE METERI:

Nobiscum DEVS, quis contra nos?

Cvius opem imploras? hominum cui credis in Orbe.
    Emanuel? Quæ te sustinet oro salus!
Quum mundo sit nulla fides: Pendentia filo
    Pelignus verè cuncta Poëta canit.
Ingenio confide sagax: frustrabere formæ:
    Crede datis, anceps forma venusta bonum.
Fidat equis alius, pedibus pernicibus alter.
    Mars equitem Bello, Mars peditemque premit.
Spes armis nec certa, licit triplice firma
    Robore, glans mixto sulphure transit ea.
Et quæ præsidio comitum fiducia? Salvo
    Milite sæpè ipsi desperiére Duces,
Viribus ast fidis, Goliath à Davide victus,
    A puero validus dux superante perit.
Gratia te Regum spes est sublimet in altum?
    Non se, non alios sæpe juvare queunt,
Ergo istis alius fidat. Tu dulce secutus
    Emanuel nomen, fidere perge Deo.
Quem si tecum habeas, in eo si Spemque reponas
    Certior Ausonio vivere rege queas.

The Flavour

HE CAXTON CELEBRATION EXHIBITION WAS OPENED at South Kensington on the thirtieth of June and closed on the first of September, 1877. During these nine short weeks the public had a rare opportunity afforded it of having some of its old popular notions respecting printing dissipated, others corrected, and not a few new ones inculcated. It is only fair, however, to the intelligent British public to state here frankly in their behalf that only a select few appear to have had any well defined ideas, convictions, notions, sentiments or intelligence, whatever, respecting the origin, development, progress, and present state of this 'Art preservative of all Arts,' especially as it exists, and has existed in this country during the last four centuries.

This circumstance is probably owing to the fact that in dear old merrie England reading and writing come by nature, while printing is no more considered an art or invention than breathing or drinking. We know it and that is enough. All these things are so familiar from infancy that one scarcely ever thinks of accounting for them, or looking into their origin.

As pleasure is said to be the absence of pain, darkness the absence of light, so printing may be simply the absence of primitive ignorance. The mind reads the newspapers and the Bible, feels, thinks, and knows intuitively. Like the eye the press sees not itself, yet is the organ by which all other things are seen, known, and organized.

It was therefore a happy thought of Mr J. S. Hodson, Secretary of the Printers' Pension Corporation, to celebrate the four hundredth anniversary of the introduction, in 1477, of the art and mystery of printing into England, by a "Caxton Celebration" in the year 1877, just for a moment to hold the mirror up to printing, to let the eye see the eye, and the press the press.

The Secretary and his happy thought were particularly lucky in having

Mr William Blades, Caxton's eminent biographer, to resort to for the needful historical foundation and literary coping of his proposed edifice.

But it is not intended to give here the history of the Caxton Exhibition of 1877, for it is itself already a matter of history. Suffice it then to say, in passing, that in more meanings than one it was a success, and in no sense a failure. The Caxton Exhibition Catalogue as finally revised and published before the close of the Exhibition, with all its faults (and none knows them better than the writer), is a bibliographical record, taken as a whole and of its kind, that has never been surpassed in any country or period. Much of it is crude, ill-digested, and unfinished, yet the honest, intelligent, painstaking, and sharp-witted bibliographer will find recorded in it, though perhaps a little too hastily, materials for the history of books, printing, and printers, not alone of England, but all foreign countries, from the earliest period to the present time, which he will find no where else so well told and so conveniently packed.

The results of the Caxton Exhibition, therefore, as booked in this Catalogue, are manifold and important, though they may perhaps have to be picked out, like the meat of the hickory-nut, with patience and discretion. At the same time it is to be remembered that by the Campanellan rule, as given by Master Prynne, generally such

'Books either miss or hit,   By scale of reader's wit.'

If the critic, historian, bibliographer, or simple reader, any of them, lack the capacity or wit to pick out and appreciate the new, true, and important matters recorded in the Caxton Catalogue respecting rare and beautiful books, early and fine printing, eminent printers, and kindred topics, it may be some consolation to somebody to know or to be told that it is not necessarily the fault of the Catalogue.

On the other hand if the capacity or wit of the critic be better adapted to pick out the flaws, errors, mistakes, blunders, omissions, false statements, and ignorances buried in the Catalogue, be its merits never so great, and if he be inclined to smack his lips over them in the *Weakly* as if he had found the very blue-mould of Stilton, or viewed the centre of decay, God help him and give him a long life, for what we, who are not critics, don't know is immense and immeasurable, in comparison with what we do know and can state correctly.

In making these general and particular remarks, the writer excepts, of course, his own portion of the Caxton Catalogue, that is Class C, Printed Bibles, lest it may be too apparent that he is publicly crying an axe hammered on his own anvil. He is not unmindful, however, of the great interest expressed by many, and the commendations expressed by some, in his treatment of this department of the Catalogue.

Nevertheless, it will be remembered that the department of Bibles in the Caxton Exhibition received more adverse criticism from some of the intelligent London press, than all the other classes put together. This may be partially owing to the great, general, and blind interest felt in England, above all other countries, in reference to the Bible, the divine book, about which every one presumes to know so much, and of which, really, so few know anything. It is the commonest and most familiar of all our books. Wherever dust can penetrate, there is our Bible, but too many of us are like the swine seeking beechnuts among the fallen leaves of the forest, devouring them with a relish, but seldom looking up to see whence they came, what their origin, or how preserved for us.

The subject of Bibles in the Caxton Exhibition, as a distinct Class, was really an after-thought. It required some stretch of the original plan of a *Caxton* Exhibition to include Bibles in all languages, though some few editions would naturally have fallen in as specimens of early and fine printing. The Exhibition, however, grew upon the hands of the Executive Committee, as did, also, the various departments of it grow upon the hands of the several Sub-Committees.

Finally, notwithstanding the long list of distinguished names that graced the several committees, the real work, and all the work, by its own gravity, fell into the hands of some half dozen men, who, at first, having volunteered their free services, had not the courage, at last, to back down as many did in the critical moment when it was almost an even balance between uncertain success and certain failure.

All this, I know, is indefinite and gossipy, and was intended to be so, but those who desire to pursue the subject further can. It is, however, only just and fair to my colleagues and collaborators to say here so much, and to relieve them as far as possible of any personal responsibility for the deficiencies and shortcomings of that department of the Catalogue, which was wholly mine and not theirs. I have, therefore, decided to separate my own portion of the work, as far as it relates to Class C, Printed Bibles, as given in the Catalogue of the Caxton Exhibition, and issue it separately under my own name, so that the work may stand or fall by itself without marring the good work of my colleagues in other departments. I say deliberately 'good work,' for where can the lover of short-cuts to knowledge find in the English or any other language, the information so well arranged and so clearly expressed about Caxton and the typographical productions of himself and his contemporaries in England, as in the first thirty pages by Mr William Blades, under Class A, sections i—v, of the Catalogue of the Caxton Exhibition? The great mass of conjecture of previous writers is abolished, and the whole interesting story of all England's earliest printers, with the titles of their books, and where the books now exist, is briefly and clearly told by Mr Blades, in a masterly and modest manner never excelled. Sections vi and vii upon the subsequent development of printing in England and Scotland, both metropolitan and provincial, are chiefly by Mr

R. E. Graves. One may hereafter enlarge the story to any extent, but after all, the enlargement will be only a bill of particulars. The vii Sections of Class A cover pretty much the whole ground.

Almost the same may be said of Class B, filling pages 44—72 of the Catalogue, containing a brief history of Block Books, and the development of the art of printing in foreign countries. Never probably was such a rich collection of rare books brought together as that described in sections i—iv of this Class, and so far as I know, no single writer has before had so good an opportunity of covering the whole field of typography outside of Great Britain, in a single essay. How concisely and clearly Lord Charles Bruce has presented this important department of the Exhibition in the brief space of less than thirty pages, is manifest. He had at hand, it is true the whole bibliographical resources of Earl Spencer's library, as well as extraordinary facilities afforded by the British Museum and its custodians. He therefore made this road for the future historian direct, true, royal and roman. The curious reader will find his lordship's name modestly placed at the bottom of page 72.

It will be noticed that there is a great difference in the modes of arranging the materials and presenting the history of printing in Classes B and C. It may as well perhaps be explained here as any where else. This divergence was fully discussed beforehand by Lord Charles Bruce and myself, and we came to the conclusion that it would be better, as our materials were abundant, and in some important cases duplicate, to present in the Catalogue, at one and the same time, two distinct views of the progress and development of printing. Accordingly it was agreed that while in Class B he should arrange and describe his materials under countries and towns geographically and chronologically—each taking precedence by the dates of the introduction of printing into each, I, on the other hand, having only *the* One Book to deal with, was to present it in all languages and countries (including England) in one consecutive chronological list. This arrangement I strictly carried out, as the reader may see in the present volume. I submit that this arrangement between us was a happy thought, as it gave the historian two distinct views instead of one. Each system has unquestionably its own objections, but these melt away when both are used. It is a vast aid to the historian of the Bible, and a leveller to the patriotic scribbler, to have before himself in one chronological list the entire biblical work of all languages and countries, by which he can see at a glance what translation, commentary and printing were going on at the same time elsewhere, as well as the comparative progress of Bible printing in different countries.

I desire here publicly to acknowledge aid, comfort, sympathy, and cooperation from my colleagues, especially Mr William Blades, Lord Charles Bruce, Mr George Bullen, Mr G. W. Porter, Mr R. E. Graves, Mr W. H. Overall, and Rev. W. H. Milman, who rendered our weekly bibliographical meetings of Sub-Committee N° 1 so agreeable, friendly, instructive, and unforgetable. While giving them my cordial thanks, I should be very sorry to make any of them responsible for any of the many defects in my portion of the Catalogue, which the printers tell me, because of the quantity of small type in the notes, was spun out to nearly one-third the composition of the entire Catalogue. It might easily have been doubled, owing to the great and unexpected liberality of the exhibitors, but I had some little conscience left about overloading Caxton with the Bible, inasmuch as it was a Caxton and not a Bible Exhibition. At another time, and that not far distant, I trust that we may have a Bible Exhibition.

However, my colleagues were tolerant and patient, and the printer found type to put up my long introduction and bibliographical notes scattered throughout the work, without grumbling. Only one note, an essay of two pages sent in by me was suppressed by the Executive Committee (goodness knows why), but that is now printed in full under N° 1450 in this edition, being a brief and circumstantial history of the Oxford Caxton Memorial Bible, at my suggestion printed at the University Press in Oxford and bound in London in twelve consecutive hours, on the morning of the 30th of June. These pages were struck out by somebody probably for other reasons than the want of space.

The whole of Class C is, therefore, re-made up, repaged, and here reissued separately from the same type as the Catalogue, but with above three hundred corrections, alterations, and improvements in the list from N° 611 to 1450, together with some forty pages of new matter not in the Caxton Exhibition Catalogue. I trust that these additions will give some flavour to this separate work and apologize for its separate appearance. This present edition is, I believe, the tenth revision of my portion of the Catalogue, and yet there are left many errors and oversights, which would have been emended but for my wholesome dread of 'printer's corrections.' I cannot, however, afford to carry this, my summer's plaything, any further.

I admit that the motto of a well-arranged Exhibition Catalogue should be 'If 'twere done when 'tis done, 'twere well it were done quickly.' In consequence of a severe illness of three weeks immediately after the opening of the Exhibition, when only the 'Rough Proof' of the Catalogue had seen the light, I confess that I failed on the 'quickly;' but by the 25th of July my proofs had been read, omissions supplied, additions made, and the copy was in the hands of the printer, including the historical Introduction and many long bibliographical notes. Great pains had been taken to ascertain the true or approximate time of printing the several editions bearing no date so that the whole might fall into a strictly chronological series, according to the well-digested plan agreed upon with the accomplished editor of Class B. I respectfully submit that my arrangement of the Bibles in Class C of the Catalogue was fairly up to the mark. The issue of it herewith presented, though somewhat polished and improved since August, will, I trust, corroborate this statement. This admitted, the arrangement of the Bibles in the cribs under glass and locks was of far less consequence. I never intended to assume or monopolize this part of the arrangement, having enough on my hands already, but working volunteers were scarcer than talking ones, and so, notwithstanding only half the space required could be had, I sorted out the folios and placed them open under glass on the north side of the gallery, in the order of their dates of printing, beginning at the far end with 1450 and coming down to the left of the entrance with the 1611 English Bible, the first edition of our present version. This was a simple arrangement such as even the uninitiated might grasp, but unfortunately the pressing want of room, the great value of the books, and the absence of safe lock-ups elsewhere in the galleries, compelled me to distribute the quartos, octavos, and smaller books among the folios, regardless of date and every other consideration except size. Every crevice was filled. The duplicates and extra volumes were placed in the cases unopened, no other safe place presenting itself. Well, some painfully orderly eyes could not stand this mixture, while others found consolation in the Catalogue. Each book being distinct and fully described, the rest was left to the general intelligence of the visitors. It seemed to appear to most of them to be a matter of little importance whether the 'bugge Bible' was on the right or left hand of the 'wicked Bible,' or whether printed before or after.

At first I consented only to arrange the Bible titles for the catalogue and prepare them for the printer, but later on, however, when I saw that many gentlemen whose names had been placed high up on the several Committees were doing but little; and when my friend Mr Blades had bravely taken upon his own shoulders the work of the Executive at their request, I willingly placed my spare shoulder thereto and volunteered, as far as my abilities extended, to help him through. For nearly a month I did what a slow and busy man could do in twelve or fifteen hours a day and night, building up and furnishing the department of Bibles alone, and looking after nothing else.

I do not ask or expect any special credit for what I then did prior to the opening of the Exhibition, and for a month subsequently, the hardest labour I ever undertook or underwent, but it is fair that I should, if possible, parry false criticism wherever I find it, and decline to receive as gospel the unjust and inconsiderate censure of the Saturday Review, for not performing the many other labours ignorantly and wrongfully assigned to me by it. My catalogue of the Bibles will, I trust, be taken as evidence of no little honest and voluntary work; and that my summer leisure was not wholly thrown away. In making, correcting and working up the Catalogue of Bibles and parts of Bibles I endeavoured to render it a book of permanent reference, as far as it goes, and one that would be useful after the Exhibition was over. I decided, after some hesitation, to use part of the materials I had been collecting for a larger work for more than a quarter of a century, with opportunities that have fallen to the lot of few bibliographers. Some of these materials I worked up into an elaborate Introduction presenting a comprehensive view of the history of the printed Bible, in all languages and countries, from 1450 to 1535; and in numerous long and short bibliographical and historical notes under various titles and languages from 1535 to 1877. All these the reader has before him re-issued in the present volume. The collations of the rarer Bibles in many languages are elaborate, and I trust generally correct and carefully done. They cost me a vast amount of labour, and I flatter myself that true bibliographers will find them useful. In the notes, as well as in the Introduction, many new points are brought forward and discussed, wherein a great deal of the slop and conjecture of the historians of the Bible, even our latest ones, is spotted and, it is believed, for ever consigned to oblivion.

Again, in the Introduction and notes I gave briefly the results of long and patient investigation respecting Coverdale and our first English Bible, and, I believe, to a great extent cleared up one of the most interesting mysteries lurking in English history and literature. Indeed, for the last three hundred years the good old Augustine monk Coverdale had been lost in a tangle of misconception and conjecture, insomuch that the last two or three historians of our dear old English Bible have asserted positively, without a particle of decent historical evidence, that the Coverdale Bible was printed by Christopher Froschover at Zurich. It has been my good fortune to discover where, by whom, and under what circumstances it really was printed. I showed on unimpeachable authority that Coverdale went abroad in 1534, and that the Bible was printed by or for Jacob Van Meteren at Antwerp; that Coverdale was not himself the translator, but that probably Van Meteren was, Coverdale aiding him, at his employer's cost, as a learned reviser, editor, proof reader, and general manager, with great prudence and discretion, and at the imminent peril of his life, both from the authorities of the Netherlands and of his own country at home. Any future historian of the English Bible must hereafter reject whole pages of conjecture, assumption, misconception, and frivolous speculation that fill the pages of Lewis, Anderson, Lee, Eadie, Westcott, and others, not alone in these matters pertaining to Tyndale, Coverdale, and Matthew, but many other points pertaining more or less to them and their times.

With all its faults, this Catalogue is now given to the public. But in justice to the public, the most patient beast of burden known to the press, and in justice to myself, I must notice here the *Notice* with which my old friend, the *Saturday Review*, honoured me. It is the last of five articles which that eminent review devoted to the Caxton Exhibition. They are all of like excellence, and could manifestly have come from no other periodical. The first was upon Mr Gladstone's opening speech, and appeared in the number for July 7. The others, divided into four parts, covering the entire Exhibition, appeared in the four numbers of July 28, August 4, 11, and 18. As the last mainly concerns me, and the Exhibition of the Holy Scriptures as described by me in the Catalogue, I have pleasure in reproducing it here verbatim and entire, simply adding a few small figures for convenience of reference in the subsequent pages of this Flavour.

From the SATURDAY REVIEW *of the* 18*th August*, 1877.

THE CAXTON EXHIBITION. IV.

Though the Exhibition has now reached what may, with probable safety, be called "positively the last fortnight," the Bibles remain unarranged.[1] This will be a great disappointment to many ardent bibliographers; but it may allay their regret[2] to know that, unless the present collection[3] had been largely supplemented,[4] it could not have been considered in any sense representative[5] of the history of Bible-printing. Mr. Stevens,[6] to whom the arrangement[7] of this part of the Exhibition was entrusted,[8] has neither done[9] it himself nor commissioned[10] any one else to do it. He has, however, published an "Introduction,"[11] in which he claims for Jacob van Meteren, an Antwerp merchant,[12] who is said to have learned to print[13] early in life, the honour of being the printer and translator of Coverdale's Bible. The passages quoted from Emanuel van Meteren's *Historia Belgica* do not justify these conclusions,[14] and, without further evidence[15] we must withhold our judgment.[16] Meanwhile, as Mr. Stevens's Introduction is not before us,[17] we may pass on to notice the Bibles actually displayed[18] in the Exhibition; since, whatever the shortcomings of the Committee[19] in their arrangement, they form an interesting collection, especially, if we include[20] among them the early specimens already described[21] from the German, the Roman, and the Paris presses.

The first complete English[22] Bible, as is well known, was the edition of 1535, printed in all probability at Antwerp.[23] It is so scarce that no perfect copy is known, and one of the six[24] examples in the Exhibition, Lord Spencer's,[25] has a title-page inserted from a different edition.[26] Her Majesty's[27] copy has part[28] of the title, but is very imperfect[29] in other places, as is Lord Leicester's,[30] which, however, has the whole title,[31] and is therefore unique. It[32] was finished, says the colophon, in 1535, "the fourth day of October." The Althorp[33] copy has a title from a Bible almost equally[34] rare, Raynalde and Hyll's,[35] 1549, of which no[36] copy seems to be in the gallery. The New Testament of Tyndale's version, lent by the Dean and Chapter of St. Paul's and almost unique, is perhaps[37] as much as ten[38] years older than Coverdale's first Bible. Mr. Fry and others are of opinion that it was printed by Peter Schoeffer at Worms in 1526. This[39] would add to its interest, as Schoeffer was the successor[40] of the Peter Schoeffer of whom we have already made frequent mention as the partner of Gutenberg[41] and Fust. A part,[42] at least, of the old Testament was printed in London from Wycliffe's version in or about 1532, by Robert Redman,[43] and a copy is in the Lambeth Library, and might perhaps have been lent for the present Exhibition if asked for, but the managers do not seem[44] to have been aware of its existence.[45] Tyndale's Pentateuch[46] is here, however,[47] printed at "Malborow in the land of Hesse," and lent by Mr. Fry. There are several other[48] Tyndale Testaments, including, according to the "preliminary issue"[49] of the Catalogue, that of 1535,[50] "whereunto is added an exhortacion to the same of Erasmus Rot, with an Englysshe Kalender and a Table, necessary to fynde easly and lyghtely any story contayned in the iiii evangelistes and in the Actes of the Apostles." The book itself is,[51] however, not to be found "easly and lyghtely" by a visitor; and is, we suspect, among the closed[52] volumes in a bookcase which occupies the centre of the gallery. The "preliminary issue" has become permanent,[53] a not unaccustomed fate of South Kensington[54] Catalogues.

Next[55] in interest after these—the first English versions—comes the first,[56] perhaps we should say the only[57] authorized edition—that of Henry VIII., printed by[58] Grafton and Whitchurch in 1539, and celebrated in history as the Great Bible. Of this there are several copies, and the wood-cut title[59] said to have been designed by Holbein,[60] is worth studying. At the top the King is seated on a throne,[61] ensigned[62] with his arms, and surrounded by his courtiers, to whom he distributes copies of the book. At either side Cromwell and Cranmer, each also identified by his shield, are similarly employed; and round[63] the head of each person is a scroll, on which we read "Vivat Rex,"[64] or, where the person represented is a child,[65] "God save the King," for children of course could not be expected to cheer in Latin.[66] There is a tragic interest, too, about these curious pictures.[67] Among the copies exhibited is one in which the circular space previously filled with Cromwell's arms is left blank. The shield has disappeared in the interval between the issue of the two[68] copies;[69] and, in the same interval, the great Vicar-General had lost not only his shield, but his head. There are copies of several later editions, but we fail[70] to find any special[71] notice of the sole[72] English issue of Queen Mary's reign. In 1553 Edward Whitchurche published a Bible which would recommend itself to some of our modern educational agitators. It is literally "without note or comment," all the preliminary matter printed with the Great Bible, including the Calendar and the Table of Lessons, being omitted. At least one[73] copy appears in the Catalogue. Strange to say, those days of bigotry[74] seem to have been favourable to Bible-printing; for the same year, 1553, witnessed the appearance of the first Spanish edition,[75] of which a copy, printed at Ferrara, comes from Althorp, and another is lent by the Bible Society. In 1557 William Whittingham, afterwards Dean of Durham, but then an exile at Geneva, published a New Testament of his own translation, the first[76] divided into verses, and three years later came out the famous "Genevan," or "Breeches Bible," which for nearly a hundred years continued to be the popular version. Copies of the first edition are very rare, but two[77] at least are in the Gallery. It is adorned with maps, and has "moste profitable annotations upon all the hard places." It went through about two hundred editions, and was not superseded[78] in the estimation of the Bible-reading public until the profitable annotations, and even the headings of the chapters, appeared in an edition of King James's version published in 1649 by the Stationers' Company,[79] and made no doubt on purpose to look as like the old favourite as possible.[80] Many liberties were taken with both text and notes, among which perhaps the most serious dealt with the heading of Psalm cxlix.,[81] the same psalm from which Obadiah[82] Bind-their-kings-with-chains-and-their-nobles-with-fetters-of-iron took his memorable surname. In the Genevan Bible[83] this psalm was headed "An exhortation to the church to prayse the Lord for his victory and conquest that he giveth his saints against all man's power." In the Authorized Version[84] a very different meaning was given to the psalm:—"The prophet exhorteth to praise God for his love to the Church, and for that power which he hath given to the Church *to rule the consciences of men.*" The new edition,[85] printed in the very year which saw the downfall of all supremacy[86] but that of the saints, was altered ingeniously; the power given to the Church was "for the conversion of sinners."[87] And, strange to say,[88] there has ever since been a certain doubt about the form of this heading, and it now stands in ordinary Bibles in a form which differs alike from King James's and the saint's, for it breaks off short at the word "Church."[89]

We do not recognize[90] a copy of the quarto of 1649 in the Gallery, nor—and this is a much more serious omission—do we find a single perfect copy of the first issue of the so-called Authorized Version.[91] One, near the door, seems only to have its New[92] Testament title; but in the Catalogue there is a long paragraph about "Hee" editions or "Shee"[93] editions which calls for some notice.[94] Two issues at least took place in 1611, and their differences are easily seen; but, except in the preliminary leaves,[95] it is seldom that the two issues are found separate.[96] Sheets from one were constantly[97] mixed with sheets from the other; and any attempt to say that one set of sheets belongs wholly to the first issue and another to the second ends not only in confusion,[98] but in something worse.[99] When it has been arbitrarily[100] determined which set belongs to each issue, the next thing is to make existing examples conform; and a process takes place exactly analogous to that by which an enthusiastic architect is sometimes tempted to falsify the record in restoring an old building.[101] The collection of editions of the Authorized[102] Version is wretchedly poor,[103] containing in fact only one volume of any importance[104]—the Bodleian copy of the famous Bible of 1631[105]—an octavo in which the "not" was omitted from the Seventh Commandment.[106] We failed to find a first Oxford[107] Testament, a first Cambridge[108] Testament, a Lloyd's[109] folio, a Blayney's[110] quarto, a first Irish,[111] a first American,[112] an "immaculate" Bible of 1811,[113] or, in fact, with the one exception,[114] anything of great note[115] in this department. There is a poor[116] copy of the Scots Bible in octavo, with the plates by Bolswaert which were such an offence to the Puritans, and were specially charged against Archbishop Laud. The Psalm-books, too, are not remarkable for their rarity[117] except the American "Bay Psalm-Book," which enjoys the credit of being the first book printed in British North America, and of which the present copy, lent from the Bodleian, is unique on this side of the Atlantic. The Queen's Printers, the two University presses, and the Bible Society make great displays on the staircase, where copies may be seen of the "Gladstone Bible,"[118] printed and bound at Oxford[119] in twelve hours. The public was informed[120] at first that the type had been set up within that time, and the curious in this kind of literature were on the look-out for a valuable crop[121] of misprints and the speedy suppression of the whole edition. But the type has been long standing, and the volume is of the ordinary[122] kind, and does not even, we believe, contain the Translators' Preface or the Apocryphal books.

The machinery is apparently the most attractive part of the show.[123] Where is Mr. Buckmaster[124] that he does not lecture on it? All[125] the processes of paper-making, type-casting, composing, distributing, electrotyping, printing, and folding are carried on here. There are specimens of ancient types and woodcuts, and paper made on the old system is printed with a memorial of the Exhibition in a press of the slow,[126] awkward[127] kind which Caxton[128] must have used. The various attempts at setting up type by machinery occupy some space, and are examined with great interest. Hattersley's machine appears to be very convenient, but it is only by a practical printer[129] that its merits or faults can be justly appreciated.[130] The Clowes method differs from the Hattersley in the use of electricity; but it is open to objections which, as far as we can judge,[131] must be fatal to its extensive use.[132] In fact, of six systems here exhibited—the Mackie steam composer, the Clowes electric composer, the Hattersley, the Kastenbein, the Muller, and the Heinemann—it may safely be said that not one[133] is likely to come into extensive use in a printing house, although the Hattersley may be suitable for amateur work, and the others are all very pretty as toys.[134] The room in which the various processes of stereotyping are carried on will be found very attractive, especially as the plates cast are for actual use. Among the curiosities of the Exhibition are the machines[135] of various kinds for arranging sheets of paper for the press, some of them seeming to be furnished with a human finger and thumb, and much more than human accuracy and regularity. It is perhaps[136] a pity that the machinery could not have formed a separate exhibition, perhaps[137] in combination with bookbinding,[138] as it is, the staid bibliographers[139] above stairs complain much of the noise and the smell,[140] caring evidently very little as to how a book is produced so that it is produced; and perhaps going on to think, since they set so much store by rarity, that when a press has issued a single copy of a book, the more seldom it repeats the process[141] the better.

Thus spake the great public Umpire of Southampton Street. Not a question of any moment in law, manners, customs, religion, literature, history or politics turns up but this Oracle delivers its learned charge and pronounces judgment for its readers. 'When our Oracle speaks let no dog bark' has been the bye-law of the community for years. To reply to a preacher-man, in his own tub, by the law of the land is, I believe, sacrilege; while to attempt to answer the Saturday Review, by the law of custom and its own rules, not less binding, is, I suppose, scarcely anything short of blasphemy. Still a duty in behalf of the public is thrust upon me per force of circumstances, to try and bring to this great self-elected Umpire with a blank cartridge and examine its papers.

The Caxton Celebration and Exhibition was, probably, deemed a sufficiently important event for the Saturday to call together its faculty of wiseacres to set the community right upon the whole subject of Printing and Books. One sees at a glance how these important topics must have taxed all the literary, antiquarian, historical, critical, judicial, biblical and bibliographical powers of the establishment. I have no idea who was the Head Centre or chief delegate chosen to superintend and work up these powerful pronunciamentos, but manifestly no one man of the staff could have done it alone. The five articles are in the highest and most elaborate style of the Saturday, and possess all the peculiar characteristics of that Review. Prick this article iv and one will do the public a service by letting its acrid midnight-oil out of it, and perhaps at the same time also out of the whole ambitious concern, for this privateering Weakly, it appears, is not constructed on the bulk-head principle.

At first I confess that I felt even a sort of pride in being extinguished by such an all-powerful luminary, but on revising my portion of the Caxton Catalogue and re-reading the five articles, I soon perceived that this attractive light was only moonshine, thin, borrowed, and pale: and that so far from feeling myself demolished, demoralized and scorched, I could still afford, so far as the Saturday is concerned, to hold up my head and re-issue my little book. I, therefore, with some confidence, appeal from the Saturday to the general intelligence of the community, a judge on a higher level, and not at present under the spell of anonymous, irresponsible, reverend, and self-made critics.

Biblical history and bibliography have run long enough in their present narrow groove, passing hand-in-hand from head to head down through many reverend and able writers since the days of Anderson, if not Lewis, without a particle of new and original investigation, until they have drizzled into the Saturday Review, and been summed up in a nutshell of common errors and commonplaces. This, perhaps, is rather strong, but the circumstances, as the reader will soon see, require something strong. By this article iv, here reprinted in full, I was either bound hand and foot in the meshes of these critics, fixed and fast, or the article is made of rotten tissues. Unless, therefore, I can manage to davenport-brothers myself from these mortal coils of theirs, I feel that I am done for. Now without further preliminary let us proceed to business and examine the examiner, and test the statements with our own critical litmus-papers. When the war between Acid and Alkali ceases, then and not till then, should one submit to this Saturdalian dribble of biblical stuff and nonsense built upon frivolous speculation.

The opening of the Saturday's fourth broadside, 18th August, 1877, against the Caxton Exhibition, Class C, is a charge that up to about the middle of August 'the Bibles remain unarranged.'[1] This is only about half true. There were two ways of arranging the Bibles, first, in the printed catalogue, as described above on page six, and second, in the thirty-five cases along the north and south sides of the gallery; the first for a permanency and future reference, the second for a hasty peep of the multitude during the nine weeks of the Exhibition.

We are told that many 'ardent bibliographers'[4] were disappointed at first sight, but comforted themselves with the reflection that if the 'present collection'[3] of Bibles had not been largely supplemented[4] it could not have been considered in any sense representative[5] of the history of Bible printing; which I suppose means, if it can be interpreted to mean any thing, that if the arrangement of the Catalogue had not been completed by reading the proofs, enlarging and correcting the titles, there would have been a very poor catalogue and a worse collection, but as it was made all right and representative there was really very little left to grumble about.

The critic, who it is presumed is the 'ardent bibliographer' himself, now grows personal and complains that 'Mr. Stevens,[6] to whom the arrangement[7] of this part of the Exhibition was entrusted,[8] has neither done[9] it himself nor commissioned[10] any one else to do it.' Now Mr Stevens[6] was never entrusted[8] by the Executive Committee 'to do the arrangement[7] of this or any part of the Exhibition,' nor had he[9] ever the power to commission[10] any one else 'to do it.' In fact the Saturday Reviewer is manifestly under some misapprehension as to the character of Mr Stevens' connection with the Caxton Exhibition, for he gives it a prominence which Mr Stevens has no right to accept without protest. The simple truth is that Mr Stevens goodnaturedly consented, at the request of Committee N° 1, Mr George Bullen of the British Museum, Chairman, (which with Mr Blades from the Executive really did the literary work of the Executive Committee,) to arrange the Bible titles for the Catalogue, and prepare them for the printer. He undertook no responsibility whatever in the Exhibition, incurred no risk, and received no emolument. Nothing was entrusted[8] to him officially: he did what he undertook to do[9] cheerfully and at his own expense, and had no power, right, or desire to commission[10] any one else to do work for him. Yet this Saturday afternoon critic passes lightly over the Introduction[11] with a sneer, calls Van Meteren an Antwerp merchant,[12] 'who is said to have learned to print[13] early in life;' says, also, that the authority I quoted 'does not justify these conclusions,[14] and without further evidence[15] he must withhold his judgment.'[16] All this new historical matter the learned critic of the Saturday Review dismisses contemptuously in three lines. This may be all the room he had at his disposal, but he may be reminded that it takes no more space to tell the truth than it does to tell the other thing. Perhaps if he will condescend to re-read the Dutch extracts given on the back of the dedication of this volume he may come to a different conclusion. Meanwhile, what his judgment is worth will be better understood further on when we have weighed it. If the patient reader will kindly follow us through our numerical objections to this writer's loose statements and looser opinions, he will see that his judgment is just the light stuff balloons are filled with. I did not ask him to stop his press to notice and pat my dog, but if he stops it voluntarily, and goes out of his way to give him a kick, he need not be surprised if he in return gets for his pains a bite such as Isaac Walton never fished for.

The next sentence, completing the first paragraph, is in the highest style of Saturday Reviewing, piquant, off-hand, self-asserting, and overwhelmingly egotistical. 'Meanwhile, as Mr. Stevens' Introduction is not before us,'[17] we may pass on to notice the Bibles actually displayed[18] in the Exhibition;' why, these[18] were the very ones one would expect him to notice, and if he had found time to read the Introduction[11] before displaying his ignorance about the matters contained in it, and pronouncing his free verdict against it, he might possibly have saved his credit, if that was of any consideration.

It was no fault of mine that the Introduction was not before him. It had been some days previously fully noticed by the *Times* and the *Athenæum*. But it is not necessary, I believe, for an experienced critic to see[17] a book he reviews. In this case, however, a cursory glance at the Introduction might have prevented our 'ardent bibliographer' displaying the profundity of his shallowness. The Introduction, filling pages 25-42 of the present volume, is still commended to his perusal. In the second clause of the sentence he alludes to the 'shortcomings of the Committee'[19] in their arrangement,' apparently forgetting that he had already[7] castigated me for the same negligence. However, with becoming condescension, he pronounces it an interesting collection of Bibles, 'especially if we include[20] among them the early specimens already described'[21] in article i, ii, and iii, in the S. R. Why not include them? Does the mere fact that the reviewer in his previous articles had briefly alluded to (but not described) some half dozen out of hundreds of early Bibles in the Exhibition, fully described in the Catalogue, lift them out of the collection? But this egotistic, pedantic and empty allusion to past services of self and partners is an old trick of these Saturdamalion critics to fill up their vacuums and to make all knowledge appear to cluster exclusively about their own brows.

I now introduce our lofty Scholastikos, with his eyebrows above his temples, and with his historical brick, as the specimen of his house, the Coverdale Bible,[22] which he owns was 'printed in all probability at Antwerp.'[23] This statement is precisely the chief item of the mysterious history of our first English Bible which a little above he declines to receive without further evidence.[15] I had discovered that it was printed at Antwerp by or for Jacob Van Meteren, instead of Zurich by Froschover, as generally accepted. It is not, I believe, an uncommon practice for reviewers who cut up historical books first to clip out for their own use the little telling historical points before they destroy their victims. However, I am glad that S. R. adopts Antwerp as the place of printing, for that fact simplifies and reconciles much. This point admitted, I have no fear as to Van Meteren's claims being also sooner or later acknowledged.

The reviewer speaks learnedly of the 'six[21] examples' of the Coverdale Bible of 1535 in the Exhibition. There are seven copies described in the Catalogue, viz. N° 765, the Earl of Leicester's, from Holkham; 766, Earl Spencer's, from Althorp; 767, from Sion College Library; 768, from the B. and F. Bible Society; 769, W. Amhurst Tyssen-Amhurst's copy; 770, Dr Gott's; and N° 771, lent by the Earl of Jersey.

These seven fine books were among the chief glories of the Exhibition, and should have awakened the latent intelligence of our 'ardent bibliographer.' But behold what a learned muddle he makes of them. First he says that Lord Spencer's[25] copy has a title-page inserted from a different edition.[26] The reader is referred to N° 766 of the present volume for a corrected description of it. The title-page is made up in manuscript, like many other copies, by using the woodcut border of the title of the Petyt and Redman Bible of 1540, or that of 1549, both from the same woodcut as the original title of 1535, insetting blank paper in the cartouch and putting in by hand the title in facsimile. The copy is on the whole a very fine one.

Scholastikos next informs us that 'Her Majesty's[27] copy has part[28] of the title, but is very imperfect[29] in other places, as is Lord Leicester's,[30] which however has the whole title,[31] and is therefore unique.' This is a lovely historical muddle, such as one rarely sees anywhere but in the columns of the Saturday Review, where ignorance is bliss and history is apparently taught by rote. It is indelicate perhaps to tell the naked truth after this, but to develop the smile it must be told that Her Majesty's copy of the Coverdale Bible was not at the Caxton Exhibition at all, nor was it even asked for, for the good reason, that we had already copies that exhibited all the variations known except one, viz. the title-page in the copy belonging to the Marquis of Northampton. But I have seen Her Majesty's copy at Windsor Castle, and am able to say that it is a good one, far above the average in condition, quite complete in the text, and having all the preliminary leaves as they came from the press of Nicolson of Southwark. It wants the map, has no part[31] of the original title, but the title is made up, like Earl Spencer's, by inserting a facsimile or manuscript title in the cartouch of the woodcut border from the edition of 1540 or 1549 from the original Antwerp block of 1535. Every statement therefore respecting Her Majesty's copy is erroneous.

For an account of the Earl of Leicester's fine and very nearly perfect copy see Nº 765. It is the only copy known with the original Antwerp title-page quite perfect. The text is complete and the copy contains the last of the original Antwerp preliminary leaves, the counterfoil of the title, in this respect also unique. The map and the other preliminary leaves are in facsimile by the elder John Harris. The only other copy known with even a part of the original title-page is that in the British Museum. 'It[32] was finished' does not apparently mean Earl Leicester's copy, as one might suppose, but the Coverdale Bible generally. Our critic here is a little mixed in his grammar, as well as in his history, and does not seem to improve in the next sentence, beginning 'The Althorp[33] copy has a title from a Bible almost equally[34] rare, Raynalde and Hyll's 1549 of which no[34] copy seems to be in the gallery.' The reviewer here is manifestly trying to outdo himself in blundering ignorance, but he succeeds better farther on. He does not seem to be aware that the Althorp[33] copy is Earl Spencer's;[25] one and the same; see Nº 766, and the remark[20] above about the title. He is mistaken also about the comparative rarity of the Coverdale Bible of 1535 and that by Raynalde and Hyll,[31] 1549. The latter is not a very rare book, and usually may be purchased complete for one tenth the usual cost of an imperfect Coverdale. This Solon is also mistaken about there being no[36] copy of the 1549 edition in the gallery. There were two copies there from the opening of the Exhibition, both described in the Catalogue under Nºˢ 853 and 853*.

So much for the seven Coverdales, of which our sublime blunderer mentions only two, Earl Spencer's and the Earl of Leicester's, both with disparaging comments which are not true. The other five he pretermits though not intentionally.

We now come to our critic's sage remark that the Tyndale's Testament of 1526 'is perhaps[37] as much as ten[38] years older than Coverdale's first Bible' of 1535. We let him off on the 'perhaps.' But when in the next sentence he speaks of Schoeffer[19] who printed at Worms as the successor[40] of the Peter Schoeffer of whom he has already made frequent mention (in his previous papers on the Caxton Exhibition) as the partner of Gutenberg[11] and Fust, he is manifestly beyond his historical and biographical depth. Fust took his son-in-law, Peter Schoeffer, as a partner after the famous lawsuit which terminated in the business being transferred from Gutenberg the inventor to Fust, who had lent him money. Schoeffer was not therefore, I take it, ever a partner of Gutenberg.

The next four lines embody as many errors in one sentence perhaps as any man living, not an old stager in Saturday reviewing, could reasonably be expected to write out. It is moreover beautifully funny, irrelevant, pedantic, officious, and startling. It is to the effect that there exists in the Lambeth Library a part[12] of the Old Testament of Wycliffe's version, printed by Redman[13] about 1532, which 'might perhaps have been lent for the present exhibition if asked for, but the managers do not seem[14] to have been aware of its existence.'[15] I am not able to speak for the managers, or the Executive Committee, but I may say that this little book alluded to is perfectly well known and was well described by the Rev Dr S. R. Maitland more than a quarter of a century ago in his 'List of some of the Early Printed Books in the Archiepiscopal Library of Lambeth,' London, 1843, 8º, Nº 529, p. 237, a work with which most English 'ardent bibliographers' are familiar. The little book, however, is not of Wycliffe's version, is not of much bibliographical importance, and would not probably have been accepted by the managers if offered, unless perhaps the Archbishop of Canterbury, as one of the prominent Patrons of the Caxton Exhibition, had particularly requested it. So much having been said, however, it is perhaps as well to give the title of the book, and some account of it here—
" Prayers of the Byble takẽ out of the olde testament and the newe, as olde holy fathers bothe men and women were wont to pray in tyme of tribulation, deuyded in vi. partes. Imprynted at London in Fletestrete by me Robert Redman. Cum gratia et priuilegio Regali." In this Lambeth copy, otherwise fine, part iii is wanting, 'An exposcayõ vpõ the psalme of Miserere .... made by Hierom Sauonarole.' The book first appeared in Italy under the name of Savonarola, and was afterwards printed in English by François Regnault at Paris without date, probably in 1538, while Coverdale and Grafton were with him superintending the printing of the 'Great Bible.' It was reprinted by Redman in London about 1538 or 1539. Being all Scripture in English it would not, of course, have been licensed in 1532, but in 1538 or 1539, as the language is modern and good, there would then have been no difficulty about the translation. The word not is uniformly spelled nat, as in [Redman's?] Testament of 1536, folio. The separate parts, being without title-pages, but with new signatures, are sometimes found attached to service books. Regnault had a house in London from about 1498 to 1540, and supplied many of the English Roman Catholic Service Books used in various Cathedrals. This little fetch about Wycliffe is one of

the Saturday's stock pieces of recondite lore, having appeared before and will probably appear again. What put this little irrelevant reprint into the head of Scholastikos no fellow can probably ever find out. It is one of those learned surprises, I suppose, that so abound in the columns of this review, put there to astonish us with by-path knowledge, to make fools ask questions and the uninitiated to stare.

But the grammarian will stare sufficiently when he reads in the two following clauses that 'Tyndale's Pentateuch[16] is here however,'[17] and 'several other[18] Tyndale Testaments.'

This little slip is not so bad as one of my own which he brings home to me with the genuine tact and skill of a Saturday critic. In Nº 779 of the revised Catalogue, the most splendid copy known of Tyndale's New Testament of 1536 in octavo, lent by Earl Spencer, the date in the 'rough proof' and 'preliminary issue' was erroneously printed 1535.[50] In my first-proof reading it was corrected to 1536, and has so stood in the last six or seven editions of the Catalogue. The precious little volume had a prominent place assigned to it among the rarest books, and as the date appeared on the title, which was exhibited, there should have been no difficulty in an 'ardent bibliographer's' "easly and lyghtely" finding the volume. However, this typographical error in the early editions of the Catalogue marked 'preliminary issue'[19] made him feign that the book itself was not[31] to be found by a visitor, and he suspected that it was among the closed[52] volumes in a bookcase near by. In his disappointment he declares that the 'preliminary issue' has become permanent[51]—'a not unaccustomed fate of South Kensington[51] Catalogues.' Now all these erroneous statements are based on an unworthy quibble, a known typographical error, known to have been corrected. The revised and corrected Catalogue had been issued some days before this article iv appeared, and hence it was necessary for the critic to go back to the 'preliminary issue.' Had his common sense been rubbed up a little he might have perceived, or been informed, that the 'closed volumes'[52] in the unused bookcase were duplicates, or spare volumes of sets not required, and were locked up for safe keeping till they could be returned with others to the exhibitors. It was very natural and boy-like to overlook what was before him and to wish to look over what was not intended to be seen. But the fling at 'a not unaccustomed fate (whatever that may be) of South Kensington[51] Catalogues' is constitutional and a chronic matter of course with a Saturdalian. It is well known that South Kensington with its Museum is the *bête noire* of the Saturday Review. No knight of the quill is qualified for its staff until he has had a successful tilt at S. K. The proprietors are presumed to keep an office Rosinante in their Southampton Street editorial stables with which each staff writer must from time to time try his hand, or do his best to donquixote the South Kensington Windmill. If our unpractised witling has not here exactly hit the mark, it is to be hoped that he may live to fight another day. Meanwhile the South Kensington Mill stands!

It is suspected that our Scholastikos in this last tilt against S. K. lost a leaf out of his note-book, for a distressing and damaging hiatus appears here in the most important part of his biblical disquisition. Notwithstanding his words 'next[55] in interest after these,' before coming to the 'Great Bible,' he wholly omits to mention the first folio and the first quarto English Bibles printed in England by James Nicolson of Southwark, dated 1537. See N[os] 790 and 791. Nor has he thought to mention the first edition of Matthew's Bible, also of 1537, N° 779, or the Taverner of 1539, N° 811. Then there lies neglected N° 779, the first edition of Tyndale's New Testament printed in England in 1536 in small folio, to say nothing of the other editions of Tyndale's and Coverdale's Testaments printed in England and abroad in the years 1536 to 1539, mostly described in this Catalogue. All these are too interesting and important to have been omitted probably for any cause short of accident, a slip of fortune, to which we are all liable. He is therefore here credited with good intentions while he is charged with careless practice in his tilting. We are told that where ignorance is bliss it is folly to be otherwise, but in this case our critic cannot be congratulated on his bliss. The dropping of these important stitches in the meshes he was weaving for another is doubtless a pure mistake. It is always well, however, in this naughty world that something of our doings should be scored as pure.

We come now to the veritable pons asinorum[56] of the English Reformation before which so many of our historians have shied or broken down; I mean the 'Great Bible' of 1539-1541, sometimes also called Cranmer's Bible, which, to use Mr Gladstone's language on another occasion, was the 'climax and consummation of the art of printing' in England up to that time. Indeed, considering the times and state of the market, that it was wholly a private, individual, and mercantile enterprise, carried on at great personal peril and commercial risk by Marler, Grafton, Whitchurche, and other City merchants, in spite of ecclesiastical bigots not yet all dead, it may be considered the greatest effort of the press even to the present day. It was the culminating point of a great struggle for reform and civil liberty. When we contemplate the several steps of progress during the seven preceding years, we see now just how much this Great Bible was required to carry on, concentrate, and consummate the Reformation.

These Great Bibles are the milestones that mark the advance of the English nation in civil liberty, civil law, refinement of language, personal freedom, statute law, popular election and legislation, the science of Government, public education, national self respect, domestic prosperity, and foreign influence. With the seven distinct editions, 1539-

The Flavour

1541, of these great and magnificent volumes scattered throughout the land, fifteen or twenty thousand copies, in the families of the nobility and gentry as well as in most of the eleven thousand parish churches, to say nothing of the precious seed planted on good ground by Tyndale, Coverdale, Rogers, Cranmer, and Cromwell, it was impossible for the English nation not to advance, though it might from time to time require a Philip and a Mary to steady its progress. We therefore hug these Great Bibles to our bosoms, and count them as the choicest gems of our libraries. It is for these reasons that I gave so much space to them in the Catalogue, Nos 813-825, and made such prominent display of them in the Caxton Exhibition.

There were certain preliminary steps, never to be forgotten, which contributed to this inestimable boon of free Scriptures, such as the fall of Wolsey, the divorce of Catharine of Aragon, the separation from Rome, the Royal Supremacy backed by Act of Parliament, the paving the road with the hardest and best heads, of More, Fisher and others; the destruction of the monasteries, the force of royal proclamations, the Act of the Six Articles, the drawing of the fangs of Convocation; and finally the Act of 1538 directing that all books of Scripture should have the sanction or licence of the King, the Privy Council or a bishop, which threw the whole matter, in spite of Convocation, into the hands of Cranmer and Cromwell. Some of these motions may at first sight appear retrograde, but if so, it was only the drawing back for a harder blow.

The seven[64, 65] distinct editions of the 'Great Bible' are identified and known by the several dates in their colophons. These are the editions, 1, of April 1539; 2, April 1540; 3, July 1540; 4, November 1540; 5, May 1541; 6, November 1541; and 7, December 1541. Besides these, the two November editions of 1540 and 1541 were both reissued with large portions of the volumes reprinted, thus making two more editions which I number 8 and 9. Five of these editions are very nearly alike and make up each other, viz. N° 1, 2, 3, 5 and 7. They are in large black letter, 62 lines on a full page, and on strong thick paper. The other editions of November are on thinner paper, 65 lines. The whole nine editions[64] have a fine showy woodcut border to the first title, all alike from the same cut, except that in the 4th[64] edition[65] of November 1540 and all subsequent editions the arms of Cromwell, who was beheaded on the 28 July 1540, are obliterated.[67] It is the aim of true bibliographers to find copies pure and distinct, with no leaves of other editions mixed. Mr Francis Fry's elaborate book on these nine editions is the best and surest guide. The wood-cut first title-page has generally hitherto been ascribed to Holbein, but Wornum in his life of Holbein,[60] and others have recently so strongly pronounced against this opinion, that it is now generally abandoned. I give on p. 21 a reduced facsimile of it, 4 by 3 inches, the original measuring 14 by $9\frac{3}{8}$ inches.

Let us now see how our learned Scholastikos treats this subject. His remarks, as usual, are worth quoting: "Next[55] in interest ..... comes the first,[56] perhaps we should say the only[57] authorized edition—that of Henry VIII, printed by[58] Grafton and Whitchurch in 1539, and celebrated in history as the Great Bible. Of this there are several copies [in the Exhibition], and the woodcut title,[59] said to have been designed by Holbein,[60] is worth studying. At the top the King is seated on a throne,[61] ensigned[62] with his[63] arms, and surrounded by his courtiers, to whom he distributes copies of the book. At either side Cromwell and Cranmer, each also identified by his shield, are similarly employed; and round[63] the head of each person is a scroll, on which we read 'Vivat Rex,'[64] or, where the person represented is a child,[65] 'God save the King,' for children, of course, could not be expected to cheer in Latin.[66] There is a tragic interest, too, about these curious pictures.[67] Among the copies exhibited is one in which the circular space previously filled with Cromwell's arms is left blank. The shield has disappeared in the interval between the issue of the two[68] copies.[69]"

This is a masterpiece of packing—a dozen crammers in a dozen lines! and yet so cleverly told that it requires an expert to detect the deception. When a gentleman describes to us beautiful flowers as *blue* which we know to be *red* we generally let it pass, for we know that he is colourblind. In like manner, when a gentlemanly clergyman or Saturday reviewer tells us a string of historical facts which we know to be fictions, we either mentally wish Dogberry to write down his proper designation, or we regard him as truth-blind, and so let him parrotize at will.

In this case it may be remarked that there is probably no evidence that the first edition of the 'Great Bible' of April 1539 was ever 'authorized'[57] beyond the words 'cum privilegio,' etc. The book was a private mercantile venture, and the licence to print was as much a protection against rival printers as a privilege to publish. Great influence was used then and for the next four years to obtain royal recommendation to secure purchasers in families and churches. Again it was not printed by[58] Grafton and Whitchurche, although their names be on the title, but it is known to have been printed by François Regnault in Paris in 1538 under the editorship of Coverdale. Grafton and Whitchurche probably paid most of the expenses and sold the books for their own profit. The April 1540, or second edition, printed in London (Anthony Marler advancing the money for printing, etc. and Grafton and Whitchurche, together or separately, acting as publishers), bore for the first time on the title the words 'Apoynted to the vse of the churches.' The 3rd, 4th, 5th, 6th, and 7th editions of 1540 and 1541 had also the same line 'Apoynted,' etc. Yet these words cannot be construed to mean 'authorized.' They simply mean that in the almanac for every day in the year, and in the tables for Salisbury or other use, one may find the psalms, lessons, epistles and gospels, etc. pointed out or appointed for the use in churches. The Bishops' Bibles after 1572 bore both the words 'authorized' and 'appointed,' but never, I believe, was the word 'authorized' so used before 1574.

As to the description of the woodcut border of the title [59-60], a mere glance at the annexed reduced facsimile will show the incorrectness of it. Above the king the Almighty is seen among the clouds; and the King, Henry VIII, with the royal arms at his feet,[62] seated in a large arm-chair,[61] is distributing the word of God, with his right hand to the archbishops and bishops (known by their mitres) representing the Church; and with his left hand to the nobility, known by their coronets. Below in the centre of the inner margin is Cranmer, designated by his arms at his feet, giving out the word of God to the clergy, while on the other side of the title, just opposite, stands Cromwell, at foot his arms, distributing the Bible to the gentry. So far, among all these figures there is not one 'Vivat Rex.'[63]  But in the double compartment at the bottom of the page under the title are crowds of the people both men and women standing and sitting between the two emblems of civilization, the pulpit and the prison, both fully occupied. The pulpit, apparently at Paul's Cross, is on the left side, occupied by a preacher with many listeners, mostly seated in the foreground, and standing crowded in the background. Among these are several scrolls with 'Vivat Rex,'[64] but not round [63] the head of each person. Over the crowd of men and women at back is a single scroll with 'God save the King.' On the right, opposite the pulpit is the prison, perhaps a tower of Newgate, across the precincts, with several prisoners looking at the crowd mostly facing them, some with 'Vivat Rex' as before, and in the foreground two youths [65] seated on the ground and a man kneeling, underneath a scroll with 'God save the King.' There are no children, and therefore the poetic expression 'for children of course could not be expected to cheer in Latin' [66] is a stroke of the imagination worthy the palmy days of the Saturday Review. Lest our Scholastikos may attempt to shield himself at the expense of confessing that he had savoyed this whole account of the 'Great Bible' from a contemporary historian, even to the pretty fiction about the children cheering in Latin, I venture to give him the friendly advice that he had better not do that, because it will not look well, as a matter of taste, for his patron the Saturday to print beauties plagiarized from a writer whom it is never tired of abusing, misquoting, and savagely reviewing.

The reader will by these comments and the facsimile perceive how utterly void of truth is the whole of the reviewer's description of the 'Great Bible' and its title, to say nothing of its many editions. It seems at first sight inconceivable that any writer can go on thus writing sentence after sentence crammed with error, deceit, and all uncharitableness. I can account for it only on the supposition that if he be a parson or pastor he may have caught from his flock the foot and mouth disease, because as Williams of the Crown says, he has it bad, leastwise, it is apparent that every time he opens his mouth he puts his foot in it.

But lest my porch to this little catalogue may be mistaken for one intended for the Saturday Review itself, it becomes necessary to hasten to a conclusion. The reviewer now proceeds nearly a whole line without anything exceptional, until he stumbles into a hornet's nest of errors; 'but we fail [70] to find any special [71] notice of the sole [72] English issue of Queen Mary's reign.' He then proceeds to say that in 1553 Whitchurche published a Bible "without note or comment," 'all the preliminary matter printed with the Great Bible, including the Calendar and the Table of Lessons, being omitted.' 'At least one [73] copy appears in the Catalogue.' 'Strange to say, those days of bigotry seem to have been favourable to Bible-printing;' [74] for the same year, 1553, witnessed the appearance of the first Spanish edition,' [75] etc. In reply, the reader is referred to N[os] 874 and 875 of this Catalogue for special [74] notices of two copies of this very Bible, both of which were in the Exhibition, and displayed from its opening. Indeed, our critic seems not to have failed [70] to notice one [73] copy, and so contradicts himself. But the odd part of the joke is, that this plain and cheap edition of the Great Bible was issued by Whitchurche

The Flavour

in Edward VI's reign and not in Mary's. It must have appeared before the 6th of July, 1553, when Edward died, for it is professedly a Protestant Bible, since we find at the end of it a table to find the Epistles and Gospels usually read in the Church, according to the boke of Common-Prayer. Scholastikos has thus managed, as usual, to misstate every fact, and then expresses surprise that in those days of bigotry[74] in England, a Bible should be printed in Spanish[75] at Ferrara!

Of the notice of the Geneva New Testament first[76] divided into verses, 1557, he should have added 'in English,' for this division into verses is copied from Stephens' Greek and Latin Testament of 1551. Pagninus had also divided the whole Bible into verses as early as 1528, see N° 746. Three[77] copies of the Breeches Bible, first edition, were exhibited, one on large paper, see N°s 909, 910, 911. I must here plead guilty to having led our critic into error as to the number of 200 distinct editions[78] of this work. In writing my note under N° 909, not remembering the number of editions and for the moment not having time to look up my memoranda, I wrote the round number 200, charging my memory to count up the editions and correct the figures in the proof. The printer set it up in full and I never thought to correct the error. The true number cannot, I think, be more than 170. The critic has thus obtained this fact from the authority he disputes.

For want of space I must omit to notice as it deserves the long rigmarole of errors and irrelevant nonsense about the edition of 1649 by the Stationers' Company.[73-89] There is nothing new in this long paragraph and very little that is true. There was a copy[90] of this edition belonging to myself exhibited, but by some mistake it failed to be entered in the Catalogue, a matter however of little consequence, inasmuch as it was a sole edition and a failure. I do not believe that this mixed edition had any influence in superseding the Genevan version or marking the period of its going out of use. The whole passage however is a fine display of useless information and might appear rather astounding to any one who did not know whence it was filched.

Scholastikos next informs us with the air of a martyr that he does not 'find a single perfect copy of the first issue of the so-called Authorized Version.'[91] 'One, near the door, seems only to have its New[92] Testament title;' wrong again, for the copy next to the door was Earl Spencer's fine and perfect copy with not only the New[92] Testament title but the original first title, with the woodcut border, and before the words "Appointed to be read in churches" were added. This is N° 1036 of the present Catalogue. By its side was another fine and every way perfect copy of the same first issue of the 1611 version having the engraved copperplate title, N° 1035, exhibited by myself. I refer the reader to my revised note under N° 1035 for a full answer to the critic's sneers and arbitrary,[100] foolish and ridiculous dicta respecting the first two editions in 1611 of the present version of our Bible. I have nothing to retract in that note and therefore the intelligent reader will see by my references[99-100] that the learned critic is floundering worse and worse in his egregious, bumptious, and random misstatements. It is indeed tiresome work this demolishing his old Spanish Castles[101].

We come now to the very marrow of our Scholastikos's reasoning, ipse dixit upon ipse dixit ! Egotism and London Assurance run mad, all at the expense of our Weakly which is made, if possible, more than ever ridiculous and that too without appearing to know it ! It is stated that the collection of editions of the Authorized[102] Version is wretchedly poor.[103] On the contrary, it was very rich, embracing with few exceptions all the prominent and best editions, according to the expressed opinions of trustworthy biblical bibliographers and critics. Indeed if any man challenge this statement I appeal to the Catalogue. Scholastikos however in his broad sweep admits one exception and says that the collection contains 'in fact only one volume of any importance,[104] the Bodleian copy of the famous Bible of 1631,'[105] that is, the 'Wicked Bible' (see N° 1075), with the word *not* left out of the seventh commandment. This remarkable statement simply proves, I think, that this remarkable critic, Scholastikos, must be a clergyman of the high and palmy state and a Fellow of the Society of the Holy Cross. None but a parson carrying such odour of sanctity about him would be likely to pronounce the 'Wicked Bible' (reading, by purely typographical error in the seventh commandment, 'Thou shalt commit adultery,') an edition of importance !

We are next informed that Scholastikos failed to find a first Oxford Testament,[107] a first Cambridge[109] Testament, a Blaney's[110] quarto, a first Irish,[111] a first American,[112] etc. or in fact, with the exception of the Wicked Bible,[113] any thing of great note in this department. I answer that the *first* Oxford Testament is as yet an unascertained fact, as far as I know. I am inclined to think that the New Testament of 1673 in small quarto, issued with the first Oxford Bible of 1675, was first issued separately. If so, this was the first Oxford Testament, a copy of which is N° 1167. If this be not admitted then there were two editions of 1679 in octavo, both in the Bodleian, and both scarce. I know not which of the two was the earlier. I am sorry to disparage our witling's little conundrum about the first Oxford Testament, but one is really getting tired of it, for he has asked it four or five times during the past season in various articles in the Saturday Review with as yet no reply. He before asked it in his comments on Mr Gladstone's speech at the opening of the Caxton Exhibition, and since in his remarks on Mr Jones's address at the opening of the Librarians' Convention, page 419, of Oct. 6, in connection with Hamilton's Genealogies, which we are somewhere informed is wanting in the library of the British Museum. As to the first Cambridge Testament, if the reviewer means the little Geneva version of

[1590?], in 48mo, it could not be borrowed, only two copies being known to me, both inaccessible. If he means the small edition of 1628 it was there, see N° 1066. For the first Blaney's folio and quarto see N[os] 1261 and 1262. The first Irish[114] was there from the opening of the Exhibition and is described under N° 1216*, dated Dublin, 1714. If these corrective hornets do not sting our Saturday critic then he may be classed among the pachydermatous.

We are next told that 'There is a poor[118] copy of the Scots Bible in octavo,' etc. On the contrary, this was perhaps the finest book that came to the Exhibition from Scotland, a fine clean and beautifully bound copy, in the original richly tooled binding, the pride of Mr David Laing's collection. It is described under N° 1078 of this catalogue. Who but a critic that is truth-blind could coolly record such false statements? and if he could what is the object of such criticism? It is beyond our comprehension. There seems to be a moral squint in the eye of this writer. You never know when it is looking at you or telling the truth. It is painful to be thus placed on one's guard all the time against rampant ignorance, distorted conceit and warped knowledge. No honest University education, one would think, could possibly have turned out in this country such a master of the long-bow! He is manifestly a graduate of Nature's University, a genus, if not a genius, of his own kind,—a self-made man—who adores his maker—and sees no good in the handiwork of any other Author. I confess that I am tired of commenting upon the prolific misstatements of this critic, and though I have numbered them from 1 to 141 in this single page of the Saturday Review, I must remind him and my readers that all this false criticism relates exclusively to the English Bibles, which formed only a small and later portion of the Bible Exhibition. One trembles for him and the Saturday when he undertakes to discourse upon the early Bibles in Latin, Greek, Hebrew, French, German, Bohemian, and many other languages, to say nothing of the Great Polyglots, parts of Bibles, etc. which are collated and described in this our little Catalogue—nearly a thousand selected out of about thirty thousand. But I leave the last score or two of my references untouched, having exhausted myself rather than the subject. The Saturday has had its fling and I have now fired my blank cartridge as promised, and come what may, shall continue to read the Review hoping in the future to find as in the past, now and then, an article of sterling merit, true, fair, noble, manly and generous. There are occasional articles in it that refresh one like the balmy breath of the south wind in springtime, and make one forget all these mountains of stuff and nonsense like the writings of Scholastikos and his kind. I ask no remedy, knowing that the Saturday Review is seldom brought to its apologetic knees as it was in italics by the Daily News on the 13th of October last, on its page 467. But I confess I should like to see in it hereafter a little less smartness, with a good deal more truthfulness. Its egotism and conceit might be lowered a peg with advantage to itself and the community. If there be virtue in this prescription for the Saturday's present weak Ies let us be content with the old saw, 'virtue is its own reward.' It is not that I like the Saturday Review less that I have squeezed this flavour into my little book, but because its erroneous criticism afforded a good opportunity to expose some of the common errors entertained by recent historians and more recent writers concerning our printed Bible, that drifted into it. If I have failed this time, a little grape on the next occasion may perhaps suffice.

HENRY STEVENS of Vermont.

4 Trafalgar Square, Charing Cross,
   London February 3, 1878

Σχολαστικὸς ἴς τίλτ ἀγαλιστ Σοὐθ Χέψουγτον

INTRODUCTION.

THE HISTORY OF PRINTING

AS ILLUSTRATED BY

THE PRINTED BIBLE,

1450—1877.

HE secular history of the HOLY SCRIPTURES is the sacred history of PRINTING. The Bible was the first book printed, and the Bible is the last book printed. Between 1450 and 1877, an interval of four centuries and a quarter, the Bible shows the progress and comparative development of the art of printing in a manner that no other single book can; and Biblical bibliography proves that during the first forty years, at least, the Bible exceeded in amount of printing all other books put together; nor were its quality, style, and variety a whit behind its quantity.

The honour of producing the first, and, as many think, the most perfect book, is now ascribed to Gutenberg alone, Fust not coming in for a share of the credit of the invention until after his famous lawsuit in 1455, when the Bible had been finished. We call it, therefore, the GUTENBERG BIBLE, and have no sympathy for any French name given to it simply because a copy found in a Paris library had the honour of being described by a French bookseller. After this suit, when Fust took over the business and associated Schoeffer with himself, there was probably a dispersion of the craft from Mentz to Bamberg, Strasburg, and other places, just as there subsequently was when Mentz in 1462 was besieged and taken by Adolphus, Duke of Nassau.

As the Art spread from Mentz throughout Germany, Italy, France, and the Low Countries, the Bible was generally the first, or among the first books printed by each of the early printers, though unquestionably during the progress of these great volumes through the press the several presses threw off a variety of smaller pieces, especially *Indulgences* and other typical or typographical aids of the Church, some of which perchance might bear dates earlier than the Bibles themselves, which were on the anvils at the same time.

Some half-dozen huge folio Bibles in Latin and German, besides the magnificent Psalters of 1457 and 1459, had appeared in type before a single volume of the Classics saw the "new lamp for the new learning." First and foremost of the ancient Classics came forth Cicero's *De Officiis*, in 1465, a little volume about the size of the Book of Genesis, followed soon after by his *De Oratore* and *Epistolæ ad Familiares*. Then came the ever-popular Virgil and Cæsar in 1469, and Pliny the Elder the next year. Ovid followed in 1471, and Valerius Maximus in 1472. Petrarch, Dante, and Boccaccio were fortunate enough among the modern classics to be set in type in 1470, 1471, and 1472, while the *Canterbury Tales* of Chaucer appeared some five or six years later from the press of Caxton. The first book in Greek came from the Milan press in 1476, followed by the first Greek classic author, dear old Æsop, in 1480, while the great Homer himself (reminding one of his own grim joke of Polyphemus) was held back and not devoured by the press till 1488.

In a word, up to the time of the discovery of America, in 1492, Columbus might have counted upon his fingers all the old classic authors (including Ptolemy and Strabo in their unbecoming Latin dress) who could throw any geographical light on the questions which the Great

Discoverer was discussing with the theologians of Spain; while, covering the same period, the editions of the Bible alone, and the parts thereof, in many languages and countries, will sum up not far less than one thousand, and the most of these of the largest and costliest kind.

We have been endeavouring for the last quarter of a century or more to compile as complete a list of printed Bibles and Parts of Bibles as possible from the earliest period to the present time, and the remarkable result is a table of some 30,000 titles, representing about 35,000 volumes. By throwing all this vast store of Biblical bibliography into one strictly chronological list, we see at a glance what Biblical work was going on in every part of the world under each year, or any given year, and comparatively how the production of the Holy Scriptures in one country or language ranged with those of another. We see, for instance, that all the earliest printed Bibles were in the Latin Vulgate, the first complete edition of the Septuagint not having been issued from the press of Aldus till the year 1518, the very year of the 14th German Bible.

The earliest printed Bibles in the modern European languages were the first and second German Bibles by Mentelin and Eggesteyn, of Strasburg, of rather uncertain date, but certainly not later than 1466. In 1471 appeared at Venice two translations into Italian—the one by Malermi, printed by Vindelin de Spira, and the other by Nicolas Jenson. In 1477 was printed the first New Testament in French by Buyer, at Lyons, and the same year appeared the first edition of the Old Testament in Dutch, printed at Delft by Jacob Jacobs zoen and Mauritius Yemants zoen. In 1480 was published the splendid Bible in the Saxon or Low German language, from the press of Heinrich Quentel, of Cologne, followed by a second edition in 1491, and a third in 1494. The Psalms, in Dutch, first came out in 1480, in small octavo, and in Greek and Latin in 1481, while the first Hebrew Pentateuch appeared in 1482. The entire Bible done into French paraphrase was published by Guyard de Moulins in 1487. A full translation appeared in the Bohemian language, printed at Prague in 1488. The same year appeared the entire Old Testament in Hebrew from the press of Abraham ben Chayim de' Tintori, at Soncino.

This chronological arrangement shows us also many noteworthy points, such as that nearly all the earliest Bibles were huge folios; that the first Bibles printed at Rome and Venice appeared in 1471, and that the sixth

German Bible by G. Zainer, in 1475, at Augsburg, was the first with the leaves folioed or numbered; that the first quarto Bible appeared in 1475, printed by John Peter de Ferratis at Placentia, which was also the first book printed at Placentia; that the first of Coburger's celebrated Bibles appeared in Nuremberg in 1475, and that by the end of the century no less than thirteen large folio Bibles had come from this house alone; that the four splendid Bibles printed in 1476 all bear the printers' signatures, though it is difficult to say with certainty which was the first —viz., that of Moravus at Naples, Jenson at Venice, Gering, Crantz, and Friburger at Paris, or that of F. de Hailbrun and N. de Frankfordia at Venice; that the first Bible with a distinct title-page was printed at Venice, by George de Ravabenis in 1487, in small quarto; and that the first Bible in small octavo, or "the poor man's Bible," was the earliest, or among the earliest books, from the press of Johann Froben, of Basle, in 1491, and is certainly one of the neatest and tidiest Bibles in our Collection. This splendidly illuminated and bound copy is lent us from the Bodleian Library.

Prior to the discovery of America no less than twelve grand patriarchal editions of the entire Bible, being of several different translations, appeared from time to time in the German language; to which add the two editions by the Otmars of Augsburg of 1507 and 1518, and we have the total number of no less than fourteen distinct large folio pre-Reformation, or ante-Lutheran Bibles. No other language except the Latin can boast of anything like this number.

As the discovery of America was the greatest of all discoveries, so the invention of the Art of Printing may be called the greatest of all inventions. But no sooner had Columbus reported his grand discovery through the press than the Pope assumed the whole property in the unknown parts of the earth, and divided it all at once between the two little Powers in the Peninsula, wholly disregarding the rights and titles of the other nations of Europe. The same little game of assumption has been tried, from time to time, with regard to this great invention, but the press has a protective power within itself, which the Church can smother only with ignorance and mental darkness.

From this rapid survey it will be apparent that our earliest Bibles, many of them printed most sumptuously on vellum, must have each cost the price of a farm. Later they could be had for a cow, but now a morning's milking of a cow will procure for a farmer a first-class well-bound Bible in his own language.

At this late day it is difficult to arrive at the precise dates of several of the earliest and most important printed Bibles, most of the dates having been first assumed by bibliographers without sufficient authority, and subsequently followed by others without inquiry. From an inscription by one Cremer, the illuminator and binder of the Gutenberg Bible, now in the National Library of Paris, we know positively that the book was printed before August, 1456. From another inscription in a copy of Pfister's Bible, also in the Paris Library, the work is assigned to Bamberg, before 1461, but the church register of Bamberg shows that this Bible was printed prior to March, 1460. More recently it has been announced and confirmed that the copy of the first of Mentelin's Latin Bibles, in the Library of Freiburg in Breisgau, bears an inscription by the rubricator showing that these important volumes had been printed prior to 1460 and 1461.

With these new data, and a new scrutiny by the light of recent bibliography, and new comparisons of our undated Bibles with books of positive dates and known printers, brought together, like the present Caxton Memorial Collection, to say nothing of the great aid derived from our recent photo-bibliography, or means of safely comparing books in one library with those of another, it is to be hoped that the day of more exact bibliography is at hand. It will not surprise us to find that the order of printing of the first seven of the great German Bibles, all of which are without dates, may be hereafter somewhat modified, or that our new scrutiny may even yet develop new or unrecognized editions in every department of Biblical research.

We therefore, for the extraordinary opportunity afforded us for comparing and collating rare Bibles and other valuable books in this unique Caxton Memorial Collection, tender herewith our warmest thanks to each and all of our contributors, and more especially to Her Majesty the Queen, His Grace the Duke of Devonshire, the Earl Spencer, Earl of Jersey, Earl of Leicester, the Archbishop of Canterbury, the Curators of the Bodleian Library, the University Library, Cambridge, the University Library, Edinburgh, Sion College, the British and Foreign Bible Society, the Advocates'

Library, Edinburgh, the Signet Library, Edinburgh, Mr. W. Amhurst Tyssen-Amhurst, Mr. Francis Fry, Mr. David Laing, Mr. Thomas Longman, Mrs. Jolyffe, the Rev. Dr. Gott, Vicar of Leeds, the Dean of St. Paul's, Mr. Henry White, Rev. Dr. Ginsburg, Mr. M. Ridgway, Mr. E. S. Kowie, Mr. C. D. Sherborn, Mr. J. Mathers, Mr. George Tawse, Rev. L. B. Kaspar, Sir Charles Reed, Mr. H. Cleaver, the University Press, Cambridge, the University Press, Oxford, Mr. Thomas Stapleton, Mr. A. Gardyner, Messrs. Bagster and Sons, Messrs. Spottiswoode and Co., and others; but still more are our thanks due to Mr. Henry J. Atkinson, who has liberally lent us above four hundred editions of the Bible in all languages. Some of these editions are of very considerable rarity and value, while others, though not of the choicest or rarest kind, are, very many of them, of the middle class of Biblical Bibliography, which are so difficult to meet with and which are of such immense importance to the student in arriving at a clear history of editions, versions, and translations. Scores of these editions are not in our national library, and we know not where else to lay our hands upon them.

Our collection boasts of nearly all the earliest and most famous Bibles and Psalters, together with representative editions of the later revisions, translations, versions, and languages down to the present time, to the extraordinary number of above one thousand editions. This unexpected and overwhelming liberality of our patrons has very nearly overwhelmed and buried the arranger and cataloguer, but he trusts that great bibliographical good will eventually result from this rare opportunity of comparison, collation, and scrutiny. Rare Bibles, early New Testaments, the Psalms, and other parts of the Scriptures are, it is well known, scattered all over the country; and we trust that people who possess them will bring or send up these lost children, and have them identified and properly registered. We shall willingly undertake this additional labour for the sake of the opportunity of discovering new and hitherto undescribed editions.

The famous collection of Bibles in the Royal Library of Stuttgard is said to exceed eight thousand editions; but by comparison of the catalogue of our present Caxton Celebration Collection with the catalogue by Adler, printed in 1787, the patient and curious reader will see that more than one-half of our collection is not represented at Stuttgard. So likewise of the extraordinarily rich collection of some five thousand titles of Bibles in the library of Wolfenbüttel. The collection of Bibles and parts thereof in the Lenox Library of New York in all languages, is probably unsurpassed in rare and valuable editions, especially in the English language, by any library, public or private. Mr. Francis Fry, of Bristol, the indefatigable collector, has succeeded in bringing together above one thousand editions of the English Bible, Testaments, Psalms, &c., most of them prior to 1700, to say nothing of above one hundred editions in ancient and foreign languages. The Rev. Dr. Ginsburg, of Wokingham, possesses a unique collection, astonishingly rich in early and rare Latin, German and Hebrew Bibles and parts thereof, including, we believe, the whole fourteen pre-Reformation German Bibles, and almost every edition of Luther's early Bibles and parts, the genuine as well as the counterfeit editions. Besides these his collection contains many other editions in other languages, both ancient and modern, to the extent, in all, of between two and three thousand editions; and, what is of infinite importance to Bible and bibliographical students, the Doctor makes his collection as free to them as to himself. But the Library of the British Museum to-day contains probably by far the richest collection of Bibles and Parts thereof in the world, numbering at present above sixteen thousand titles; but even this our Caxton Celebration Collection, so hastily brought together, contains very many editions not to be found in our national library.

Notwithstanding the active research of many eminent scholars for the last three centuries, Biblical Bibliography is even now but in its infancy. The subject is so vast that no general bibliographer can more than indicate certain special and prominent editions. It is now more than one hundred and fifty years since Le Long published in Latin the last edition of his bibliography of the Bible. The work was excellent in its day, but very imperfect in many departments, especially English. About a century ago Masch re-edited and vastly improved certain parts of Le Long, especially the editions of the Bible in the ancient languages. He left the work, however, unfinished; so that for Bibles in most of the modern languages we have still to refer to Le Long.

In this brief sketch of the History of Printing, as illustrated by the reproduction of the Bible by moveable types, we have left ourselves space merely to allude to the first five editions of Erasmus's New Testament in Greek and Latin, 1516-35, a work which marks the beginning of a new era in Biblical bibliography; to the Psalter of Giustiniani in five languages, printed at Genoa in 1516, with the first life of Columbus in the long note on the nineteenth Psalm, in which are given some important particulars of Columbus's second voyage along the southern coast of Cuba, nowhere else to be found; to the first Bible in Greek, the Septuagint from the press of Aldus of Venice, in 1518; and above all to the first Great Polyglot Bible of Cardinal Ximenes, printed at Alcala in six large folio volumes between the years 1514 and 1517, though not published till 1520, the most memorable monument of typography the world had yet seen. Nothing less than the inpouring wealth of the Indies, combined with the overbearing power of Ximenes, at that time could have collected the manuscripts, collated and edited them, and printed these splendid volumes in such a sumptuous manner in the short space of fifteen years! While Ximenes was building up this great monument in Spain, Wolsey was about building Hampton Court. Two Cardinal virtues! It would be curious to inquire which cost the more money, the Polyglot or the Palace, and which won the greater honour!

This brings our running narration down to the time of Luther, Protestant Germany, and Scripture-hungry England. The presses of Caxton and his successors had been more than half-a-century in operation, and yet not a chapter of the Bible had ever appeared, as such, printed in the English language. It is true that in his *Golden Legend* Caxton had printed in 1483 in English nearly the whole of the Pentateuch, and a great part of the Gospels, under the guise of the lives of Adam, Abraham, Moses, the Apostles, and others; but all was mingled with so much of priestly gloss and dross that though probably read in churches it was never recognized as the Holy Scriptures. The *Liber Festivalis* of 1483 contained also some Scripture paraphrases; and in 1509 Wynkyn de Worde printed a fine edition of the Apocryphal Gospel of Nicodemus. These were the nearest approaches that the English people made to the printed Bible in our own tongue. It is true that many copies of the Bible and New Testament translated into English by Wycliffe and his followers were scattered throughout the country in manuscript, and had given educated people and persons of quality a taste of the Book of Books.

It is not unlikely that had not the bones of Wycliffe, buried in the little churchyard of Lutterworth, been dug up and burnt, and his ashes cast into the Swift, by order of the Council of Constance, under the pious protective benevolence of the Church and priesthood, in the first quarter of the fifteenth century, Caxton in the last quarter of the same century might have begun in England his great work of printing, like most of the great printers of the Continent, with the Bible in his native tongue, and thus have modernized Wycliffe's Bible, and cast it into another and a rapider Swift.

But Caxton was prudent and wise, as well as a man of business. He had witnessed the storm, and recognized the obstructive and selfish power which gloried in mental darkness, and taught ignorance as the peculiar knowledge and birthright of the people. It was a part of the same piece of priestly wisdom that a few years later gave itself utterance in a sermon at Paul's Cross, in these ever-memorable words: "We must root out printing, or printing will root out us." So Caxton and his successors, taking the prudent and business-like course, printed what was most likely to sell in peace; and so the Scriptures in our vernacular tongue saw not the dawn in England, but awaited the broad daylight of the Reformation, in the second quarter of the sixteenth century, long after they were familiar to the Germans, the Italians, the Dutch, and the Bohemians.

The educated of England, however, were not ignorant of the Scriptures, for Coburger of Nuremberg, and probably other continental printers, had established warehouses in London, for the sale of Latin Bibles, as early as 1480, and perhaps earlier. There is an instructive letter in the Public Record Office from Coverdale and Grafton to Cromwell, written from Paris the 12th of September, 1538, in behalf of their host, Francis Regnault, who was then printing the "GREAT BIBLE" for them: "Where as of long tyme he [Regnault] hath bene an occupier into England more than xl. yere, he hath allwayes provyded soche bookes for England, as they moost occupied, so y^t he hath a great nombre at this present in his handes as Prymers in Englishe, Missoles w^t other soche like: wherof now (by ye company of ye Booksellers in London) he is utterly forbydden to make sale, to the utter undoying of the man. Wherfore most humbly we beseke yor lordshippe to be gracious and favourable unto him, y^t he may have lycence to sell those which he hath done allready, so yt hereafter he prynte no moo in the english tong, onlesse he have an english man yt is lerned, to be his correcto{r}. . . . . Yf yor l. shewe him this benefyte we shall not fare the worse in the readynesse and due expedicion of this yor l. worke of the Byble, which goeth well forwarde, and within few moneths will drawe to an ende," etc.

From the time of Luther the Continent was filled with new and cheaper issues of the Bible and every part of it, not only in Latin and Greek, but in the modern languages. The history of Bible printing in Germany, Switzerland, and the Low Countries, though in many instances opposed and even prohibited, remains no secret or mystery. The French and Italians printed extensively in the ancient languages, but the Church managed to have small call for the Scriptures in the vulgar tongues which the people could read and comprehend. The history of Luther's own translations and publications of the Scriptures, 1522-34, first by instalments as fast as he could get the parts ready, then by revisions and complete works in 1534, is well known. But the bibliography of Luther's early pieces, counterfeits, reprints, &c., requires careful revision. Again, much is to be still settled in the Biblical bibliography of the many editions of the Bible and parts thereof, in various languages, printed by Froschover of Zurich, from his little 16mo Swiss-German Bible, in five vols, 1527-29, and his folio revision of Luther in five parts, 1525-29, the Prophets and Apocrypha done by Leo Jude, Zwingle, and others.

The story of the learned Robert Stephens and the printing of his Bibles and New Testaments in Paris, as told by the late M. Firmin Didot, is one of the most interesting in the literary history of printing and printers. Yet though encouraged, protected, and favoured by Francis as far as any king could protect a subject against the wiles of the Church, at last poor Stephens was driven in exile to Geneva for his Bibles and Testaments; so that to this day the Bibles and Testaments of Robert Stephens remain the glory and the shame of France.

Germany was not only boiling over for liberty and free Scriptures, but scholars of advanced thoughts flocked thither from all parts of the world. But Flanders was the paradise of printers, and Antwerp, at this time, the very centre of it, because it enjoyed some special privileges for its citizens within their own dwellings, by which the Burgomaster could resist imperial authority, and disregard imperial emissaries. Any

Belgian could print what he liked, and sell it if he could at home and abroad. Hence, disregarding the counsel of St. Paul, according to an old translator, against "making marchandize of the Word of God," it became an extensive and lucrative business of the Low Countries to supply England and France with printed Bibles and Testaments in their own languages. Besides this, the Flemings themselves fanned the Reformation by producing a very large number of Bibles in their own language, for their own consumption, between 1520 and 1550, though the Emperor's Ordinance of 1529 was very stringent against heretical or Lutheran books and anonymous printing of all kinds, especially the Holy Scriptures in the vulgar tongues.

Finally the high tide of the Reformation reached England in 1526 in the shape of a beautiful New Testament in English by William Tyndale. The people soon got a taste of the Word of God in their own language, and a Christian Association was formed in London to read and circulate the Scriptures even in the Universities. Here read the stories of Garret and Dalaber. Within the first ten years probably as many as fifteen distinct editions of Tyndale's New Testament in English, of not less than three thousand copies each, were printed and sold. Tyndale himself living abroad ran the gauntlet of persecution as few men had done, being driven from place to place for six or seven years, till he was found out and hunted down in 1534, imprisoned in May, 1535, and burnt in 1536. The public demand for his Testaments was very great, and no power could check their importation, sale, and consumption. Edition after edition appeared silently in England, but from whence nobody cared to inquire. They were certainly not printed in England. Tyndale himself was scented and ferreted out by English emissaries sent abroad for the purpose, and run down like a wolf. Even his friends and followers in England who could be proved to have read or to possess even a New Testament were also hunted through London and the Universities as the greatest of criminals; and this, too, even after the King had replaced the Pope and become the chief head of the Church of England. But all this raid and tirade of the learned doctors of divinity against Scripture readers only lowered the Church whilst it raised the people. Bibles, Psalms, Testaments, and other parts of the Bible thenceforth increased in England to an extent wholly unknown in any other country or nation. Though late in getting possession of themselves and their liberties, the people of England succeeded to a surprising degree; basing their rights and liberties more on their Bibles than anything else. No wonder, then, that the editions of the Bible in English, since 1535, have not only outnumbered those of any other nation, but in the aggregate, including America, exceed those of all other languages.

With all these vast accumulations of Bibles and Biblical history, what is at present the extent of our positive knowledge concerning the history and production of our early English Bibles and Testaments prior to 1550, or even later? More than a hundred industrious writers from the time of Lewis to to-day, have ransacked every corner of Christendom in search of facts respecting Tyndale, Coverdale, and Rogers. In a wonderfully small degree they have gleaned a few items respecting the persecuted Tyndale and his New Testaments, but many of these facts require confirmation. As to Coverdale and our first Complete English Bible, finished the 4th of October, 1535, THE MOST PRECIOUS VOLUME IN OUR LANGUAGE, what do we know? Absolutely next to nothing. The volume itself tells us the day it was finished, but where it was printed, or by whom, or for whom, or under what circumstances, no historian or bibliographer has as yet given us any trustworthy information. No literary mystery for the past three centuries has elicited so much inquiry, or so many investigators, especially of late and latest years; yet up to the opening day of this Caxton Celebration, the 30th of June, 1877, all is but mere conjecture. Some have assigned the production of the volume to Lubeck, others to Frankfort, still others to Zurich, Hamburg, Cologne, Worms, Strasburg, and even Marlboro in the land of Hesse; while some say that it came from the press of Egenolph, others detect in it the master hand of Froschover, and still others attribute it to Quentel or some one else; but all to no purpose. The very variety of these conjectures proves their falsity, and shows that they are really and truly mere conjectures, without the slightest base or foundation.

The woodcuts used in the "Coverdale Bible" have indeed been traced into the possession of James Nicolson, printer in St Thomas's Hospital, Southwark, in 1535, but not a scrap of the type used in that first English Bible has ever yet, so far as we can learn, been seen or identified in any other book printed at home or abroad. We have ourself, for more than a quarter of a century, spent much time in comparing translations, type, cuts, initial letters, and the general and particular style and make-up of various Continental printers, mousing and groping among old books of all sorts, in search of traces of Coverdale in 1534 and 1535. The results are numerous, but entirely negative. We have had the satisfaction, from time to time, of narrowing down the field of research, and positively convincing ourself, first, that the book could *not* have come from the press of Egenolph, then of Froschover, and so on, but never a bit of positive testimony has greeted our eyes in favour of the true story. But at last, when all our researches for new bibliographical fields to explore had been exhausted, and just as we were forced to the conclusion that no analytical exploration was ever likely to reward us, the long-kept secret dropped into our open mouth of its own mere motion and ripeness, as if it desired to be in time for the Caxton Celebration. We comprehended the whole story in a minute, and realized it instantly with a thrill of delight we can never attempt to describe, though it showed us how utterly vain and unprofitable all our researches and comparisons of type, cuts, paper, watermarks, inks, and other printer's etcetera had been. The naked facts were before us in all their simplicity and truthfulness before we had time to understand how far away our historical and antiquarian investigations, primed by our so-called human reason, had drifted us.

Let us now return to Coverdale and his Bible. In his Preface to the Reader, Coverdale says, "For the which cause (accordynge as I was desyred anno 1534) I toke the more vpon me to *set forth* this specyall translacyon." This important date, "anno 1534," was interpolated in Froschover's [Hester's] edition of 1550, no doubt on good authority. Coverdale also informs us, in the first paragraph of his Preface to the Reader, after alluding manifestly to Tyndale, or perhaps to George Joye, "which were not onely of rype knowledge, but wold also with al theyr hartes haue perfourmed that they beganne eyf they had not had impediment," etc. "These and other reasonable causes considered, I was the more bold to take it in hande." He then tells us that various translations were put into his hands which he was glad to "followe for the most parte, accordynge as I was requyred. But to saye the trueth before God, it was nether my laboure ner desyre to haue this worke put in my hande; neuertheles it greued me y^t other nacyōs shulde be more plenteously prouyded for with yᵉ Scripture in theyr mother tongue then we; therfore whan I was instantly requyred, though I coulde not do so well as I wolde, I thought it yet my dewtye to do my best." Again, in his Dedication to King Henry VIII, Coverdale says, "as the holy goost moued other men to do the cost herof, so was I boldened in God, to laboure in the same." These and several other expressions and explanations of Coverdale—in some of which he speaks of the translation as his own, and in others of himself, as being employed or required to "set forth," that is, to see the translation through the press—have been commented upon scores of times, but always without satisfaction.

But all these mysterious extracts will read much clearer when we add that there was at that time a certain young man of position living in Antwerp, a great linguist, of good education and natural endowments—so high indeed as to enable him "to distinguish well light from darkness," that is, to be a Protestant, who was the "begetter" of this "specyall translacyon." In his youth he had been taught the art of printing; and in manhood his chosen profession or business, in which he manifested great zeal, was in producing at Antwerp a translation of the Bible into English "for the advancement of the Kingdom of Christ in England," says his biographer; "and *for this purpose he employed a certain learned scholar named* MILES COVERDALE."

This simple statement, which we believe to be perfectly authentic, and which has been lying under our noses in most of our libraries for two centuries and a half unnoticed, narrows the matter down to ANTWERP, and assigns the honour of producing our first English Bible to that city, an honour which will be acknowledged by coming generations of Englishmen as well as Americans, who, while they inquire, with guide-book in hand, for the pictures of Rubens, will not forget the home of JACOB VAN METEREN, the probable translator of our first Bible, who employed Miles Coverdale to "set forth" and father "this specyall translacyon." All honour to Miles Coverdale, the learned scholar, the modest self-sacrificing student, the earnest simple-hearted Christian, who was unquestionably the best proof-reader and corrector of his age; to whom, perhaps, more than any other one man of his time, William Tyndale himself not excepted, the English language owes a debt of gratitude for its clearness, pointedness, and simplicity. That he left in this our first complete

English Bibles some few *foreignisms* and some inverted English is not surprising when we find that the dozen corps of revisers since have not seen fit or been able to exclude them.

Coverdale's duties and responsibilities in revising and setting forth this special translation at Antwerp in 1534-35, at the cost and charges of Jacob van Meteren, who was also, we believe, its original translator out of "Douche and Latyn" into English, were, we take it, precisely the same as when in 1537-38 he revised and set forth the Great Bible in Paris at the cost and charges of Grafton and Whitchurch. In the latter case he was the nominee of Thomas Cromwell, and similarly, we suppose, when he was "instantly required" at Antwerp in 1534, he received his appointment through Cromwell, who, it is well known, since 1510 had been in close and confidential personal connection with affairs of the English Company of Adventurers at Antwerp. From 1527 to 1539 we know that Coverdale was on the most friendly and cordial terms with Cromwell, yielding his mind, his services, and his judgment to that great statesman, so much so that in 1535 he was probably the only man who would have been allowed to put his name to a dedication to the King, and Preface to the Reader of an English Bible. He was employed and required not only to revise and see the Bible through the press, but to father the translation.

There are a few interesting circumstances which we may not omit even here, respecting Jacob van Meteren, his family and connections. About the year 1480 William Ortelius and his family, on account of their religion, removed from Augsburg to Antwerp, where the family became one of the most distinguished. Not long after there removed from Breda to Antwerp Cornelius van Meteren and his family. Jacob, the son of Cornelius van Meteren, married in 1534 (?) Ottilia, the accomplished daughter of William Ortelius, and aunt to the afterwards famous Abraham Ortelius, the Geographer.

These two Protestant families were very intimate, and were soon after joined, by intermarriage, by an Englishman named John Rogers, *alias* Thomas Matthew. Rogers had nominally taken the post of Chaplain to the English Company of Adventurers, which had been held by Tyndale, and perhaps by Coverdale. Tyndale having had, as all the world knows, "impediment" in producing the Bible, Coverdale " was the more bold to take it in hande." But Van Meteren soon found new and greater impediment. The London bookbinders and stationers, finding the market filled with foreign books, especially Testaments, made complaint in 1533-34, and petitioned for relief; in consequence of which a statute was passed compelling foreigners to sell their editions entire to some London stationer in sheets, so that the binders might not suffer. This new law was to come into operation about the beginning of 1535. In consequence of this law, Jacob van Meteren, as his Bible approached completion, was obliged to come to London to sell the edition. We have reason to believe that he sold it to James Nicolson of Southwark, who not only bought the entire edition, but the woodcuts, and probably the punches and type; but if the latter, they were doubtless lost in transmission, as they have never turned up in any shape since. All the copies of the Coverdale Bible, in the original condition, as far as we know, have appeared in English binding, thus confirming this law of 1534.

While Van Meteren was absent in England, in 1535, the Imperial authorities, instigated probably by some of the English emissaries at Antwerp, went to the house of Van Meteren to search it, ostensibly for the person of Leonard Ortelius, the father of Abraham, and the uncle of Ottilia, to arrest him as a Lutheran, but really to search for forbidden books, such as English Bibles and New Testaments. The searchers, who were harsh and cruel, gave Madame Ottilia great alarm. She prayed fervently to Almighty God that they might not find what they were in search of, and promised that if she and her's were protected, she would so mark this great providence of God by naming the child she was about to give birth to, if a son, as to commemorate the circumstances. Though the searchers frequently laid their hands on the very chest that contained the hidden books, they did not find them. On the 9th of July, 1535, a son was born to her, and keeping her promise she named him EMANUEL, that is, "GOD WITH US." This boy, twin brother of the Coverdale Bible, became a distinguished man, a scholar, and an historian. He passed most of his life in London as merchant and Belgian Consul. He died the 18th of April, 1612, in his 77th year. He never forgot the circumstances preceding his birth, and frequently wrote his name "Emanuel Quis-contra-nos?" "If God be with us, who can be against us?" For this fitting appendage to his name he was indebted to his cousin, DANIEL ROGERS, the distinguished diplomatist and Latin poet, the eldest son of John Rogers, the proto-martyr, who, in 1536-37, "set forth" again at Antwerp for Jacob van Meteren, under the assumed name of Thomas Matthew, a splendid edition of the Bible, called now Matthew's Version, the whole edition of which was sold to Grafton, as before the Coverdale Bible had been sold to Nicolson. A mystery has long hung over "Matthew's Version," since it is well known that part of it is Tyndale's, part Coverdale's, and only a portion revised by Rogers himself. Matthew's New Testament has recently been proved by Mr. Francis Fry, of Bristol, to be a reprint of Tyndale's last revision, the edition of 1535-4, with the combined initials of Tyndale and Van Meteren on the title page. Mr. Francis Fry, under his No. 4, calls this edition G H, but has hitherto been unable to explain the monogram. Our suggestion is that the G H means the translator, GUILLAUME HYTCHINS, the assumed name of William Tyndale; the other letters being the initials of the printer and proprietor, I v M, that is, JACOB VAN METEREN. If this be true, the fact reconciles much. The property or copyright belonged to Van Meteren, who, employing Rogers, had the right to produce Matthew's Bible by combining in it parts of Tyndale and Coverdale, which were his own property.

These are only a few of the circumstances that have come to light. Further and more careful investigation may compel us to somewhat modify some of these details, and to qualify others; but, on the whole, we trust that our hurried account is substantially correct. We are indebted for the larger part of our statement to the Rev. Symeon Ruytinck, the bosom friend of our EMANUEL Quis contra nos? who was, we believe, for a time connected with the Dutch Church of Austin Friars in London. It is contained in a brief biographical notice by him of Emanuel van Meteren, appended to that distinguished writer's *History of Belgium*, published in the Flemish language at the Hague in 1614, and in French at the same place in 1618.

In the precious volume of some 400 autograph letters, addressed by many of the learned of the world between 1560 and 1595 to Abraham Ortelius, belonging to this Dutch Church, and now preserved in the Guildhall Library, are two very long autograph letters of our Emanuel van Meteren, once or two of Daniel Rogers, and something of Rev.

Symeon Ruytinck. Honour to them all, however remote and small the light they throw on our dear old Coverdale Bible, and treble honour and blessing on the memory of Jacob and Ottilia van Meteren, to whom we owe our first Bible. They lived together happily, finished their great work together, and perished together. Let their names become household words in England, and let them be loved and honoured together as long as the language of the Coverdale Bible lasts. Towards the end of the reign of Edward VI, finding Antwerp unsafe for them on account of their religion, they resolved to remove with all their effects and penates to London, and live under the young King, who had offered them an asylum. On their passage from Antwerp the ship that bore them was attacked by a French cruiser, burnt, and sunk; and so perished Jacob and Ottilia van Meteren. Though the sea holds their bones, their names are now given up to be recorded with honour in England and America this Caxton Memorial Year.

HENRY STEVENS.

4, *Trafalgar Square, London,*
July 25, 1877.

Postscriptum.—For the continuation of these bibliographical Notes on the printed Bibles in English and other languages from 1535 to 1877, and for the fuller Notes on Bibles and parts of Bibles prior to 1535, of which the above is but an epitome, the courageous reader is referred to our forthcoming little book entitled OUR PRINTED BIBLES, 1450-1877.

THE COMPARATIVE DEVELOPMENT OF THE ART OF PRINTING

IN ENGLAND AND FOREIGN COUNTRIES, ILLUSTRATED

BY SPECIMENS OF THE PRINTED BIBLE

CHRONOLOGICALLY ARRANGED, 1450-1877.

No. 611.

BIBLE (Latin). *Begin.* [With the prologue of Saint Jerome.] [F]Rater ambrosius tua michi munuscu-/la perferens. detulit siml' 't suauissimas litteras : etc. [Genesis begins Fol. 5 recto col. 1 at the top. I]n principio creauit deus ceūl et terram. *End.* [Fol. 641 verso, col. 2] Gratia dñi ñri ihesu cristi cū omnib; vobis amē. [Mentz, Joannes Gutenberg, 1450-55?] Gothic letters, first edition, 2 volumes, measuring 15¾ by 11⅓ inches. Folio. *Lent by Earl Spencer.*

Without title-page, pagination or signatures ; 641 leaves printed in double columns, 42 lines to a full column ; the initials and rubrics are in MS. throughout. The earliest book known, printed with moveable metal type; was formerly styled, unjustly to Germany, the "Mazarine Bible," but is now properly called the Gutenberg Bible. Some copies, which may be called a second issue, have 40 lines on the first eight pages, forty-one on the ninth, and the rest forty-two, like the present copy. In this latter issue the three lines in red at the beginning are in type, and not in manuscript, as in the 42 line issue.

612. PSALMS (Latin). Psalmorum Codex. Presens Psalmorum Codex venustate capitalium decoratus, rubricationibusque sufficienter distinctus, ad inventione artificiosa imprimendi ac caracterizandi absque calami ulla exaracione sic effigiatus, et ad eusebiam dei industrie est consummatus, per Johannem Fust civem maguntinum et Petrum Schoffer de Gernszheim anno domini MCCCCLVII. In vigilia Assumpcionis. [Mentz], 1457. Folio.
Lent by Her Majesty the Queen.
The Mentz Psalter on 138 leaves, the first book printed with a date and names of the printers. This large and sumptuous volume, probably the most magnificently printed book known, is on pure vellum. Indeed, we believe no copies are known printed on paper. It measures 16½ by 12 inches.

613. PSALMS (Latin). *Begin.* Beatus vir qui nō abijt in cōsilio impioꝝ. [The Psalms, with the sacred canticles, creeds, prayers, and ecclesiastical Hymns.] *End.* PResens psalmoꝝ codex: venustate capitaliũ. decoratus. rubricationibusꝗ sufficienter distinctus. adinuencōne artificiosa imprimendi ac caracterizandi: absꝗ ulla calami exaracōne sic effigiatus. et ad laudem dei ac honorē sancti Jacobi est ɔsuat'. Per Joh'em fust civē magūtinũ. et Petrũ Schoifher de Gernssheym clericũ Anno dñi Millesimo cccc.lix. xxix. die mensis Augusti. Large Gothic letter. On vellum. [Mentz], 1459. Folio. *Lent by the Earl of Leicester.*
The second edition of the Mentz Psalter, without pagination, signatures or catchwords. 136 leaves, 23 lines in a page, with the plain chant noted throughout. The large ornamental capitals are printed in two colours, the smaller in red only. Nearly all the known copies of the first and second editions have minute variations, especially in the subscriptions, which appear to have been adapted to the particular church or monastery for which they were intended. This volume contains the earliest printed text of the Athanasian Creed.

614. BIBLE (Second Latin). *Begin.* [F]Rater ambro-/sius tua michi munuscula p/ferens. etc. [Genesis begins Fol. 6 verso, col. 1. at the top. I]n principio creauit deus celũ ꝛ terram. *End.* [Fol. 882 verso, col. 2. lin. 6] bis amen. Gothic letter. [Bamberg: Albert Pfister, 1460?] Folio. 15¾ by 11 inches. *Lent by Earl Spencer.*
Without title-page, pagination or signatures; 882 leaves printed in double columns, 36 lines to a full column. A copy in the Paris library has the rubrication dated 1461, proving that this Bible was printed prior to that date. But the cover of the Church Register of Bamberg being composed partly of waste leaves of this Bible, and the Register beginning with 21 March, 1460, it follows that these leaves were printed prior to this latter date.

615. BIBLE (Third Latin). *Begin.* [F]Rater ambrosius tua etc. [Genesis begins fol. 3 verso, towards the bottom of col. 2. I]N principio creauit deus celũ et tĕram. *End.* [Fol. 477 recto col. 1.] Gratia dñi nr̃i ih'u xp̃i cũ oñibs vobis amen. Gothic letter. 2 vols. [Strasburg: Jo. Mentelin, 1460 and 1461?] Folio. 15¾ by 11¾ inches. *Lent by Earl Spencer.*

Without title-page, pagination, or signatures; 477 leaves, printed in double columns, 49 lines to a full column. The rubrics and initials are in MS. throughout. A copy of this Bible is preserved in the library of Freiburg in Breisgau, with the rubrications of the volumes dated 1460 and 1461, ranking this edition as the third Latin Bible.

616. BIBLE (Fourth Latin). *Begin.* Incip̄ epl'a sci iheronimi ad paulinū p̄sbiterū : de om̄ib' diuine historie libris. [Fol. 4 recto, col. 1. lin. 7.] Expl'. plogus. Jncip̄ liber bresith quē no$ genesim dicimis. [Fol. 242 verso, col. 2. *end*] laudet dominū. Alleluia. [Vol. 2. *Begin.*] Epistola sancti ieronimi . . . . de libris salomonis. *End.* [Fol. 239 recto, col. 2.] Gr̄a dn̄i nr̄i ihesu cristi cū om̄ib' vobis amē. [followed by the Colophon in seven lines.] Pn̄s hoc opusculū Artificōsa adinuentione imp̄mendi seu caracterizandi. absq̄ calami exaracōn etc. 2 vols. Gothic letter. Per ioh'ez fust et Petrū schoiffher de gerns'heym, in ciuitate Maguntū. 1462. Folio. 16⅓ by 12¼ inches. Magnificent copy on pure vellum.
Lent by Earl Spencer.

Without title-page, pagination or signatures; vol. 1 has 242, and vol. 2, 239 leaves, printed in double columns, 48 lines to a full column. The first edition of the Bible having date, name of printer and place. From a collation of this with other copies on paper and vellum it appears that many of the leaves were reprinted, as for example, the first five in vol. 1, and fol. 90-96, 207-216, and 227-242; in vol. 2, fol. 1, 51 recto, 121-124, and 233-239, etc. This magnificent copy is richly illuminated throughout in gold and colours.

617. BIBLE (Fourth Latin). *Begin.* Incip̄ epl'a sci iheronimi ad paulinū p̄sbiterū, etc. Another copy printed on pure vellum. Per ioh'e$ fust et Petrū schoiffher de gerns'heym, in ciuitate Maguntū, 1462. Folio.
Lent by Earl Jersey.

This magnificent copy, a duplicate of No. 616, with some variations, is also splendidly illuminated throughout in brilliant colours, but the style of the illuminations of the two copies, though both exceedingly well done, is widely different.

618. BIBLE (Fourth Latin). *Begin.* Incip̄ epl'a iheronimi *etc.* Per ioh'e$ fust et Petrū schoiffher de gerns'heym, in ciuitate Maguntū, 1462. Folio. 16½ by 11½ inches. A superb copy printed on paper.
Lent by Henry Stevens, Esq.

This third copy is placed here as a good contrast with Nos. 616 and 617, printed on pure vellum. As many of the leaves have rough edges, they show that no copy on paper can be much taller or wider than this one, which is only a large fragment of this first Bible, with date, names of printers, and place.

619. PSALMS (Latin). Psalterium, etc. 126 leaves, twenty long lines in a full page, no signatures, catch-words or numbering. Large fine type resembling [Albert Pfister's, Bamberg, 1462?]. 4to.
Lent by the Bodleian Library.

620. BIBLE (First German). *Begin.* [B]Ruder Ambrosius der hat, etc. [Genesis commences fol. 4 recto, in col. 1. I]n dem anegang

geschieff got etc. *End.* [fol. 400 verso, col. 2.] Die genade vnsero herren ihc/su cristi sey mit vns allen Amen. [followed by five leaves containing the titles and arguments of the Psalms] *End.* in nach d'menig seiner grössung. Amen. [Strasburg: Joannes Mentelin, 1466?] Folio. 15½ by 11½ inches.
Lent by Her Majesty the Queen.

Without title-page, pagination or register, 405 printed leaves in double columns, 60 lines to a full column ; there is a blank leaf at the end of the Gospels. A magnificent copy, richly illuminated in gold and colours.

621. BIBLE (First German). *Begin.* [B]Ruder Ambrosius der hat, *etc.* Another very fine copy. [Strasburg: Joannes Mentelin, 1466?]. Folio. *Lent by Earl Spencer.*

405 printed leaves, 2 columns, 60 lines in a full column. This is also a splendid copy, beautifully illuminated in gold and colours, but in a style quite different from No. 620, lent by Her Majesty the Queen.

622. BIBLE (Second German). *Begin.* [B]Ruder Ambrosius d'hat vns bracht ein deine gab etc.[preceded by two leaves containing the table of rubrics. Genesis begins in col. 1 on the recto of fol. 6. A]N dē angang beschüff got den hymel vn̄ die erde. *End.* [fol. 400 verso, col. 2.] . . . Die genad vnsers herren jhesu cristi sey mit vns allen. Amen. [followed by five leaves containing the titles and arguments of the Psalms] *End.* in nach d'meing seiner grössung. Amen. [Strasburg: Heinrich Eggestyn, 1466?] Folio. 16 by 11½ inches. *Lent by Earl Spencer.*

Without title-page, pagination or register. 405 leaves printed in double columns, 60 lines to a full column ; foll. 2, 103, and 157 have the verso blank.

623. BIBLE (Latin). *Begin.* [F]Rater ambrosi' tua etc. [Genesis begins fol. 4 verso, col. 2, lin. 10. I]N principio creauit deus celū ⁊ terrā. *End.* [Fol. 631 verso, col. 2.] vobis amen. [Followed by a table of rubrics occupying four leaves.] Gothic letter. [Strasburg: H. Eggestein, 1468?] Folio. *Lent by Earl Spencer.*

Without title-page, pagination, or signatures ; 635 leaves, printed in double columns, 41 lines to a full column. The rubrics and initials are in MS. This is the first edition of the Latin Bible by Eggestein. This copy wants the four leaves of the table of rubrics.

624. BIBLE (Latin). *Begin.* [F]Rater ambrosius tua mi/chi munuscula perferens, etc. [Genesis begins fol. 4, col. 2. I]N principio creauit deus celū ⁊ terrā. *End.* [Fol. 493 verso, col. 2, lin. 7.] mini n̄r̄i ihesu cristi cū omnibus vobis amē. Gothic letter. [Strasburg: H. Eggestein, 1469?] Folio.
Lent by Earl Spencer.

Without title-page, pagination, or signatures ; 493 leaves, printed in double columns, 45 lines to a full column ; the verses of foll. 124 and 330 are blank ; the initials and rubrics are in MS. throughout. This edition is sometimes attributed to J. Baemler of Augsburg ; but the type is the same as that of the edition generally attributed to Eggestein. The book contains the same paper-mark as that which is undoubtedly Eggestein, and is one of the marks ascribed to him by Sotheby in the Typography of the fifteenth century.

625. BIBLE (Third German). *Begin.* Hie hept sich an die vorred oder die epistel des heiligen priesters sant Jeronimi zu paulinum von al en gotlichen historien d' brüder vnder der Biblē Das erst capitel. *End.* Die genade vnsers herrn ihesu cristi sei mit vns allen. Amen. Deo Gracjas *End.* Hie hebt sich an ein Register über die bücher d Biblen, etc. [Augsburg? J. Pflanzmann? or C. Fyner? Eslingen? 1470?] Folio. 15½ by 10¼ inches.
Lent by Earl Spencer.
Without title-page, signatures, or pagination. Printed in double columns, 54 lines in a full column.

626. BIBLE (Latin). *Begin.* [T]Abula omniū diuine scpture seu biblie libroɤ [occupying twenty-eight leaves. Fol. 29 begins] Incipit epl'a sācti iheronimi ad paulinū etc. [Fol. 33 recto, col. 2.] Explicit plogus. Incipit liber bresith quem nos genesim dicim'. *End.* [Fol. 724 recto, col. 2.] Explicit liber apocalipsis beati Johannis apostoli. Gothic letter. 2 vols. [Cologne: Ulric Zell, 1470?] Folio. 11½ by 8½ inches.
Lent by Earl Spencer.
Without title-page, pagination, or signatures; 724 leaves, printed in double columns, 42 lines to a full column.

627. BIBLE (Latin). Another edition. [Cologne: Ulrich Zell, 1470?]
Lent by the Bodleian Library.
Two columns of 42 lines to a full column.

628. BIBLE (Italian). *Begin.* [Fol. 7 recto.] Prologo. Qvi comincia la solemne Epistola di Sancto Hieronymo . . . . reportata per prologo sopra tutta la Biblia. [Foll. 1-6 are occupied by tables of the books of the old Testament, and a table of chapters to the first part. Fol. 11 verso.] Biblia in lingva volgare tradutta : lo primo libro secondo la lingva Greca etc. [Fol. 316 verso.] Finisse il l'salterio di David. [Part 2, fol. 1. *Begin.*] Prologo. di. San. Jeronimo. supra. ilibri. Disalomone. *End.* [Fol. 331 verso.] Qvivi finisse Lapocalipsis et e il fine del novo testamento M.CCCC.LXXI. In Kalende. de Octobrio. [followed by one leaf, containing on the recto : Tabula de testamento nouo.] Two parts. [Venice : N. Jenson,] 1471. Folio. 16¼ by 11 inches.
Lent by Earl Spencer.
Without title-page, pagination, or signatures; part 1 contains 316, and part 2, 332 leaves, printed in long lines, 50 lines to a full page ; the initial letters are either left blank, or printed in small characters throughout. Foll. 1 and 6 of part 1 are blank on the recto and fol. 5 on the verso. Foll. 206 and 232 of part 2 are blank on the verso.

629. BIBLE (Latin). [The Bible, *Lat.*, Edited by J. Andreas.] *Begin.* [Vol. 1, fol. 1, recto.] Io. An[dreæ] Episcopi Alerien ad Paulum II. Venetum Pon. Max. epistola [verso]. Sequitur tabula, etc. [Fol. 2, verso]. Paulo II. Veneto summo Pont. Mathias Palmerius fœlicitate. [Line 30.] Aristeas ad Philocratem fratrem per Mathiam Palmeriũ Pisanũ e Grẽco in Latinũ cõversus [Fol. 17, recto]. Incipit epistola sancti Hieronymi ad Paulinũ presbyterũ de omnibus divine historie libris [Fol. 20, recto, last line]. Incipit liber Bresith quem nos Genesin dicimus I. [*End.*] Finis Psalterii. [Vol. 2, fol. 1, recto.] Epistola sãcti Hieronymi p̃sbyteri ad Chromatiũ et Heliodorum Episcopos de Libris Salomonis [Colophon] Aspicis illustris lector quicunq̢ libellos/ Sicupis artificum nomina nosse : lege./ Aspera videbis cognomina Teutona : forsun/ Mitiget ars musis inscia uerba uirum./ Cõradus suuçynheym : Arnoldus panartzq̢ magistri/ Rome impresserunt talia multa simul/ Petrus cum fratro Francisco Maximus ambo/ Huic operi aptatam contribuere domum/ M.CCCC.LXXI. [On the recto of the following leaf], (Incipiunt interpretationes Hebraicorum Nominum). 2 vols. Rome : Sweynheym and Pannartz, 1471. Folio. 15½ by 11½ inches. *Lent by Earl Spencer.*

<small>Without title-page, register, catchwords, or pagination. In vol. 1 there are 279 leaves, and in vol. 2, 341. The preliminary matter in vol. 1 occupies 18 leaves, foll. 15 and 16 being left blank. The "Interpretationes Hebraicorum Nominum" at the end of vol. 2 occupy 62 leaves. The first Bible printed in Rome ; only 275 copies were printed.</small>

630. BIBLE (Latin). *Begin.* Incip̃ expl'a sci iheronimi ad paulinũ p̃sbiterũ oñibs divine historie libris. *End.* Pñs hoc opus p̃clarissimũ. Alma in urbe magũtina. . . . . Artificiosa quadam adinvencõe impremẽdi seu caracterizãdi absq̢ ulla calami exaracõne sic effigiatũ. et ad eusebiam dei industrie ẽcsũmatũ p Petrũ schoiffer de gernshez, etc. 2 vols. [Mentz]: Schoeffer, 1472. Folio. *Lent by the Bodleian Library.*

<small>Without pagination, register, or catchwords ; 471 leaves ; printed in double columns, 48 lines to a full column. This edition very closely resembles that of 1462, but they are not identical, as has been supposed.</small>

630*. BIBLE (Fourth German). 2 volumes, 408 and 104 leaves, in two columns of 57 lines in a full column. [Nuremberg : Sensenschmidt und Frissner, 1470-73. Folio.] *Lent by the Rev. Dr. Ginsburg.*

631. BIBLE (Fifth German). 2 vols., 553 leaves, 2 columns of 58 lines in a full column. Augsburg : [Gunther Zainer ?] 1473-75. Folio. *Lent by Earl Spencer.*

632. BIBLE (Latin). *Begin.* [F]Rater ābrosi' tua mi, etc. [Genesis begins fol. 3 verso in the middle of col 2. I]N principio creauit de' celū et terrā. *End.* [Fol. 436 verso, col. 1.] nostri ihesu cristi cū omnib' vob' amen. Gothic letter. [Basle : Berthold Rodt (?) and Bernard Richel, 1473 (?).] Folio.
Lent by the Rev. Dr. Ginsburg.

Without title-page, pagination, or signatures ; 436 leaves printed in double columns, 50 and 48 lines to a full column. The first part, as far as the end of the Psalms, fol. 220 verso, is printed in a type used by Berthold Rodt, and the remainder in one used by Bernard Richel. The initials and rubrics of the first part are in MS., while some of the initials in the second part are from wood engravings.

633. BIBLE (Latin). *Begin.* Incipit epistola sancti iheronimi ad paulinum etc. [being the commencement of the table of rubrics, etc., which occupies four leaves, the verso of the last blank. Fol. 5] *begin.* [F]Rater ambrosi' tua mi, etc. [Genesis begins fol. 8 recto, in the middle of col. 2. I]N principio creauit deus celum et terrā. *End.* [Fol. 537 recto, col. 1.] Gra-/cia dñi nr̄i ih'u xp̄i cū omibs vobis amen. Gothic letter. [Basle : Berthold Rodt (?), 1474 (?)]. Folio. *Lent by the Rev. Dr. Ginsburg.*

Without title-page, pagination, or signatures ; 537 leaves, printed in double columns, 47 lines to a full column. The rubrics and initials are in MS. throughout.

634. BIBLE (Latin). *Begin.* Incipit epistola sancti iheronimi ad pauli-/num presbiterum de omnibus divine historie libris. [Fol. 3 verso, col. 2, lin. 11 from the bottom.] Incipit liber bresich q̄; nos genesim dicim'. *End.* [Fol. 461 verso, col. 1] mini nostri ihesu cristi cum omnib' vob' amen. Et sic est finis. [Fol. 462 recto.] VEnerabili viro do-/mino. Jacobo de ysenaco. Menardus, etc. [A general notice of the Bible, ending fol. 465 verso, col. 2, with seven Latin verses, *begin*] Qui memor esse cupit librorum bibliotece. [Fol. 466 recto]. Incipit tabula canonum, etc. Gothic letter. [Basle : Bernard Richel, 1474 (?).] Folio.
Lent by Henry White, Esq.

Without title-page, pagination, or signatures ; 460 leaves, printed in double columns, 48 lines to a full column. The initials are from wood engravings.

635. BIBLE (Sixth German). *Begin.* [Fol. 1.] ¶ Hie höbet an die Epistel des heyligen priesters sant Jheronimi, etc. [preceded by one leaf, containing the register of the books on the verso. Fol. v. recto, col. 1.] ¶ Eyn end hat die vorred vnd hebet an das būch Presith oder Genesis, etc. *End.* [Fol. cx.] ¶ Diss durchleūchtigost werck der gantzen heyligen geschrifft. genandt die Bibel fūr all ander vorgedrucket teutsch biblen. lauterer. klārer.

vnnd warer. .... hat hie ein ende, etc. Gothic letter. Augspurg: [Gunther Zainer, 1475 (?)] Folio.
Lent by Henry J. Atkinson, Esq.

Without title-page or register; numeration—Old Testament, i-ccccxxj; New Testament, i-cx. Printed in double columns, 58 and 59 lines to a full column. The first Bible with the leaves folioed (?)

636. BIBLE (Sixth German). Another copy, very fine, measuring 18½ by 13 inches. [Gunther Zainer, 1475?] Folio.
Lent by Earl Spencer.

637. BIBLE (Latin). *Begin.* Incip epl'a scī hieronimi ad paulinū p̄sbiteȝ de oib̵s divine historie libris. [Fol. 4 recto, col. 1, lin. 7.] Expt plogus. Incipit liber bhresit quē nos genesim dicimus. *End.* Opus veteris nouiq̨ testamēti. Impressum ad laudez & gloriam sancte ac indiuidue trinitatis, etc. Gothic letter. Per Anthoniū Coberger, in regia ciuitate Nurmbergēn, 1475. Folio.
Lent by Earl Spencer.

Without title-page, pagination, or signatures; 481 leaves printed in double columns, 48 lines to a full column. Koberger in 26 years printed 13 editions of the Bible, of which this is the first.

638. BIBLE (Latin). Another copy. A. Coberger. Nuremberg, 1475. Folio.
Lent by Henry J. Atkinson, Esq.

639. BIBLE (Latin). *Begin.* Prologus in Genesim. Incipit epl'a sancti Hieronymi, etc. [Fol. 3 verso, col. 1, at the bottom.] Explicit p̄fatio. Incipit liber Genesis qui dicīt hebraice bresith. *End.* [Fol. 421 verso, col. 2.] Explicit Biblia impressa Venetijs, etc. [Fol. 422 recto.] Incipiūt interp̄tatiōes hebraicorū nominū, etc. Gothic letter. p Frāciscū de hailbrun & Nicolaū de frankfordia socios, Venetijs, 1475. Small folio. *Lent by Earl Spencer.*

Without title-page, pagination, or signatures; 454 leaves printed in double columns (except the table of Hebrew names, which has three columns), 51 lines to a full column. The initials are in MS, and the verso of the last leaf is blank. This is the first Latin Bible printed at Venice.

640. BIBLE (Latin). *Begin.* Quia vestigia seq̄mur Joann. An. Ep̄i Aleriensis quē nihil reliq̄sse cōperium' quod ulteriori emendatione egeat, preter pauxilla q̄ vicio compositorum litterar, viciata sunt. Ideoq̨ epistolā quā ip̄e pposuit omittere nolium, ne cuj' doctrinā imitamur, ejus ədignā laudē videamur supprimere. Joann[is] An[dreæ] Episcopi Alerien[sis] ad Paulū secūdum Venetum Pon. Max. epistola. (Aristeas ad Philocratē fratrem per M. Palmeriū e Greco in Latinum conversus. Interp̄tationes hebrai-

corum nominū.) Gothic letter. 2 vols. A. Frisner et J. Sensenschmit ī nuremberga, 1475. Folio. *Lent by Earl Spencer.*

Without title-page, register, or pagination ; printed in double columns, 60 lines to a full column. The preliminary matter, including the prefaces of Saint Jerome, occupies 11 leaves. The " Interpretationes," etc., are placed at the end, after the imprint. Splendid copy on large paper, measuring 19 by 13 inches.

641. BIBLE (Latin). *Begin.* [F]Rater ambrosius tua mihi munuscula perferes : etc. [Fol. 3 recto, col. 1, lin. 8 from the bottom] Explicit p̄fatio Incip̄. Liber Genesis qui dicit' hebraice bresith. [Fol. 284 verso, col. 2. *End.*] Vet' testamētū a religiosis uiris ac prudentissimis correctū atq̷ p me iohāne petrū d'ferratis cremonēsē placētic imp̄ssus. Anno dn̄i Mcccc.lxx quinto felicit' explicit. [Fol. 285 recto, col. 1. *Begin.*] Incipit epistloa sancti hieronimi . . . sup. libro quatuor euāge-/lioɋ [Fol. 357 verso, col. 2. *End.*] Explicit liber actuum apostoloɋ cum reli- quis noui libris testamenti etc. *End.* [Fol. 391 recto, col. 2.] Biblie uocabuloɋ interpretationes expliciūt. Gothic letter. p iohāne petrū d' ferratis, placētie, 1475. 4to. *Lent by Earl Spencer.*

Without title-page, pagination, or signatures ; 391 leaves, printed in double columns, 60 lines to a full column. This is said to be the first printed book at Placentia, and is believed to be the first Bible printed in quarto.

642. BIBLE (Latin). *Begin.* [F]Rater Ambrosi' tua mihi munus-/cula perferens : etc. [Genesis begins fol. 3 verso, col. 1. lin. 14 from the bottom—I]N principio creauit de' celum & tr'ā. *End.* [Fol. 425 recto, col. 1.] domini nostri ihesu xp̄i cū om̄ibs vobis amē. [Strasburg ? 1475 ?] Folio. *Lent by the Rev. Dr. Ginsburg.*

Without title-page, pagination, or signatures ; 425 leaves, printed in double columns, 56 lines to a full column ; the initials and rubrics are in MS. throughout ; fol. 7 verso, at the bottom of col. 2 two lines omitted in printing are supplied in MS. and fol. 300 verso, one line is similarly supplied at the bottom of col. 2. The versos of foll. 117 and 213 are blank.

643. BIBLE (Latin). *Begin.* [Sig. A i.] Prologus in Genesim. Feliciter incipit. Incipit epl'a sancti Hierony-/mi etc. [preceded by one leaf, containing on the verso : an epistle to Thomas Taqui, from Blasius Romerus, with the answer of the former.—Sig. A iii verso, col. 1.] Explicit p̄fatio. Incipit liber genesis qui dicit' hebraice bresith. [eighth leaf of sig. tt. verso]. Explicit Biblia. Incipiūt interp̄tationes he-/braicorū nominū, etc. *End.* Editum opus & emēdatū accuratissime ac deligēter, etc. Gothic letter. Impressit M. Morauus . . . In urbe Neapoli, 1476. Folio. Printed on vellum. *Lent by Earl Spencer.*

Without title-page or pagination ; sign. A—z & aa—ll, lm, mm—yy, and z. Printed in double columns, except the table of names, which is in three columns. Query, is not this the first Bible with printer's signatures ?

644. BIBLE (Latin). *Begin.* [Sig. A 2.] Prologus. Incipit epl'a sācti Hieronymi ad Paulinū etc. [Genesis begins sig. A 5.] Incipit liber genesis q dicitur hebraice bresith. *End.* Biblia impressa Venetijs opera atq̄ impensa Nicolai Jenson Gallici etc. (interpretationes hebraicorū nominum etc.) Gothic letter. Printed on vellum. Venetijs: N. Jenson, 1476. Folio.
Lent by Earl Spencer.
Without title-page or pagination; sig. a 2—z. & 3, 4, A—X. The first leaf of sig. A and the last of sig. II are blank; at the end is a table of the register on one page in the copies on paper, but generally wanting like this one when printed on vellum. This copy, printed on the thinnest and purest vellum, is splendidly illuminated with gold and colours, including miniatures of high art.

645. BIBLE (Latin). Another copy. Same edition as No. 644, but printed on paper. Venetiis: Nicolas Jenson, 1476. Small folio.
Lent by Henry White, Esq.
This copy has the rare end leaf containing the register. It is still a question whether this, No. 646, the Naples or the Paris Bible, all of 1476, was the first Bible with printer's signatures. They all appeared with signatures the same year.

645*. BIBLE (Latin). *Begin.* Epistola beati hieronymi ad paulinū p̄sby-terū de ōnibus diuine hystorie libris incipit. [Fol. 4 recto, col. 2. lin. 7.] Incipit liber Bresith. quē nos Genesim dicimus. *End.* [Fol. 482 recto, col. 2]. Finit liber apocalipsis beati iohannis apl'i. [followed by twenty Latin verses beginning:]
Me duce carpe viam! qui celū ascendere gestis.
[and ending]
Jam tribus vndecimus lustris francos Ludouicus.
Rexerat! vlricus martinus itemq̄ michael.
Orti teutonia, hanc mihi composuere figurā.
Parisij arte sua-me correctā vigilanter.
Venalem in vico iacobi sol aureus offert.
[Fol. 483. sig. A. j.] Interpretationes hebraicorum nominū feliciter incipiunt. Gothic letter. Ulricus [Gering] Martinus [Crantz] Michael [Friburger]. Parisij, [1476]. Folio. 14¼ by 11 inches.
Lent by Earl Spencer.
Without title-page or pagination; sign. to the table of names only, A—C. 509 leaves, printed (except the table of names) in double columns, 48 lines to a full column; the table of names is printed in treble columns, 60 lines to a full column. The initials are printed in small characters, the verso of fol. 482 is blank. This is the first Bible printed in Paris.

646. BIBLE (Latin). *Begin.* [sig. A 2.] Prologus in bibliam—Incipit epl'a sancti Hieronymi ad Paulinū etc. [Sig. A 4 verso, col. 2 at the bottom.] Explicit p̄fatio. Incipit liber Genesis qui dicit hebraice bresith. *End.* Explicit biblia ip̄ressa Venetijs etc. (interp̄ta-

tiones hebraicorū nominū etc. Gothic letter. p Frācis̄cū de hailbrun ꝟ Nicolaū d'frankfordia socios, Venetijs, 1476. Folio.
Lent by Henry White, Esq.
Without title-page or pagination; sign. A 2—y, j, 2—18. A—C. Printed in double columns, 51 lines in a full column. The first Bible with a date having printers' signatures? see Nos. 643, 645, 645*.
Another copy, *Lent by Henry J. Atkinson, Esq.*

647. BIBLE (Latin). Aurea Biblia. 1476. Folio.
Lent by Henry White, Esq.

648. BIBLE (Seventh German). *Begin* [Fol. 1, recto]. Die epistel Iheronimi zu Paulinum. *End.* [Fol. 332 recto] Diss durchleicht igest werck d gantz en heyligen geschrift genandt die bibel ... hat hie eyn ende. Augspurg: [Gunther Zainer], 1477. Folio. 2 vols. 321 & 332 leaves. *Lent by Earl Spencer.*
Without title-page, register, and catchword. Printed in double columns, 51 lines to a full page. The first German Bible with a date.

649. BIBLE (Italian). [The Holy Bible, with the history of the Septuagint by Aristeas, translated into Italian by N. de Malermi.] Pt. 1. *Begin.* Registro de la prima parte de la Biblia. Pt. 2. *Begin.* Registro del secondo libro. 2 pt. Venetia: Antonio Bolognese, 1477. Folio. *Lent by Henry White, Esq.*
Printed in double columns. Each part has a distinct register, without title-page or pagination. Aristeas is at the end of part 1: part 2 commences with the Proverbs.
Another copy, *Lent by the Bodleian Library.*

650. BIBLE (Latin). *Begin.* Incipit epl'a sancti hieronimi ad paulinū etc. [Fol. 3 verso, col. 3. lin. 8 from the bottom]. Incipit liber bresith quem nos genesim dicimus. *End.* [Fol. 461 verso, col. 2. lin. 3.] Finit liber apocalipṣ beati iohānis apl'i. followed by the Colophon. Fol. 462 recto. *Begin.* V]Enēabili viro dño iacobo de ysenaco. Menard' solo noie monachus etc. [A general notice of the Bible, followed by the Canons of Eusebius: the whole occupying six leaves.] Gothic letter. p Antonium Coburger. In regia ciuitate Nurnbergñ, 1477. Folio.
Lent by the Rev. Dr. Ginsburg.
Without title-page, pagination, or signatures; 467 leaves printed in double columns, 51 lines to a full column.

651. BIBLE (Latin). *Begin.* Epistola. Incipit epistola sācti hieronimi ad paulinū presbiteꝛ de oib' diuine historie libris. [Genesis begins fol. 3 verso, col. 1.] Incipit liber bresich q̄ nos genesim dici'. *End.* [Fol. 390 recto, col. 1] omibs vob amen.—Et sic est finis. [same page, col. 2—V]enerabili viro dño. Jacobo de ysenaco. Menard' solo no-miē monach' etc. [A general notice of the Bible, extending to the verso of fol. 393, col. 1, and

ending with seven verses. *Begin.*] Qui memor esse cupit libroꝗ bibliotece [and *End.*] credentes verbis sacris saluare paratus I ☙A3. Gothic letter. [Nuremberg? Jo. Sensenschmidt?], 1476. Folio.
Lent by the Rev. Dr. Ginsburg.

Without title-page, pagination, or signatures, 393 leaves printed in double columns, 57 lines to a full column; between fol. 17 and 18 half a leaf is inserted with part of a single column printed on the verso, to supply an omission at the end of fol. 18, col. 2.

652. NEW TESTAMENT (French). *Begin.* Cy commence la table du nouuau testament. *End.* Cy finist lapocalipse et samblablement le nouueau testament [translated by G. des Moulins] veu et corrige par venerables personnes frēs iullien macho et pierre sarget [sic. *i.e.* Farget.] etc. Bartholemieu buyer, lion, [1477?] 4to.
Lent by Earl Spencer.

Without title-page or pagination, sign. a—c; a—t and A—I. 299 leaves printed in long lines, 28 lines to a full page, and two blank leaves, one at the end of the table and another at the end of the book. The first edition of the New Testament in French.

653. OLD TESTAMENT (First Dutch). *Begin.* Hier beghīt dat prologus vāder biblē des ouersetters te duytsche vtē latine. [Fol. 2, recto, I.]Nden beghin sciep god hemel ēn aerde, etc. *End.* Hier eyndt de prophect malachias, etc. Jacob iacobs soen ēn Mauritius Yemants Zoen van middelborch. Delf, 1477. Small folio. 2 volumes. *Lent by Earl Spencer.*

The Book of Psalms was omitted in this edition, but appeared separately three years later. Without title-page, register, catchwords, or pagination; printed in double columns, 38 lines to a full column. This is the first edition of the Old Testament in the Dutch language. See No. 669.

654. OLD TESTAMENT (First Dutch). Hier beghīt dat prologus, *etc.* Another fine large copy. Jacob iacobs soen ēn Mauritius Yemants Zoen van Middelborch, Delf, 1477. 2 vols. Small folio.
Lent by the Dutch Church in Austin Friars.

655. BIBLE (Latin). *Begin.* [Sig. A 2.] Prologus in bibliam. Incipit epistola sancti Hieronymi etc. [Genesis begins Sig. A 4 verso, col. 2 at the top. I]N princi-pio crea-uit deus celū & terrā. (interp̄tationes hebraicoꝗ nominū etc.] Gothic letter. per Leonardum vuild de Ratisbona expensis Nicolai de franckfordia, Venetijs, 1478. Folio. *Lent by the Rev. Dr. Ginsburg.*

Without title-page or pagination; Sign. A 2—y, j, 2—i S, A—C; at the end is a table of the register on one page.

656. BIBLE (Latin). *Begin.* [Fol. A 2] Prologus in bibliam. Incipit epl̄a sancti Hieronymi ad Paulinū p̄brem d' oı̄b' dine historic

libris. *End.* Biblia impressa Venetiis, etc. (Interp̄tationes hebraicorū nominū sedm ordinem alphabeti). Gothic letter. Opera atq̄ impēsa T. de Reynsburch ⁊ Reynaldi de Novimagio. Venetiis, 1478. Folio. *Lent by the Rev. Dr. Ginsburg.*

<small>Without title-page or pagination ; the " Interp̄tationes hebraicorū nominū " are at the end after the imprint.</small>

657. BIBLE (Latin). *Begin.* Incipit epla sancti Hieronimi ad Paulinū presbiteȝ de oīb' diuine historie libris. *End.* Anno incarnatōnis dñice. Millesimo-quadringentesimoseptuagesimo octavo Mai v̄o Kl' octauo decimo. Q̄ȝ insigne veteris nouiq̄ testamenti opus. Cum canonibs euāgelistarumq̄ concordantiis, etc. Gothic letter. Per Antoniū Coburger, In oppido Nurnbergñ. Mai vo Kl. 18. 1478. Folio. *Lent by the Rev. Dr. Ginsburg.*

<small>Without title-page or register. Preceding the Epistle of Saint Jerome is a leaf containing a table of the books ; the canons are placed after the imprint and have no pagination. This is Coberger's third Latin edition.</small>

658. BIBLE (Latin). *Begin.* [Fol. j.] Incipit epl'a sancti Hieronimi ad Paulinū, etc. [preceded by one leaf containing an index of the books on the verso.—Genesis begins fol. iiij.] Liber Genesis. *End.* [Fol. ccclxj.] . . . . insigne veteris nouiq̄ testamenti opus. cum canonibs euāgelistarumq̄ concordantijs . . . . finit feliciter. [Then follows : V]enerabili viro domino Jacobo de ysenaco. Menard' . . monachus . . Rogatus nuper a vobis . . . q̄tenus aliquā generalem 't ɔpediosam libroȝ biblie ɔscriberem notitia etc. [and afterwards] Incipit tabula canonū, etc. Gothic letter. Per Antoniū Coburger, in oppido Nurnbergñ. IV. Id. Nov. 1478. Folio.
Lent by the Rev. Dr. Ginsburg.

<small>The collation of this, Coberger's fourth Latin edition, is the same as the third, but it is a distinct edition.</small>

659. NEW Testament (Latin). Signature in eights. 2 cols. 1478 ? 8vo. *Lent by the Bodleian Library.*

660. BIBLE (Latin). *Begin.* [Sig. A 2] Incipit epistola beati Hieronymi ad Paulinum presbyterum de omnibus divine historie libris. *End.* " Fontibus ex Grecis hebreorum q̄ 93 libris." " Emendata satis et decorata simul. / Biblia sum p̄ns supos ego testor et astra. / Est imp̄ssa nec in arbe mihi similis. / Singula q̄ loca cū concordantib' extāt. / Orthographia simul q̄; bene p̄ssa manet." Gothic letter. [1479?] Folio. *Lent by the Rev. Dr. Ginsburg.*

<small>Without title-page or pagination. This is supposed to be the first of the editions distinguished by the appellation " Fontibus ex Græcis," in which case it is of the date of 1479, or still earlier.</small>

661. BIBLE (Latin). *Begin.* Incipit epl'a Hieronimi ad Paulinū presbite*r* de oĩbs diuine historie libris. *End.* Anno īcarnatois dominice. Millesimo-qdri gē tesimo septuagesimonono sexto die augusti. I*r* īsigne veteris nouiq̨ testamēti op' cū canonibs euāgelistarūq̨ *r* cordātiis, etc. (Interpretationes Hebraicorum nominum.) Gothic letter. Per Antoniuz Coburger, In oppido. Nurnbergñ, 1479. Folio. *Lent by the Rev. Dr. Ginsburg.*
    Without title-page or register. Printed in double columns, 51 lines to a full column. The "Canons" and "Interpretations" are without pagination. This is Coberger's fifth Latin Bible.

662. BIBLE (Latin). *Begin.* [Sig. A 2.] Prologus. Incipit epl'a Hieronymi ad paulinum, etc. [Genesis begins sig. A 5.] Incipit liber genesis qui dicit hebraice bresith. *End.* Biblia īpressa Venetiis, etc. [Then follows, sig. Q] Incipiunt interpretationes hebraico*r* nominum, etc. [and on the last leaf] Registrum biblic. Gothic letter. Opera ... Venetus: Nicolai Jenson, 1479. Folio.
    Lent by the British and Foreign Bible Society.
    Without title-page or pagination, signatures A—Z, *r*, ɔ, *2/*. A—V.

663. BIBLE (Eighth German). *End.* Diss durchleuchtigest werck d'gancẓen heiligē geschrifft. genannt die Bibel für all ander vorgedruckt teutsch Bibeln. lauterer. klärer. vnd warer nach rechtem gemeynē teutsch dañ vorgedruckt. hat hye ein ende, etc. 2 Th. Augspurg: Anthoni Sorg, 1480. Folio. *Lent by the Rev. Dr. Ginsburg.*
    Without title-page or signatures; each Th. is preceded by a register or index.

664. BIBLE (First German, low). *Begin.* [D] Ic born der ewyger wijsheyt dat wort gœdes i dē hogestē sprekz: etc. [Fol. 4 recto.] (Hijr beghynt Genesis dat erste boeck der vijf boeckere Moysi, etc.) *End.* Een salich ende hefft dat boek der hemelikē apenbaringe. sent Johans des ewangelistē .. vñ dar mede de gantse bybel. dar van gade dank unde loff sy in ewicheyt. Amen. [Cologne, 1480?] Folio. *Lent by the Rev. Dr. Ginsburg.*
    Printed in double columns, without title-page, register, or pagination; 57 lines to a full column.

665. BIBLE (Latin). *Begin.* Prologus in bibliam. Incipit epistola sancti Hieronymi ad Paulinum presbyterum: de omnibus diuine historie libris. (interpretatioēs hebraicorū nominū, etc.) Gothic letter. Venetijs: per Franciscum de hailbrun, 1480. 4to.
    Lent by the Bodleian Library.
    Without title-page or pagination. Signatures a—y, j, z. 7, 4-18, A—D.

666. PSALMS (Greek and Latin). *Begin.* [Fol. 3, recto] ΔΑΥΙΔ ΠΡΟΦΗΤΟΥ ΚΑΙ ΒΑϹΙΛΕΩϹ ΜΕΛΟϹ. David prophetæ et regis melos. [Preceded by Ioannes [Crestonus] placentinus

Monachus Reuerēdo patri & domino. D. Ludouico Donato Episcopo Bergomensi, S. p. d. commencing on the verso of fol. 1.] *End.* ποδας ἡμῶν εἰς ὁδὸν εἰρηνης. pedes nostrum in uiam pacis [Edited by J. Crestonus]. Mediolani, 1481. Folio. 11¼ by 8¼ inches. *Lent by Earl Spencer.*

<small>Eighty-one leaves, sig. a i—z iii. This is the first of the editions printed at Milan in 1481, and is known by its colophon : " Impressum Mediolani anno Mcccc. Lxxxi. die. xx. Septembris." It is printed in double columns, containing 28 and 29 lines in a full column. No pagination or catchwords.</small>

667. BIBLE (Latin). *Begin.* Incipit epl'a sancti Hieronimi ad Paulinu presbitc⁊ de oïbs diuine historie libris. *End.* Anno incarnationis dūice. Millesimoquadringentesimooctuagesimo. Mai vero Kl' octauo decimo. Q⁊ insigne veteris nouiq̄ testamenti opus. cum canonib' euangelistarumq̄ concordantiis, etc. Per Antoniuz Coburger, In oppido Nurnbergn̄, 1480. Folio.
Lent by the Rev. Dr. Ginsburg.

<small>Without title-page or register. Preceding the epistle of Saint Jerome is a leaf containing a table of the books ; the canons are placed after the imprint, and have no pagination. This is Coburger's sixth Latin edition.</small>

668. BIBLE (Latin). [The Holy B. in Latin, according to the Vulgate translation, with the Glossa Ordinaria of Walafridus Strabo, and the Glossa interlinearis of Anselmus Scholasticus.] *Begin.* Epistola beati Hieronimi presbiteri ad Paulinum presbiterū ... incipit. [Fol. 3 verso :] Glossa ordinaria incipit [Fol. 5 recto :] [I]N pricipio creauit de' celum ⁊ terrā, etc. Gothic letter. 4 vols. [Venice? 1480?] Folio. *Lent by the Sion College Library.*

<small>A manuscript note in Latin on the cover of vol. I. says that in 1480 this book belonged to Giles de Bresc, Rector of S. Mary the Virgin outside Malines, and that he bought it for 26 florins.</small>

669. PSALMS (Dutch). 278 leaves, 17 lines. *End.* Hier eyndet die duytsch Souter end es gheprent te Delf, 1480. 16mo.
Lent by the Bodleian Library.

<small>278 leaves, 17 lines. Signatures a b c d e f g h i k l m n o p q r ⁊ ſ s t v w x y z A B C D E F G H in eights and I in 6 leaves, in all 35 sheets, or 278 leaves. This Bodleian copy has a separate printed title-page, added apparently some few years later. This little volume, with No. 653, completes the first Old Testament in Dutch.</small>

670. BIBLE (Latin). *Begin.* Incipit epistola sancti Hieronymi ad ... divine historie libris. Sig. a 5 recto, col. 2.] In principio creavit de' ... t'rā, etc. (Iterp̄tatiões hebraicorū nominū s'm ordinem alphabeti.) Gothic letter. 1481. Folio.
Lent by Henry J. Atkinson, Esq.

<small>Without title-page, pagination, or catchwords. Sig. a—y, A—Y, 1-13, 570 leaves, printed in double columns, 47 lines to a full column. This is one of the " Fontibus ex Græcis" editions. The Colophon, which is at the end of the Apocalypse, is followed by the Rubric of the Proper Lessons and the "Interpretationes."</small>

H

680. BIBLE (Latin). With Commentaries of De Lyra. 2 vols. Nurnbergñ: Anthonius Coberger, 1481. Folio.
Lent by Matthew Ridgway, Esq.

681. BIBLE (Latin). *Begin.* Incipit epistola sancti Hieronym ad Paulinū, etc. [Sig. a 5 recto, col. 2] i N principio creavit de' celū ī trā, etc. (Iterp̄tatioes hebraicorū nominū s'm ordinem alphabete.) Gothic letter. 1481. Folio.
Lent by Henry J. Atkinson, Esq.

> Without title-page, pagination, or catchwords. Sig. a—y, A—V, 1-13, 570 leaves, printed in double columns, 47 lines to a full column. This is one of the "Fontibus ex Græcis" editions. The colophon, which is at the end of the Apocalypse, is followed by the Rubric of the Proper Lessons, and the "Interpretationes."

682. PENTATEUCH (Hebrew). חומש עם תרבום אונקלוס ופיורש רשי. *Begin.* בראשית. On vellum. [Bologna: Abraham ben Chayim de' Tintori, 1482.] Folio. *Lent by Earl Spencer.*
> First edition of the Pentateuch in Hebrew.

683. VORAGINE (James de). The Golden Legende. [*Colophon*] Thus endeth the legende named/ in latyn legenda aurea, that is to saye/ in englysshe the golden legende, For/ lyke as golde passeth in valewe alle/ other metalles, so thys legende excedeth/ alle other bookes, wherin ben contey-/ned alle the hygh and grete festys of/ our lord, the festys of our blessyd la/dy, the lyues passyons and myracles/ of many other sayntes, and other hys-/toryes and actes, as al allonge here/ afore is made mencyon, whiche werke/ I haue accomplisshed at the commaundemente and requeste of the noble and/ puyssaunte erle, and my special good/ lord Wyllyam erle of arondel, ī haue/ fynysshed it at Westmestre the twenty/ day of nouembre, the yere of our lord/ M, CCCC, lxxxiij, ī the fyrst yere/ of the reygne of Kyng Rychard the/ thyrd **By me Wyllyam Caxton.** Folio.
Lent by the Rev. Dr. Gott.

> First edition. Four preliminary leaves, comprising the Prologue and two tables; text in double columns, folioed 1 to cccexliij.
> This book is, we think, fairly placed among Bibles, because it contains a translation into English of nearly the whole of the Pentateuch and a great part of the Gospels, and hence must have been read extensively by the people, or to the people, long before the Reformation, or the days of Tyndale and Coverdale. Historians of the English Bible appear to have overlooked the numerous editions of this work. It was no doubt read in churches, and though the text is mixed with much priestly gloss and dross, it nevertheless contains, in almost a literal translation, a great portion of the Bible; and it became thus one of the principal instruments in preparing the way for the Reformation. The people demanded the Scriptures in a purer form. The modifications and changes of the text and form of the Golden Legend is a theme worthy the bibliographer.

The future historian of our dear old English Bible should not fail to sift the matter well. The annexed passage is copied line for line and verbatim from folio 37 verso, 2nd column. This may take precedence of the Genevan Version in being called the "Breeches Bible," as that was not published till 1560, more than three quarters of a century later.

And thus they knewe then that they were naked/ And they toke figge leuis and sewed them togyder for to couere theyr membres in maner of Breechis/

684. BIBLE (Ninth German). *Begin.* Das erst Blat. Hie hebet an die Epistel des heyligen priesters sant Jheronimi etc. [fol. v. recto] Hie hebt sich an. Genesis etc. *End.* [fol. cccclxxxiij. verso.] Disz durchleuchtigist werck der gantzen heyligen geschrifft. genant dy bibel für all and' vorgetrücket teutsch biblē. lauterer. clarer vnd warer nach rechter gemeyner teutsch ... gegē dem lateynischen text gerechtuertigt ... mit vberschrifften ... Vñ mit schonen figuren ... hat hie ein ende. etc. Gothic letter. Nurenberg: durch anthonium Koburger, 1483. Folio. 15½ by 11½ inches. *Lent by Henry J. Atkinson, Esq.*

Without title-page or signatures; printed in double columns, 50 lines in a full column. The first German Bible printed at Nuremberg. With many extraordinary woodcuts.
Another copy, *Lent by the British and Foreign Bible Society.*

685. BIBLE (Ninth German). *Begins.* Das erst Blat. Hie hebet an die Epistel, *etc.* Another copy. Very fine. *Lent by Earl Spencer.*

686. BIBLE (Latin). *Begin.* [Fol. a. 2.] Incipit epistola beati Hieronymi ad Paulinum presbyterum de omnibus divine hystorie libris. *End.* Exactum est inclyta in urbe venetia⁊ sacro sanctum biblie volumen &c. (F. Moncliensis a genua in sacrosanctam ac sacratissimā bibliā Epl'a. Interpretaciones nominū hebraicorum.) Gothic letter. Caracteribus Magistri Johanis dicti magni. Herbort de Siligenstat alemani, in urbe venetia⁊, 1483. Folio. *Lent by Henry White, Esq.*

Without title-page or pagination; the epistle of Franciscus Moncliensis is on the verso of the first leaf, and the "Interpretaciones nominū hebraicorum" are at the end, after the colophon.

687. BIBLE (French). In French paraphrase by Guyard de Moulins, or Comestor, 1487. Folio, with very many curious woodcuts. *Lent by the British and Foreign Bible Society.*

688. BIBLE (Italian). La Biblia en lingua Volgare (per Nicolo di Mallermi). *End.* Venetia: per Joan. Rosso Vercellese, 1487. Folio. *Lent by Henry White, Esq.*

689. BIBLE (Latin). Venetiis : per Georgium rauabenis, 1487. 4to.
Lent by Francis Fry, Esq.
This first Bible with a separate title-page is printed in two columns of 52 lines each.

690. BIBLE (First Bohemian). [The Holy Bible in Bohemian.] *Begin.* Poežinagi Prwnie Knihy Moyziessowy. Capitola I. etc. ❡ Mjestie Starem Pražskem, 1488. Folio. *Lent by Earl Spencer.*
Printed in double columns, without numerals or catchwords, 47 lines to a full page ; register a. iii—z. v. A—Z, v. A. A.—C. C. iiii. a. a.—m. m. iiii. At the end is a register of the Epistles and Gospels, printed alternately red and black, signatures i—iiii.

691. BIBLE (First Hebrew). [תורה נביאים וכתובים.] *Begin.* [fol. 1 verso] בראשית. Editio Princeps. [Soncino : Abraham ben Chayin de' Tintori, 1488.] Folio. *Lent by the Rev. Dr. Ginsburg.*
380 leaves without pagination, printed in double columns, 30 lines to a full page. The Pentateuch is followed by the Five Rolls, which have a separate register, as also the Prophets and the Hagiographa. De Rossi, Ann. Sec. XV. p. 54. This is the first complete edition of the Bible. The whole Bible had been printed previously in portions. viz., the Pentateuch, 1482, the Former Prophets, 1485, the later Prophets, 1486, and the Hagiographa, 1487.

692. BIBLE (12th German). 2 vols., 799 leaves, 2 columns, 48 lines, woodcuts. Augspurg : Hen. Schonsperger, 1490. Folio.
Lent by the Bodleian Library.

693. BIBLE Picture Book (Dutch). Boeck van Ihesus Leven. Woodcuts. Zwolle : Peter van Os Breda, 1490. Folio.
Lent by Henry J. Atkinson, Esq.

694. BIBLE (Second German Low). 2 vols., 2 columns, 66 lines in a full column. With large woodcuts. Lubec, 1491. Folio.
Lent by Earl Spencer.

695. BIBLE (Latin). Biblia. (Epistola beati Hieronymi . . . de omnib' divine historie libris. . . Translatores biblie. Epistole et Evangelia Per anni circulum Interp̄tatiões hebriaco:/ noūm, etc.] Gothic letter. Impensis . . . Nicolai Keslers, civis Basilicū [Basle], 1491. Folio. *Lent by Henry J. Atkinson, Esq.*
Without pagination. Sig. a—z, t, & E, A—Z, Aa—G.g., a—c. Printed in double columns, 56 lines to a full column. The Colophon, which is on the verso of sig. F. f. 7, is followed by the " Translatores biblie, etc."

696. BIBLE (Latin). Biblia integra, summata ; distincta : supēmedatā utriusq̧ testameti reordātus illustrata. [Fol. a 2 recto :] Incipit epistola beati Hieronymi ad Paulinū, &c. [New Test. Fol. 1 recto.] Incipit epistola beati Hieronymi ad Damasum, &c. [Fol.

A. 1 recto.] Interpretationes Nominū Hebraico. Gothic letter. Per Johanem froben de Hammelburck, Basilee, 1491. 8vo.
Lent by the Bodleian Library.

<small>491 leaves, without pagination or catchwords; register, beginning at fol. 5, a—y, A—Z, 1-11 iiii, A— E 7 in eights, except 11 which is in twelves. Printed in double columns, 56 lines to a full column. Fol. a 1 and E 7 are blank. This is said to be the first Bible printed in octavo, or in small form, and is hence called the first edition of the "poor man's Bible." It is also the first or one of the first books printed by Froben. This copy is splendidly illuminated.</small>

697. BIBLE (Latin). In title, "Tu es Petrus," emendata per Angelum de Monte Ulmi. Venetiis: per Hieronimum de Pagininis, 1492.
Lent by Henry J. Atkinson, Esq.
<small>The earliest Bible with an illustration on the title-page.</small>

698. BIBLE (Latin). Biblia [on woodcut "Tu es Petrus."] Another copy. Venetiis, 1492. 8vo. *Lent by the Bodleian Library.*

698a. PSALMS (German). Der Psalter/ zu Deutsch./ [*Colophon*] ¶ Getruckt zu Vlm vō Cun-/rad dinckmut. Anno salutis. M./cccc. Vnnd im.xcii. Ulm, 1492. 16mo. *Lent by the Rev. Dr. Ginsburg.*

<small>Eight prel. leaves, the 7th and the recto of the 8th being blank; Text, 17 lines on a page, a to z and A to K 3 in eights. These Psalms are a literal translation from the Latin Vulgate, into High German of the fifteenth century, of a southern (Swabian) dialect. Added to the Psalms are the hymns of Isaiah, Ezekiel, Anna, Moses, Abacuck, the Three Children, Zachariah, St. Augustine, and the Athanasian Creed. This is a fine specimen of an early *pocket edition* of the Psalms in the language of the people. The size of the page is $3\frac{5}{8}$ by $2\frac{1}{2}$ in.</small>

698b. BIBLE (Latin). Biblia integra, *etc.* Finit p Johannem froben civē Basilie. 6° Kal Nov. 1495. 8°. *Lent by Sion College.*

699. BIBLE (Latin). Biblia, cum tabula noviter edita (Tabula alphabetica ex singulis libris τ capitulis totius biblie ... a G. Bruno... summa cura composita.) *End.* Exacta est biblia presens Venetiis summa lucubratione. (Interpretatiões hebraicorū nominū pm ordinem alphabeti.) Gothic letter. Venetiis: Bevilaqua, 1494. 4to.
Lent by Matthew Ridgway, Esq.

700. BIBLE (Latin). LIber uite. Biblia cum glosis ordinarijs et interlinearibus; excerptis ex omnib' ferme ecclesie sancte doctorib'; simulq̄ cum expositōis Nicolai de lyra; et cum concordantijs ī margine. (*End.* Glosa ordiaria vna cū postill' ve. f. Nicolai de lyra... feliciter finit.... emēdata... Bernardinū gadolū, etc. 4 vols. Gothic letter. Venetiis: p. Paganinū de paganinis, 1495. Folio. *Lent by Henry White, Esq.*

701. BIBLE (Latin). Biblia Correcta per Petrum Angelū de monte ulmi. Venetiis: Hieronimus de Paganini, 1497. 8vo.
Lent by the Bodleian Library.

702. BIBLE (Latin). Biblia Sacra Latina cum Glossa Ordinaria et Postillis Nicola de Lyra. 6 Parts. Basiliæ, J. Petri de Langendorff et Joan. Froben de Hamelburg, 1498. Folio.
Lent by Henry J. Atkinson, Esq.

703. BIBLE (Latin). 2 col., 52 lines. Venetiis : per Symonum dictum beuilaqua, 1498. 4to. *Lent by M. Ridgway, Esq.*
This is one of the *Fontibus ex Græcis* editions.

704. BIBLE (Latin). Liber Vitæ Biblia correcta per Petrū angelū. Venetia : Arte Paganini de Paganinis Brixiensis, 1501. 8vo.
Lent by Earl Stanhope.

705. PSALMS (English). ¶ This treatise concernynge the fruytful-Sayinges of/ Dauyde the kynge & prophete in the seuen penytēcyal/ psalmes Deuyded in seuen sermons was made and com-/plyed by the ryght reuerente fader in god Johan fyssher/ Doctour of dyuynyte & bysshop of Rochester at the ex-/ortacion and sterynge of the moost excellente pryncesse/ Margarete countesse of Rychemoūte and Derby & Mo-/der to our souerayne lorde Kynge Hēry the vij on who-/se soule Jesu haue mercy./ [*Colophon*] Here endeth the exposycyon of yᵉ .vii. psalmes. Enpryn/ted at London in the fletestrete at the sygne of yᵉ sonne/ by Wynkyn de Worde. In the yere of oure lorde. M/CCCCC. viii. yᵉ .xvi. day of yᵉ moneth of Juyn. The/ xxiii. yere of yᵉ reygne of our souerayne lorde kynge Hē/ry the seuenth./ London, 1508. 4to. *Lent by W. Harrison, Esq.*
146 leaves without folios, pagination, or catchwords. Signatures aa to zz in eights and fours alternately, and && in six leaves. Colophon on the recto of && .iv. with Wynken de Worde's device on the reverse. This edition is distinguished from the others by the initial F at the beginning of the text having the Portcullis of Westminster, and by the signatures being in double letters in lower case. There are 32 lines on a page, and the Latin text is in larger letters than the English.

706. QUINCUPLEX Psalterium. Gallicum, Romanum, Hebraicum, Vetus, Conciliatum. Parisiis: Hen. Stephani, 1509. 4to. Two copies.
One lent by Henry J. Atkinson, Esq., the other by Earl Spencer.

707. BIBLE (Latin). 6 vols. Paris : Wolfgang Hopyl, 1510. 16mo.

708. BIBLE (Latin). Biblia, Pars scunda. Josue—Psalter. Paris : Wolfgang Hopyl, 1510. 16mo. *Lent by Rev. J. B. Ebsworth.*

709. BIBLE (Latin). In Parrhisiorum vniuersitate arte Philippi pigouchet Impēsis Symonis vostre, 1512. Folio.
Lent by Henry J. Atkinson, Esq.

710. BIBLE (Latin). Lugduni : J. Mareschal, 1514. 4to.
Lent by Henry J. Atkinson, Esq.

711. BIBLIA Polyglotta. Hebr. Chald. Gr. Lat. Cardinalis Ximenez. A. W. de Brocario. In Complutensi universitate (Alcala), 1514-17. Folio. 6 vols. *Lent by Earl Spencer.*
    The first Polyglot Bible. Only 600 copies of it were printed, which were not published until 1520. The work occupied fifteen years in execution, and its cost was defrayed by Cardinal Ximenes. The first volume was completed the 10th January, 1514, and the last the 10th July, 1517. The Licence of Leo X. is dated 22nd March, 1520, but copies were not issued before 1522. The Cardinal died the 8th of November, 1517, and the hitch in the publication of the work was probably owing to this circumstance.

715. BIBLE (Latin). Lugduni per Jacobum Sacon, expēsis Anthonij koberger, 1515. Folio. *Lent by H. White, Esq.*

716. BIBLE (Latin). Lugduni in officina Jacobi Sacon, 1515. 8vo. *Lent by Henry J. Atkinson, Esq.*

717. BIBLE (Latin). Lugduni: Jacobi Sacon, expensis Ant. koberger, 1516. Folio. *Lent by Henry J. Atkinson, Esq.*

718. NEW Testament (Greek and Latin). Nouum Instrumentum Erasmi. Basiliæ: Froben, 1516. Folio. Two copies.
    One lent by *Henry White, Esq.*, the other by *Earl Spencer.*
    The first Greek New Testament accompanied by a Latin translation is reported to have been executed by Erasmus and Froben in five months. See Erasmus's twenty-sixth letter.

719. NEW Testament (Greek and Latin). Nouum Instrumentum, *etc.* Basiliæ: Froben, 1516. Folio. *Lent by Henry J. Atkinson, Esq.*
    This is generally called the first New Testament in Greek, though it had been printed two years before in the Ximenes Polyglot, but not issued till 1520. It had also been printed by Aldus, but in consequence of that printer's death, was not published till 1518. See No. 721.

720. PSALMS (Polyglot). Psalterium. Hebr. Gr. Ar. Chald. Studio Aug. Justiniani. Genuæ: P. P. Porrus, 1516. Folio. Splendid copy, printed on vellum. *Lent by Earl Spencer.*
    A note on the nineteenth Psalm gives a short account of the life of Christopher Columbus, especially of his second voyage along the southern coast of Cuba, containing details of importance nowhere else told so fully.

721. BIBLE (Greek). Παντα τα κατ'εξοχην καλουμενα ΒΙΒΛΙΑ θειας δηλαδη γραφης παλαιας τε, και νεας. Sacra Scripturae Veteris Novaque Omnia. Venetiis in ædibus Aldi et Andreæ soceri, 1518. Februarius. Folio. *Lent by Earl Spencer.*
    First edition of the Septuagint. Contains the first Greek Old Testament published, though it had been printed the previous year in the Ximenes Polyglot. This is a sumptuous copy on large paper. Aldus Pius Manutius, the projector of this work, as well as its chief editor and printer, died in 1516, before it was completed. Hence his father-in-law Andreas Asolanus' address to Cardinal Ægidius the friend of Aldus.

722. BIBLE (Latin). Lily on title. Venetiis: L. A. de Giunta, 1519. 8vo. With the earliest metal engraving (?) *Lent by Henry J. Atkinson, Esq.*

722*. NEW Testament (Greek and Latin). Erasmus's second edition. Basiliæ: J. Froben, 1519. Folio. Magnificent copy, printed on pure vellum. *Lent by the Archbishop of Canterbury.*
   In this second edition the text is considerably purified, and it contains the verse in 1 John v. 7, about the three that bear record in heaven, introduced here for the first time by Erasmus, though it had been printed in the Complutensian Polyglot in 1514.

723. NEW Testament (Greek and Latin). Erasmus's second edition. With the Annotationes. 2 vols. Basiliæ: J. Froben, 1519. Folio. *Lent by Henry J. Atkinson, Esq.*

724. BIBLE (Latin). Lugduni: J. Mareschal, 1519. 8vo. *Lent by Henry J. Atkinson, Esq.*

724*. BIBLE (Latin). Another copy. *Lent by the Earl of Beauchamp.*

725. BIBLE (French). La Bible en francois. Paris: Jehan Petit, 1520. Folio. *Lent by Edwin S. Kowie, Esq.*

726. ACTS OF the Apostles (German, Luther's). Printed on vellum. 1521. 8vo. A fragment. *Lent by Henry J. Atkinson, Esq.*

727. CONCORDANCE (Latin). Basiliæ: J. Froben, 1521. Folio. *Lent by Henry J. Atkinson, Esq.*

728. NEW Testament (Greek). Hagenoæ: Thomas Anselmi, 1521. 4to. *Lent by Henry J. Atkinson, Esq.*

729. BIBLE (Latin). Bibliorvm Opvs integrvm. Printed in Italics. Basiliæ: J. Wolf, 1522. 4to. *Lent by Henry J. Atkinson, Esq.*

730. BIBLE (Latin). Lugduni: Jacob Sacon, 1522. 8vo. *Lent by Henry J. Atkinson, Esq.*

731. BIBLE (Latin). Nurembergæ: Fredericus Peypus, sumptu Joh. Koburger, 1522. 4to. *Lent by Henry J. Atkinson, Esq.*

732. NEW Testament (Latin). 2 vols. Argent.: J. Cnobloch, 1523. 8vo. *Lent by Henry J. Atkinson, Esq.*

733. BIBLE (Latin). Lugduni: J. Mareschal, 1523. Folio. *Lent by Henry J. Atkinson, Esq.*

734. NEW Testament (French). (Transl. par Jacques le Fèvre d'Etaples.) Guilaume Vorsterman, Anvers, 1523. 8vo. *Lent by the British and Foreign Bible Society.*

735. BIBLE (German). Das Alt und neues Testaments der Martin Luther. Gedrukt zu Nuremberg durch Frederichen Peypus, 1524. 3 vols. Folio. Printed on vellum. *Lent by Earl Spencer.*
   These volumes want the Prophets and Apocrypha, which were not printed by Luther till 1532, to render this edition complete. This is the world-renowned copy printed on pure vellum, with the wood illustrations splendidly coloured like miniatures.

737. BIBLE (German). Das gantz neüw Testamēt (Luther's). Zū Strassburg durch Wolff Köpphel. 1524. 8vo.
    Lent by the British and Foreign Bible Society.

738. BIBLE (Latin). Biblia Magna. Lugduni: Jacob Mareschal, 1525. Folio.   *Lent by Henry J. Atkinson, Esq.*

739. BIBLE (Hebrew). 4 vols. Venet.: Bomberg, 1525. 4to.
    Lent by the British and Foreign Bible Society.

740. BIBLE (Latin). Sacra Biblia ad LXX interpretum tralata. Basiliæ, per Andream Cratandrum, 1526. 4to.
    Lent by Henry J. Atkinson, Esq.

741. BIBLE (Latin). Lugduni: Jacob Marischal, 1526. 8vo.
    Lent by Henry J. Atkinson, Esq.
    Curious plates at the end of Maccabæus.

742. HABACUC (German). Luther's. 1526. 4to.
    Lent by Henry J. Atkinson, Esq.

743. NEW Testament (English). [The Newe Testament in Englysshe, by William Tyndale. Worms: Peter Schoeffer, 1526?]. 8vo.
    Lent by the Dean and Chapter of St. Paul's Cathedral.
    This is one of the rarest and most precious volumes in our language, being the first complete edition of the New Testament by William Tyndale. Only two copies are known, this and the one at Bristol. This one is very imperfect, while the Bristol copy wants only the title.

744. NEW Testament (English). Tyndale's first edition, supposed to have been printed at Worms by Peter Schœffer in 1526; a facsimile on vellum, illuminated, reprinted from the copy in the Baptist College, Bristol. With an Introduction by Francis Fry. 1862. 8vo.   *Lent by Francis Fry, Esq.*
    Mr. Fry has rendered a great service in reproducing this rare volume with so much care and fidelity. We ought here also to call attention to Mr. Arber's reprint of the quarto fragment of Tyndale's first edition of 1525.

745. BIBLE (Latin). Habes in hoc libro utriusque instrumenti novam translationē æditam a Sancto Pagnino. Lugduni: Ant. du Ry, 1528-7. 4to.   *Lent by Earl Spencer.*
    With Melancthon's autograph notes.

746. BIBLE (Latin). Another copy. Lugduni: per Ant. du Ry, 1528. 4to.   *Lent by Henry J. Atkinson, Esq.*
    First Bible divided into verses, but not divided exactly, as was afterwards done by Robert Stephens in his sixth edition of 1555, subsequently adopted by our English translators first in the Genevan version.

747. BIBLE (Dutch, Protestant). Te Bibel. Gheprint Thantwerpen, Bi mi Willem Vorsterman, 1528-31. Folio.
    Lent by Henry J. Atkinson, Esq.

748. NEW Testament (German). Das New Testament, so durch L. Emser. Leyptzick durch Valter Schuman, 1528. 8vo.
Lent by Henry White, Esq.

749. BIBLE (Latin, Vulgate). Coloniæ ex ædibus Quentelianis, 1529. Folio. *Lent by Henry J. Atkinson, Esq.*

750. NEW Testament (German). ☞ Das gantz New Testament: So durch den ⚓/ Hochgelerten L. Hieronymun Emser verteütscht, mitt sampt seinen zugefüg-/ten Summarien vnd Annotationen vber yegliche capitel angezeigt, wie Mar-/tinus Luther dem rechten Text (dem Huschischen exemplar nach) seins gefal-/lens, ab vnd tzugethan, vnd verendert hab, Wie dan durch bitte etzlicher Fürsten/ vnd Herren geschehen, das er wöl dem gemeynen volck tzu nütz, das war/ vnd recht Euangelion, am trück ausz geen lassen./ ¶ Item ein new Register verordent vnd gemacht, vorstetlicher dan vor gewest./ Auch dem käuffer vnnd gemeynen man tzu gutt sindt hynden an getrückt, die/ Episteln ausz dem alten Testament, die man in der Christlichen kirchen durchs Jar helt, wöl-/che dann der Emser in seyner Translation nicht bey gesetzt hat, da mit nicht eym jeglichen/ not sey eyn gantze Bybel tzu kauffen./ Anno M. CCCC. XXIX. Am. XXIII. tag des Augstmonts./ [*Colophon*] Getruckt vnd volendet in der loblichen stat *Collen* / durch Heronem Fuchs, vnnd auffs new mit fleysz durchleszen vnnd corrigirt/ vonn dem wirdigen doctor Johan Ditenberger. Mit verlag vnnd belo-/nung des Ersamen vnnd fürsichtigen bürgers Peter Quentel. Im/ Jaer nach Christi vnsers sälichmachers geburt M.CCCC. / XXIX. Am XXIII tag des Augstmants. Collen, 1529. Folio. *Lent by Henry J. Atkinson, Esq.*

Six preliminary leaves: text folioed from 1 to 204, and paged from 205 to 227. This Translation of Emser is opposed to Luther's, which is here pronounced to be a falsification of the text.

751. BIBLE (Dutch, Protestant). Antwerp, By mi Willem Vorsterman, 1528-29. Folio. *Lent by Henry White, Esq.*

752. BIBLE (French). La Saincte Bible Françoys, translatée selon la pure et entière traduction de Sainct Hierome (par Jacques le Fèvre d'Estaples). En Anvers: par Martin Lempereur, 1530. Folio. *Lent by Henry White, Esq.*

This splendid volume was long regarded as the first complete Bible in the French language. It was translated by Le Fèvre of Estaples from the Latin Vulgate, and was so faithfully done as to become the basis of all other French translations, both Roman Catholic and Protestant. It is however now rendered certain that the entire work had previously seen the light in six small octavo volumes, between the years 1523 and 1528, which volumes are so scarce that no library, as far as we know, possesses a complete set. The New Testament was printed by Simon de Colines at Paris in 1523, and again in 1524. By an order of the French Parliament, 28th August, 1525, the work was censured and rigorously suppressed. The New Testament was in 1524 and 1525 reprinted in Antwerp by Vorsterman, and again in 1525 it was reprinted at Basle. In 1528 Martin Lempereur printed the Pentateuch and the Prophets in two volumes. The Psalms had been printed separately in 1525 by Colines at Paris. Lempereur again reprinted some of the volumes in 1529 and 1532, in octavo.

753. PENTATEUCH (English). The fyrst boke of Moses called Genesis. By William Tyndale. Marlborow: Hans Luft, 1530. 8vo.
Lent by Francis Fry, Esq.

The five books of the Pentateuch have each separate titles, and were probably issued separately. Genesis and Numbers are in black letter, while the other three books are in Roman.

754. BIBLE (German). Zürich: C. Froschover, 1531. Folio.
Lent by Henry J. Atkinson, Esq.

Translated by Leo Jude and others. Woodcuts said to be by Holbein. See distaff of Eve and cannon and armour of Paul's escort.

755. BIBLE (Latin). Paris: Robertus Stephanus, 1532. Folio.
Lent by Henry J. Atkinson, Esq.

This is Robert Stephens's second Bible, of which he edited and published eight distinct editions between 1528 and 1556-7.

756. BIBLE (Dutch). Gheprint Thantuerpen, By my Willem Vorsterman, 1533-4. Folio. *Lent by Henry J. Atkinson, Esq.*

756*. BIBLE (German). Biblia, Getruckt zū Franckfurt am Mayn, Bei Christian Egenolph, 1534. Folio. *Lent by Francis Fry, Esq.*

This very scarce Bible in the type and woodcuts closely resembles the Coverdale Bible of 1535, but from a careful comparison we confidently affirm that the type and the woodcuts are not identical with those of the Coverdale Bible.

757. BIBLE (Latin). Paris: R. Stephanus, 1534. 8vo.
Lent by Henry J. Atkinson, Esq.
This is Stephens's third Bible.

758. NEW Testament (English, Tyndale's). ¶ The ne-/we Testament, dyly/gently corrected and/ compared with the/ Greke by Willyam/ Tindale; and fynes-/shed in the yere of ou/re Lorde God./ A. M. D. ꝟ. xxxiiij./ in the moneth of/ Nouember./ Antwerp: by Marten Emperowr, 1534. 8vo.
Lent by W. Amhurst Tyssen-Amhurst, Esq.

Sixteen preliminary leaves, viz. Title within a woodcut border; on the reverse, "¶ W. T. vnto the Reader." 17 pages; "¶ A prologe into the .iiii. Euangelystes"/ (**. ii.) 3½ pp., the remaining half-page being occupied by "¶ A warninge to ye reader if ought be/ scaped thorow necligence of the prynter." Then comes, on ** .iiii./ "Willyam Tindale/ yet once more to the/ christen reader."/ 9 pages: next page blank. Then follows the second title ¶ The ne-/we Testa-/ment, ¶ Imprinted at An-/werp by Marten/ Emperowr./ Anno. M.D.xxxiiij./ On the reverse is "¶ The bokes conteyned in the/ newe Testament." 27 lines, the last 4 not numbered. The Text begins with folio 1 (so in error for folio ii.) on A. ii. with a small woodcut of St. Matthew filling the space of 10 lines, nearly an inch wide. Revelations end on the top of the reverse of folio ccclxxxiii. with "The ende of the newe/ testament."/ Then follows on, "These are the Epistles ta-/ken oute of the olde testament," ending on the bottom of the recto of folio cccc with "¶ Here ende the epistls of the olde/ Testament."/ Next come on the reverse of folio cccc. "¶ This is the Table/ whe/re in you shall fynde/ the Epistles and/ the Gospels/ after the vse of/ Salsbury." 18 pages, and 4 lines of the next page, followed immediately by, "¶ These thinges have I added to fill/ vp the lesse with all." / Occupying the remainder of that and the following page, ending at the bottom of the recto of Ee. viii. with "¶ The ende of this/ boke."/ The reverse of the last leaf Ee. viii. is blank. The woodcut borders of the two titles are alike, except that while the shield at the bottom of the first is blank, that in the second is occupied by armorial bearings between the initials of Martin Kaiser, the Flemish name of the printer, Martin Emperour. Preceding each of the four Gospels, the Acts, and most of the Epistles, are small woodcuts, representing the Evangelists and Apostles, nearly one inch wide, and one and three-eighths inches high. In the Revelations are 22 woodcuts, two and three-eights inches by 3½ inches. This is Mr. Fry's No. 3, where it is fully described.

759. PENTATEUCH (English). By William Tyndale. The fyrst boke of Moses called Genesis. Newly corrected and amended by W. T. (in roman type). [Marlborow: Hans Luft, 1534.] 8vo.
Lent by Earl Spencer.

William Tyndale's corrected copy of the Pentateuch of 1534 is usually called the second edition, but only the first book was reprinted; the other four books, all dated 1530, were not changed. The first edition of Genesis appeared in 1530 [see No. 753]. A complete copy, comprising the whole five parts, like the present, is of the highest rarity.

765. BIBLE (English). Biblia./ The Bible, that/ is, the holy Scripture of the/ Olde and New Testament, faith-/fully and truly translated out/ of Douche and Latyn/ in to Englishe./ M.DXXXV./ [Myles Coverdale.] [*Colophon.*] Prynted in the yeare of our Lord M.D.XXXV./ and fynished the fourth daye of October./ [Antwerp: Jacob van Meteren], 1535. Folio. 11¾ by 8 inches.
Lent by the Earl of Leicester.

Eight preliminary leaves. The title is in black within a beautiful border composed of four woodcuts. On the reverse, in a similar type to the text of the Bible, are "The bokes of the whole Byble, how they are named/" &c., in four columns under the headings, "Abbreuiacion," "Boke," "Chapters," and "leafe." Then comes, on +. ii. the Dedication "Vnto the most victorious Prynce/" &c. 5 pages, ending on the recto of + iiii. with "youre graces humble sub-/iecte and daylye oratour,/ Myles Couerdale."/ On the reverse begins, "A prologe./ Myles Couerdale Vnto the Christen reader."/ with the initial C, six lines deep, 6 pages ; next follows on the reverse of the leaf "The bokes of the hole Byble," occupying 2 pages ; then comes in a smaller black letter, on the reverse of the last preliminary leaf, "The first boke of/ Moses, called/ Genesis/" 1 page. The Text is in six parts, Genesis to Deuteronomy, Folios i to xc, recto, the reverse blank ; Title, "The seconde par-/te of the olde Testament./ The boke of Josua." &c., within a woodcut border composed of eight pieces, with "The boke of/ Josua./ What this boke conteyneth," on the reverse ; Text, Josua to Hester, Folios ij. to cxx. verso, Signature aa ij to vv in sixes : The third Part, without separate title-page, Job to Solomons Balettes, Folios i to lij, recto, Signatures Aa to Ii iiij. Title to the fourth Part, within a woodcut border of nine pieces, "All the Prophetes/ in Englishe./ Esay, Jeremy" &c., having on the reverse

"The Prophet/ Esay./ What Esay conteyneth," one page; Text, Esay to Malachy, Folios ij to cij verso, Signatures Aaa ij to Krr vj. Title to the fifth Part, "Apocripha/ The bokes," &c., within a woodcut border of eight pieces, having on the reverse "The transzlatoure vnto the reader." 29 lines, and "The thirde boke of Esdras./ What this boke conteyneth." one page; Text, The Third boke of Esdras to the Second boke of the Machabees, Folios ij to lxxxiij (marked lxxxi.) Signatures A ij to O v, followed by one blank leaf. Then comes the title to the sixth Part, "The new testament."/ &c., within a border of eight pieces, having on the reverse "The gospell of/ S. Mathew./ What S. Mathew conteyneth," one page; Text, Mathew to Revelation, Folios ij to cxiij verso, concluding with "The ende of the new testament." on the middle of the page. Underneath is "A faute escaped in pryntinge the new Testament," four lines; and then comes the colophon near the bottom of the page, "Prynted in the yeare of oure Lorde M.D. XXXV./ and fynished the fourth day of October." Between the first and second parts is a large woodcut map, 11⅜ by 15⅝ inches square, entitled, "The desiripcion of the londe of promes, called Palestina, Canaan, or the holy londe."/

Let no Englishman or American view this and the six following Bibles without first lifting his hat, for they are seven extraordinary copies of the COVERDALE BIBLE, containing, with one important exception (the Marquis of Northampton's copy), all the variations known of the most precious volume in our language. For the latest notes on its history the reader is referred to our Introduction to this collection of Bibles, pp. 36-42. Jacob van Meteren, of Antwerp, printer and proprietor, and probably the translator, by whom Coverdale was employed to edit and see the work through the press, having sold the edition to James Nicolson, of Southwark, that English printer and publisher seems to have had as much trouble in working off his book as Simmons had in selling Milton's "Paradise Lost," if we may judge by the number of new titles and preliminary leaves found in different copies. First, we have here in the Earl of Leicester's copy, Van Meteren's original Antwerp title, as first issued, with part of the list of "The bokes of the hole Byble," ending with Malachi on the reverse. Of course the second leaf would be a continuation of this list of "The bokes" from the Apocrypha to Revelation, and hence we may infer that the volume originally contained no dedication to Henry VIII and his "dearest iust wife," Anne [Bulleyn] or Jane [Seymour], for that would cause the dedication to commence on the verso of the second leaf. Besides, we have in this copy of the Earl of Leicester a unique leaf, containing the end of Coverdale's Prologue to the Reader, in the Antwerp type of the body of the book. If our calculations are correct, Coverdale's Prologue to the Reader would commence on the verso of the second leaf and end with this page in the Holkham copy, thus demonstrating almost to a certainty that there was originally no dedication to the King. This being the case, Nicolson, towards the end of 1535, finding the Convocation, Cranmer, Cromwell, and the King, more propitious towards free Scriptures in English than they had been in Sir Thomas More's time when he went over to Antwerp, had abundant reason for cancelling the Antwerp title and reprinting all the preliminary matter, so as to admit the long and rather fulsome dedication to Henry, which Coverdale probably concocted in London to suit the occasion and to pave the way to a royal licence. These two unique perfect leaves, the first and the last of the original four or six preliminary leaves, therefore render this (the Earl of Leicester's copy) of unspeakable importance in the bibliographical history of the Book.

Nicolson then, it seems, cancelling the originals, replaced them with eight preliminary leaves, inserting Coverdale's Dedication of five pages and leaving verso of title blank. A copy of Nicolson's first title with date 1535, the reverse blank, is in the library of the Marquis of Northampton; very important as proving that there was no delay in issuing the volume, as some writers have claimed there was. Nicolson, it is well known, possessed the original woodcuts of the work, including the map and the title. The arrangement of the title is very beautiful, and Nicolson, we think, somewhat improved upon the original. He added two lines to the last motto so as to complete the sense, instead of leaving it to end with &c. like the Antwerp title, but as his type was larger than the foreign type, and the cartouche of the wood-block was confined, he was obliged to drop one line, and hence were omitted the only words he could well omit, "and truly .... out of Douche and Latyn," about which omission pages and pages of pure nonsense have been written for and against the honour and credit of Coverdale. It is true that the words left out tell strongly in favour of the translation being done by a foreigner, but in the London dedication Coverdale having mentioned his use of "fyue sundry interpreters" in "setting forth" the work, he and Nicolson avoided a seeming contradiction by omitting these words. The omission, however, was unquestionably and simply a matter of the printer's taste and convenience, the truth having been more fully and accurately explained by Coverdale himself, in his Epistles to the King and to the Reader. Nicolson's first or separate edition of the Dedication contains the name of Queen Anne, while the Dedication in his folio reprint of 1537 has instead the name of Queen Jane, who was married to the King, May 20, 1536, showing that it was printed after this date.

Nicolson not only sold off this original edition in 1535 and 1536, but he immediately printed two other editions in English type, the one in folio and the other in quarto, both bearing the date of 1537, though probably printed mostly in 1536. It has been a much debated question as to which of these editions of Nicolson was the earlier. We are inclined to give the precedence to the folio, first because the preliminary leaves that appear in it were used to make up the Antwerp edition with a title dated 1536, like the Earl of Jersey's and the Gloucester Cathedral copies, having in the Dedication the name of Jane; and, secondly, because neither the 1536 nor 1537 folio titles bear the words "Set forth with the kinges moost gracious licence," which appear at the bottom of the title of the quarto edition. It is not unlikely that when Grafton obtained his licence to "set forth" the Matthew Bible in 1537, a similar favour was granted to Nicolson for his three editions of the Coverdale Bible, though it was too late to add these words to the titles.

766. BIBLE (English). Coverdale's. Fynished the fourth daye of October, 1535. [Jacob van Meteren, Antwerp], 1535. Folio. 12¼ by 8 inches. *Lent by Earl Spencer.*

This copy is slightly imperfect, wanting only the original title-page and the map. A title is made up in manuscript by using the woodcut border of the title of the Great Bible of 1539, reprinted in 1540 by Petyt and Redman for Berthelet, or that of Raynalde and Hyll's Matthew's Bible of 1549, both from the same block as the genuine title of 1535, but differing in the setting of the texts. The dedication leaves containing the name of Queen Jane are the same as the second edition (folio) of the Coverdale Bible printed by Nicolson, of Southwark, No. 790.

767. BIBLE (English). Coverdale's. Nearly complete. [Jacob van Meteren, Antwerp]. 1535. Folio. *Lent by the Sion College Library.*

A MS note pasted in the cover says this copy was borrowed by the British Museum, August 19, 1772, to complete their copy by facsimiles taken from it. Certain leaves then wanting in this copy have been added, since it appears now to want only the original title-page and map. The name of Queen Jane is in the Dedication.

768. BIBLE (English). Coverdale's. Another copy. [Antwerp: Jacob van Meteren], 1535. Folio. *Lent by the British and Foreign Bible Society.*
This is a good copy correctly made up with facsimiles.

769. BIBLE (English). Coverdale's. Another copy. [Jacob van Meteren, Antwerp], 1535. Folio. 12¾ by 7⅞ inches.
Lent by W. Amhurst Tyssen-Amhurst, Esq.
An excellent copy, having the title, the next three leaves, and the map in facsimile.

770. BIBLE (English). Coverdale's. [Antwerp: Jacob van Meteren], 1535. Folio. 12¾ by 7⅞ inches. *Lent by the Rev. Dr. Gott.*
This copy has the titles and map in excellent facsimile; otherwise fine.

771. BIBLE (English). ❧ Biblia ❧ / The Byble: that/ is, the holy Scrypture of the/ Olde and New Testament,/ faythfully translated in/to Englyshe./ M.D. XXXVI./ S. Paul. II. Tessal. III./ Praye for vs, that the word of God/ may haue fre passage 't be glorified./ S. Paul. Colloss. III./ Let the worde of Christe dwell in you/ plenteously in all wysdome, 'tc./ Josue. I./ Let not the Boke of this Lawe departe/ out of thy mouth, but excercyse thy selfe/ therin daye and nyghte, yt thou mayest/ kepe and doe euery thynge accordynge/ to it that is wrytten therin./ [*Colophon*] Prynted in the yeare of oure Lorde M.D. XXXV./ and fynished the fourth daye of October./ [Jacob van Meteren, Antwerp], 1535, and [James Nicolson, Southwark], 1536. Folio. 12½ by 7⅞ inches.
Lent by the Earl of Jersey.
This is our seventh copy of the COVERDALE BIBLE, and though last by no means least. It is, we believe, the only copy known, perfect as it came from the hands of the publisher Nicolson; that is, with the title, reverse blank, and the seven other preliminary leaves, together with the map as added by Nicolson; while the rest of the volume is as it came from Van Meteren. The Dedication has the name of Queen Jane, showing that the seven leaves are the same as those in Nicolson's folio of 1537. The map has the descriptive line at the top in English type and not in the Antwerp type, showing that this impression was taken off the block in England. We can trace this same block of the map as late as the Bishop's Bible of 1574. We have said before that the blocks used in the title and in the body of the book by Van Meteren at Antwerp all passed into the possession of Nicolson, and can be traced in many books for many years in England. Mr. Francis Fry, in his admirable book called *The Bible by Coverdale*, 1535, has amply proved this. We do not, therefore, credit the oft-repeated story that they are the cuts of Hans Sebald Behem of Nuremberg, or that they were the identical cuts used by Christopher Froschover of Zurich. There is a bare possibility that Froschover at Zurich got up the Coverdale type, cuts, title, and map, and having used them in his folio German Bible of 1534, sold them at once and secretly to Van Meteren of Antwerp in time for him to finish printing the Coverdale Bible by the 4th of October, 1535, and then sell the whole stock, books, type, cuts, &c., to Nicolson of Southwark, and so escape the lynx-eyed imperial emissaries and spies. But there are heaps of floating straws in the current against this argument, one of which is perhaps sufficient to show that these cuts never saw Zurich. The large cut of the Tabernacle, used twice, has the words OOST, NORD, and SAIFD (the v and the j

upside down), three unmistakable Flemish words, or such as would not have been used in Zurich, Lyons, or Frankfort, but are well suited to the latitude of Antwerp. We are rejoiced, therefore, to be privileged to place this world-renowned Osterly copy at one end of our rank of seven matchless Coverdales, with the equally celebrated Holkham copy at the other end.

It remains now to give a brief history of the several vain attempts made during the last hundred years to satisfactorily complete our first Bible. In 1772 the British Museum and Sion College copies were used to complete each other in manuscript. About 1840 the late Mr. John Harris supplied the outer border of the title of the British Museum copy by piecing it, and adding a facsimile of the cuts from the same block title used in the edition of 1549, having the centre inscription in Latin. But when the Holkham copy was brought to light, in 1846, it was found that the original inscription was in English on the right side as it was on the left. The Osterly copy confirmed this, though dated 1536. In December, 1849, Mr. Harris, having traced the Holkham title while it was in London being bound by Lewis, made an excellent lithographic facsimile of both the title and the list of books on the back of it. The late Mr. William Pickering in the meantime had a wood-cut made in facsimile of the title of the Museum copy, as first restored by Harris, with the English inscription on the one side and the Latin on the other. The fourth facsimile is an off-tract from Harris's Holkham copy, made by him for Mr. George Offor, but somewhat inferior to his own. A fifth kind of restoration is to take the title of 1540 or 1549, cut out the centre, and put in the Coverdale title of 1535, but this leaves the inscriptions all in Latin. The sixth facsimile is from Harris's original Holkham stone with the Osterly inset of 1536, the reverse being left blank. The seventh is from Harris's stone with the inset from the Marquis of Northampton's copy, with date 1535, reverse blank. Collectors, being very properly puzzled how to use these several facsimiles to make up their copies, generally insert as many as they can procure. Harris's original stone is still in existence, together with the insets of the English titles of both 1535 and 1536. Nicolson issued two sets of the Dedication, Prologue, &c., in seven leaves, one with the name of Queen Anne, and the other with that of Queen Jane. Mr. Triphook reprinted these leaves in old black letter, about 1825, in quasi facsimile. Mr. Pickering had a "seeming" facsimile of the Anne leaves printed on old paper at the Chiswick Press. Mr. Harris did them both in his best style, traced and lithographed. Mr. George Offor did them both also in his style, and both sets have more recently been reproduced in facsimile for Mr. Fry. All these issues are found in various copies, and, we believe, some copies have all of them, or as many as procurable. Still, after all is said and done, no one has yet seen of Van Meteren's original preliminary leaves any others besides the title and the last one, as described above in the Earl of Leicester's copy.

772. BIBLE (French). La Bible . . . . . en Francoys. Le Viel Testament de Lebrieu : τ le Nouveau du Grec. [By P. R. Olivetan, assisted by J. Calvin.] Neufchastel: Pierre de Wingle, 1535. Folio. Two copies.

One lent by H. White, Esq., and the other by Earl Spencer.

The first Protestant French Bible, usually called the "Olivetan," from the name of one of its translators.

774. NEW Testament (German). Das New Testament Deüdsch (Luther's). Widerumb fleissig corrigiert. Printed on vellum. Augspurg: Heinrich Stayner, 1535. 8vo.

Lent by the British and Foreign Bible Society.

774*. NEW Testament (German and Latin). C. Froschover, Zurich, 1535. 4to. *Lent by Mrs. B. F. Stevens.*
  This rare edition probably served Nicolson in 1537-38 as a model for his New Testament in English and Latin, to which with consent he put Coverdale's name. See No. 798 and 800.

775. NEW Testament (German). Luther's second edition. 153 . Folio. *Lent by Henry J. Atkinson, Esq.*

776. BIBLE (English). The History of the Bible. *circa* 1535. 8vo.
  Lent by the Rev. Dr. Gott.

777. BIBLE (Hebrew). With marginal notes in Greek. Basiliæ: Ex officina Frobeniana, 1536. 4to. *Lent by Charles D. Sherborn, Esq.*

778. NEW Testament (English). Tyndale's. London [Thomas Berthelet?] 1536. Folio. *Lent by the Bodleian Library.*
  This fine and perfect volume is believed to be the first portion of the Holy Scriptures printed in England.

779. NEW Testament (English). The newe Testament yet once agayne corrected by Wylliam Tyndall, whereunto is added an exhortacion to the same of Erasmus Rot. with an Englysshe Kalender and a Table / necessary to fynde easily and lyghtely any story contayned in the iiii. euangelistes ꝉ in the Actes of the Apostles. 1536. 8vo.
  Lent by Earl Spencer.
  At the end of the New Testament in this edition there follow the "Epystles taken out of the Olde Testament / what are red in the Church after the use of Salsburye upon certen dayes of the year." This fine, large, clean, perfect and matchless copy is fully described by Mr. Fry under his No. 10.

780. NEW Testament (English). ¶ The Newe Testament yet once agayne corrected by Willyam Tyndale. [Antwerp?], 1536. 4to.
  Lent by the Rev. Dr. Gott.
  This is called the Engraver's mark edition. A fine perfect copy, measuring 8½ by 5⅞ inches. It is Mr. Fry's No. 9.

782. NEW Testament (English). ¶ The Newe Testament yet once agyne corrected by Willyam Tindale. [Antwerp?], 1536. 4to.
  Lent by the Earl of Jersey.
  This is called the Mole edition. A very fine tall copy on paper stained yellow. Measures 9¾ by 5⅞ inches. Fry's No. 8.

783. NEW Testament (English). ¶ The newe Testament yet once agayne corrected by Willyam Tindale. [Antwerp?], 1536. 4to.
  Lent by W. Amhurst Tyssen-Amhurst, Esq.
  This is called the Blank-Stone edition, and measures 8¼ by 6¼ inches. A fine and perfect copy. It is Fry's No. 7.

784. NEW Testament (Latin). Per D. Erasmum. Coloniæ prope Diuum Lupum, 1536. 32mo. *Lent by Henry J. Atkinson, Esq.*

K

790. BIBLE (English, Coverdale's). ❧ Biblia ŋe/ The Byble, that/ is the holy Scrypture of the/ Olde and New Testament, fayth-/fully translated in Englysh, and/ newly ouersene ɫ corrected./ M.D.XXXVII./ [3 mottos as before] ❡ Imprynted in Southwarke for/ James Nycolson./ Folio. *Lent by Francis Fry, Esq.*
    It is still a question whether this folio or Nicolson's 4to is the earlier impression. They both appeared in 1537. This reprint of the Coverdale Bible has impressions of the original woodcuts and the map, but the type is the regular black-letter English. Not a particle of the original Antwerp type has yet, as far as we know, been identified in any other book. As the blocks and maps came to England it is presumed the fount of type was lost or destroyed.

791. BIBLE (English, Coverdale). The Byble that is the holye Scrypture of the Olde and Newe Testamente faythfully translated in Englysh and newly ouersene and correcte. M.Vᶜxxxvii. [the 3 texts as before] Imprynted in Southwarke in Saynt Thomas Hospitale by James Nycolson. Set forth with the Kynges moost gracious licence. 1537. 4to. *Lent by Earl Spencer.*
    This is generally considered the third edition of the Coverdale Bible, the second English Bible printed in England, but the first in the quarto form.

792. BIBLE (English, Matthew's). ❡ The Byble,/ which is all the holy Scrip-/ture: In whych are contayned the/ Olde and Newe Testament truly/ and purely translated into En-/glysh by Thomas Matthew./ ❡ Esaye. j./ ☞ Hearcken to ye heauens and/ thou earth geaue care: For the/ Lorde speaketh./ M, D, XXXVII,/ Set forth with the Kinges most gracyous lycēce./ [*Colophon*] ❡ The ende of the newe Testament,/ and of the whole/ Byble,/ ❡ To the honoure and prayse of God/ was this Byble prynted and fy-/nesshed, in the yere of oure/ Lorde God a,/ M, D, XXXVII [Antwerp? printed by Jacob van Meteren? and published in London by R. Grafton and E. Whitchurch,] 1537. Folio. Fine and perfect. *Lent by the Bodleian Library.*
    20 preliminary leaves, viz. Title, within an elaborate woodcut border, having on the reverse, "❧ These thynges ensuynge are ioyned with/ thys present volume of the Byble."/ The second leaf begins on *. ij. with " The Kalender," 4 pp., with " ❡ An Almanack for .xvi ij. yeares," at the bottom of the fourth page. The next leaf, *.iiij, begins " ❡ An exhortacyon to the studye of the/ holy Scripture," etc. 1 page, with large flourished capitals I R at the bottom nearly 2½ inches high; on the reverse is " ❡ The summe & content of all the holy/ Scripture," 2 pp. On the reverse of the fifth leaf begins " ❡ Rogers' Dedication " ❡ To the moost noble and gracyous/ Prynce Kyng Henry the eyght," etc. 3 pp., ending with "Youre graces faythfull & true subiect/ Thomas Matthew." beneath which are two large flourished capitals, H R. Then follows, on signature * *, " ❡ To the Chrysten Readers." and " A table of the pryncypall matters conteyned/ in the Byble," 26 pp.; next comes " ❡ The names of all the/ bokes of the Byble," and " ❡ A brief rehersall of the yeares passed" etc. 1 page; on the reverse of which is a large woodcut filling the whole page, representing Adam and Eve in Paradise; Text, Genesis to Solomon's Ballet, Cexlvij. folioed leaves, the reverse of the last being blank. Then comes a second title, in black and red, within a border composed of 16 wood-

cuts, "The Prophetes/ in English,"/ Esay to Malachy, having on the upper corners of the reverse R G, and on the lower corners E W, (the initials probably of Richard Grafton and Edward Whitechurch) in large flourished capitals, and in the centre a woodcut representing the angel touching the lips of the prophet with a coal of fire from the altar ; Text, folioed j to xciiij, ending at the centre of the reverse, and having the large initials of William Tyndale below. Next follows the third title, in black and red, " ❧ The Volume of/ the bokes called Apocripha."/ within a border of 15 woodcuts, having on the reverse a prologue " ❧ To the Reader," in long lines ; Text folioed ij to lxxxj. ending on the reverse, and followed by a blank leaf. Then comes in black and red, within the same woodcut border as the first title, " ❧ The newe/ Testament of/ oure sauyour Jesu Christ,/ newly and dylygently translated/ into Englyshe with annotacions/ in the Mergent to help the/ Reader to the vnderstan-/dynge of the/ Texte./ ❧ Prynted in the yere of/ oure Lorde God./ M.D.XXXVII./" reverse blank ; Text, Matthew to Revelations, folioed ij. to Cix. ending on the recto. On the reverse begins "This is the Table/ wherin ye shall fynde the Epi-/stles and the Gospels, after the/ vse of Salisbury," 5 pp. ; on the next leaf is the Colophon given above, reverse blank. Really edited by John Rogers, the first martyr under Queen Mary, 1555. It was printed abroad, the expense of the work being defrayed by R. Grafton and E. Whitchurch, two citizens of London. By Cranmer's and Cromwell's influence it received royal authority. It now appears tolerably evident that the enterprising foreign citizen of Antwerp, Jacob van Meteren, who printed Coverdale's Bible and sold the edition to Nicolson, with cuts, map, and probably the type (lost), got up and printed this Bible also, and sold the whole edition to Grafton and Whitchurch, together with the special plant thereto belonging. Rogers and Van Meteren were relatives by marriage. See our Introduction, page 39.

793. BIBLE (English). Matthew's. [Antwerp? Printed by Jacob van Meteren?] London : Grafton & Whitcherche, 1537. Another copy. Folio. *Lent by the Rev. Dr. Gott.*

794. BIBLE (English). Matthew's. Another not quite perfect copy [Antwerp? Printed by Jacob van Meteren?] London : Grafton and Whitchurch, 1537. Folio. *Lent by Earl Spencer.*

795. BIBLE (English). Matthew's. Another copy, wanting title [Antwerp? Jacob van Meteren?] London : Grafton and Whitchurch, 1537. Folio. *Lent by Samuel Hare, Esq.*

795*. BIBLE (French). Illustrated. Paris, 1537-1538. Folio. *Lent by Henry White, Esq.*

796. BIBLE (German). Zurich : C. Froschover, 1538. 4to. *Lent by Henry J. Atkinson, Esq.*

797. NEW Testament (English, Coverdale's). ❧ The new/ Testament of oure/ Sauyour Jesu/ Christ./ Faythfully translated, &/ lately correcte : wyth a/ true concordaunce in the/ margent, & many neces-/sary annotacions decla-/rynge sondry harde pla-/ces côteyned in the text./ ❧ Eympret in the yeare/ of our Lorde M.d. xxxviii./ [*Colophon*] ❧ Imprynted at Antwerpe, by Matthew/ Crom. In the yeare of oure Lorde M.D. xxxviii. 8vo. *Lent by the British and Foreign Bible Society.*

Eight preliminary leaves, viz. the Title, in red and black, in a small compartment surrounded by a beautiful and elaborate woodcut border, having on the reverse "☾ An Almanack for xxxii. yeares." The second leaf begins on *ij with the Kalendar which fills eight pages. The sixth leaf begins "☾ A Prologe vnto/ the newe Testament." 5 pp. with the running titles in red. On the reverse of the eighth leaf, above a woodcut, is "☙ A prologe of/ Saynt Matthew." The Text in long lines, black letter, neither paged or folioed, Matthew to Revelations, signatures A to Z, a to m, in eights, and ending on the reverse of m viij, with "The ende of the new Testament." Then comes "Here followe the/ Epystles of the olde Testament, whych are/ red in the Churche after the vse of Salysbury,/ vpon certayne dayes of the yeare."/ 19 pp.; ending on the recto of o ij, followed by "§☞ The Table,/ wherin ye shall fynde the Epystles and/ the Gospels after the vse of Salysbury,"/ 9 pp. and half of the following page, the rest of this and the next three pages being occupied by "☾ The summe &/ content of all the holy Scripture, both/ of the olde and new Testament," ending with the colophon; making in all 16 sequent leaves. This is one of the most interesting of all the early editions of the New Testament. It possesses many peculiarities, and little seems to be known of its history. It is Coverdale's Version of the text, with Tyndale's Prologues. The prologues of each of the Evangelists are placed before the books to which they severally belong, and Coverdale's summaries of the chapters are placed not together before each book as in the edition of 1535, but separately before each chapter. At the ends of a greater part of the chapters are Gloses, or Notes, in a smaller type, which appear here, as far as I can learn, for the first time, and add considerably to the interest of this edition. They are quite different from the Notes of Matthew as given in the first edition of 1537. The woodcut illustrations are far more numerous than in any other edition, there being nearly 200 cuts, above twenty of which fill the whole page. Many of them are very spirited and beautiful. Matthew begins on the recto of A ; Mark on the verso of E. vij. ; Luke on the recto of H. v. ; John on the verso of H. iij ; Acts on the verso of Q viij ; Romans on the recto of X. vij. ; Timothy on the recto of e. v. ; Hebrews on the verso of h. iij ; Revelations on the verso of k. i.

This copy appears to have belonged to Henry VIII, having the arms of that sovereign stamped on the covers. It corresponds in every thing but the imprint at the end with the Grenville copy in the British Museum.

It was at one time stolen from the Library of the British and Foreign Bible Society, and disposed of to a London Bookseller ; but it was afterwards recovered through information given by Mr. F. Fry to Mr. Bullen of the British Museum, who compiled the well-known Catalogue of the Bible Society's Library.

798. NEW Testament (English and Latin, Coverdale's). The newe tes-/tament both Latine and/ Englyshe ech correspondent to/ the other after the vulgare texte, com-/munely called S. Jeroms. Fayth-/fully translated by Myles/ Couerdale./ Anno. M.CCCCC.XXXVIII./ Jeremie. XXII./ Is not my worde lyke a fyre sayeth the/ Lorde, and lyke an hammer that/ breaketh the harde stone ?/ Printed in *Southwarke*/ by James Nicolson./ Set forth wyth the Kyn/ges moost gracious licence./ 1538. 4to.

Lent by the Rev. Dr. Gott.

Six preliminary leaves, viz. Title in black and red, within a border composed of four woodcuts, a column on each side supporting a head-piece containing in the centre a medallion with a male and a female head ; reverse blank : "☾ To the moost noble,/ moost gracious, and oure moost dradde so-/ueraigne lord Kynge Henry yᵉ eyght, etc. Sig. + ii. 3 pp.; On the reverse begins, "To the Reader." 3 pp.; "An Almanack for .xviii. yeares." (the 1st, 3rd, and 5th words in red) and a Kalendar, in red and black, 4 pp. in double columns, the Almanack occupying only the first half of the first column. The text in double columns, the Latin in roman type occupying the inner, and the English, in black letter, the outer column, begins "☞ SANC-/TVM IESV CHRISTI/ euangeliū secundū Matheū." (the N in the first word being printed upside down) with folio 1 [not marked] on A. i. and ends on the verso of folio 344, Vv. vi. followed by, "☞ A table to finde the Epistles/ and Gospels vsually red in the Church/ after Salysbury vse," 4 pp. in double columns. This is Nicolson's first edition of Coverdale's New Testament, printed in Southwark while Coverdale was in Paris, superintending the printing of The Great Bible. It is a sightly volume, well printed, and on good paper; but the proof reading was so exceedingly bad, and the blunders of all sorts were so numerous, that Coverdale on receiving a copy in July 1538 was so mortified and annoyed, that he at once put to press in Paris another edition more correct, which was finished in November. His dedication to the King was written in Paris in Lent, 1538, and sent to Nicolson, who issued the volume in time for Coverdale to receive by chance a copy in Paris in July following. See No. 799.

799. NEW Testament (English, Coverdale's). ☞ The new testament both in/ Latin and English after/ the vulgare texte :/ which is red in/ the churche./ Translated and corrected by My-/les Couerdale : and prynted in/ *Paris.* by Frannces Regnault./ M. ccccc. xxxviii/ in Nouembre./ Printed for Richard Grafton/ and Edward Whitchurch/ cytezens of London./ Cum gratia ꝛ priuilegio regis./ 1538. 8vo. *Lent by the Rev. Dr. Gott.*
Another Copy, *lent by Henry J. Atkinson, Esq.*

Title in red and black within a very beautiful architectural woodcut border, reverse blank; Coverdale's Dedication "☞ To the ryght honorable lorde Cromwell" 2 pages, + ij; "☞ To the Reader." + iij, 2 pages; "☞ *An Almanack for .xvii. yeares.*" 1 page; Kalender 6 pp. next page blank; in all 7 prel. leaves. Text, Matthew to Revelations, cclxxiiij folioed leaves, ending with the 18th line on the reverse. In the centre of same page begins, "☞ A table to fynde the Epist-/les and Gospels vsually red in the/ Church after Salysbury vse," etc. filling that and the four next pages, concluding on the reverse of M M iiii, with "☞ The ende of the table." This is Coverdale's revised or authorized edition, printed at Paris under his own eye, in consequence of the errors of Nicolson's edition printed in London during his absence. The English text, the running titles, the folios, and the headings of the chapters in English, are in a small black letter, while the Latin text occupying the inner column and the marginal notes is in small roman type. There are fortynine lines in English, and sixty in Latin on a full page. There are no woodcuts, except one on the first leaf of the text. In his dedication to Cromwell Coverdale gives the following interesting details respecting this and his previous editions, reprinted verbatim. "Trueth it is, that this last lent I dyd with all hūblenesse directe an Epistle vnto the kynges most noble grace: trustinge, that the boke (wher vnto it was prefixed) shulde afterwarde haue bene aswell correcte, as other bokes be. And because I coulde not be present my selfe (by the reason of sondrye notable impedimētes) therfore in asmoch as the new testment, which I had set forth in Englisch before, doth so agree wyth the latyn, I was hartely well contēt, that the latyn and it shulde be set together: Prouyded allwaye, that the correctour shulde followe the true copye of the latyn in anye wyse, and to kepe the true & right Englishe of the same. And so doynge, I was cōtēt to set my name to it. And euen so I dyd: trustinge, though I were absent & out of the lande, yet all shuld be well: And (as God is my recorde) I knew none other, till this last Julye, that it was my chaūce here in these parties at a straungers hande, to come by a copye of the sayde prynte. Which whan I had perused, I founde, that as it was disagreable to my former translacion in English, so was not the true copye of the latyn texte obserued, nether the english so correspondent to the same, as it ought to be: but in many places both base, insensyble, & cleane contrary, not onely to the phrase of oure language, but also from the vnderstondyng of the texte in latyn. Wherof though no man to this houre did wryte ner speake to me, yet for asmoch as I am sworne to the trueth, I wyll fauoure no man to the hynderaunce therof, ner to the maynteyning of anye thing that is contrary to the ryght & iust furtheraunce of the same. And therfore, as my dewtye is to be faythfull, to edifye, and with the vttermost of my power to put awaye all occasions of euell, so haue I (though my businesse be greate ynough besyde) endeuoured my selfe to wede out the fautes that were in the latyn & English afore: trustinge, that this present correction maye be (vnto them that shall prynt it herafter) a copye sufficient. But because I may not be myne owne iudge, ner leane to myne owne pryuate opynion in thys or anye lyke worke of the scripture, therfore (according to the dewtye that I owe vnto youre lordshippes office, in the iurisdiction ecclesiasticall of oure most noble kynge) I humbly offre it vnto the same, besechinge you, that (where as this copye hath not bene exactly followed afore, the good hart and wyll of the doars may be considered, & not be necligence of the worke: Specially, seing they be soch men: which as they are glad to prynt and set forth any good thyng, so wyll they be hartely well content, to haue it truly correcte, that they them selues of no malyce ner set purpose haue ouersene. And for my parte (though it hath bene dāage to my poore name) I hartely remitte it, as I do also the ignoraunce of those, (which not long agoo) reported, that at the prynting of a right famous mans sermon, I had depraued the same, at the doyng wherof I was thirtie myle from thence, neither dyd I euer set pēne to it, though I was desyred. Now as concerning this texte of latyn, because it is the same that is red in the church, & therfore comōly the more desyred of all men, I do not doute, but after that it is examined of the lerned (to whom I most hartely referre it) it shall instructe the ignoraūt, stoppe the mouthes of euell speakers, & induce both the hearers and readers to fayth and good workes?". Marke begins on the recto of E iij, Luke on the recto of H, John on the recto of M vij, Acts on the recto of Q iij, Romans on the verso of V viij, Revelations on the verso of JJ viij.

800. NEW Testament (English and Latin, Hollybush). The newe tes-/tament both in Latine and/ Englyshe eche correspondente to/ the other after the vulgare texte, com-/munely called S. Jeromes. Fayth-/fullye translated by Johan/ Hollybushe./ Anno. M.CCCCC.XXXVIII./ Jeremie. xxi./ Is not my worde lyke a fyre sayeth the/ Lorde, and lyke an hammer that/ breaketh the harde stone./ Prynted in *Southwarke*/ by James Nicolson./ Set forth wyth the Kyn-/ges moost gracious lycence./ 1538. 4to.

Lent by Henry J. Atkinson, Esq.

Six preliminary leaves, viz. Title all in black, within a woodcut border like the preceding edition, reverse blank: " ❧ To the moost noble,/ moost gracious, and oure moost dradde so-/ueraigne lord Kynge Henry ye eyght, kyng of Englāde/ and of Fraunce. Defender of Christes true fayth, and vnder/ God the chefe and supreme heade of the church/ of Englande, Irelande, 'tc. " 3 pages, signed by *Myles Couerdale;* the ⊄ at the beginning of this address is in red, while in the former edition it is black. On the reverse begins, "To the Reader", 3 pages; "An Almanack for .xviii. yeares." (These words are in black) occupying half of the first column, and the Kalendar, the rest of that and the three following pages, as in the first edition. The Text as in the first issue, begins "⊄ SANC-" (the N here printed correctly) with folio I (not marked) on A. i. and ends on the reverse of folio 342, Vv. vi. "⊄ A table to finde the Epistles/ and Gospels vsually red in the *churche*/ after Salysbury vse." 4 pages in double columns. This is Nicolson's Second Edition of Coverdale's New Testament, and so closely resembles the first, that it is difficult to distinguish them without having both before you. They are however distinct editions throughout, though, being printed generally page for page, they are sometimes used to make up each other. Nothing is known of Hollybush, whose name appears on the title page. It is probably a pseudonym adopted by the printer, in consequence of the complaints of Coverdale against the inaccuracies of the former edition. A great many changes were made in this edition, both in the Latin and English texts, yet, from new blunders, it cannot be called on the whole any more accurate than the first.

809. NEW TESTAMENT (Latin). 1538. 4to.
Lent by the Archbishop of Canterbury.

811. BIBLE (English, Taverner's). The Most/ Sacred Bible,/ Which is the holy scripture, con-/teyning the old and new testament,/ translated into English, and newly/ recognised with great diligence/ after most faythful exem-/plars, by Rychard/ Taverner./ ☞ Harken thou heuen, and thou earth gyue/ eare : for the Lorde speaketh. Esaie. i./ ☞ Prynted at *London* in Fletestrete at/ the sygne of the sonne by John Byd-/dell, for Thomas Barthlet./ ☞ Cvm Privilegio/ ad imprimendum solum./ M. D. XXXIX./ Folio.
Lent by Earl Spencer.

Title, within a border of four woodcuts, the top one having in the centre a male and female head within a circle, the whole surrounded with a double black line, reverse blank ; Dedication begins on ☞. ij. "☞ To the most noble, most mighty, and most/ redoubted prynce, kynge Henry the. VIII." etc. I page ; on the reverse, "☞ These thynges ensuynge are/ joyned w^t this present vo-/lume of the bible.", and "☞ An exhortacion to the diligent/ studye of the holy scripture/ gathered out of the Bible "/ 1 page. The third leaf begins "The Contentes of the Scriptvre" 2 pp. in long lines ; The fourth leaf begins "The Names of the Bokes of the Byble.", 1 p. in two columns ; on the reverse, "☞ A briefe rehersall of the yeres passed," etc. filling about a quarter of the page ; then comes "☞ A Table of the principal maters/ conteyned in the Bible.", filling in double columns that and the next twenty-four pages : making in all 16 preliminary leaves. Text, in double columns, Genesis to Solomon's Ballet, CCXXX folioed leaves, with signatures A to Z, Aa to Oo in sixes, and Pp in eight leaves. Then follows a title without any border, "☞ The Boke of/ the Pro-/phetes." etc. reverse blank ; Text, beginning on AA. ij. Esaye to Malachi, LXXXXI folioed leaves, sigs. AA. to PP. vij ; then comes on PP viij. a third title, also without any border, "☞ The Volvme of/

the Bokes cal-/led Apocripha."/etc. reverse blank ; Text, Third book of Esdras to Second Machabees, LXXV folioed leaves, followed by one blank leaf. Sigs. Aaa to Mmm in sixes, and Nnn in four leaves. Then comes the New Testament title, within a border the same as the first title, reverse blank ; Text, Matthew to Revelations, folios II to CI, ending near the centre of the reverse, sigs. A. ij. to R. v. Then follows " ℭ This is the Table wherin ye shall/ fynde the Epistles and the Gospels/ after the vse of Salisbury." 5 pp. in double columns, ending at the bottom of the fifth page with this Colophon, " ℭ To the honour and prayse of God, was this Byble/ prynted : and fynyshed, in the yere of/ our Lorde God, a/ M. D. XXXIX./ The last page is blank. This is generally known as Taverner's Bible, and is very seldom found quite complete. This copy, like all others I have seen, wants signature K, or folios 55 to 60 in the New Testament. This hiatus of six leaves was probably intended to be filled with a Prologue to the Epistle to the Romans.

812. BIBLE (English). Another copy. Recognised by Richard Taverner. London : John Byddell for Thomas Berthelet, 1539. Folio. *Lent by the Rev. Dr. Gott.*

813. BIBLE (English, "Great Bible"). ℭ The Byble in/ Englyshe, that is to saye the con-/tent of all the holy scrypture, bothe/ of ye olde and newe testament, truly/ translated after the veryte of the/ Hebrue and Greke textes, by ye dy-/lygent studye of dyuerse excellent/ learned men, expert in the forsayde/ tonges./ ℭ Prynted by Rychard Grafton ῆ/ Edward Whitchurch./ Cum priuilegio ad imprimen-/dum solum./ 1539./ [*Colophon*] The ende of the new Testamēt :/ and of the whole Byble, Fynisshed in Apryll,/ Anno. M. CCCCC. xxxix./ A dño factū est istud,/ Folio.

Lent by Earl Spencer.

Six preliminary leaves, viz. 1. Title, in black and red within Holbein's beautiful woodcut border, having on the reverse " ℭ The names of all the bookes of the Byble/ 't the content of the Chapters," etc. 2. * ii, "The Kalender/ January,/ hath. xxxj. dayes. The mone .xxx./ (all these words in red) 2 leaves, in red and black, having ' ℭ An Almanach for. xix, yeares./ on the last half of the verso of the third leaf, with three lines underneath in black, preceded by a ℭ in red. 4. * iiij, " ℭ An exhortacyon to the studye of the holy/ Scripture gathered out of the Byble."/ 1 page, the letter S in Scripture directly under the letter r in exhortacyon. On the reverse " ℭ The summe and content of all the holy/ Scripture, both of the olde and new testament." 2 pp. ; the fifth leaf beginning "loue to al mē,". On the reverse " ℭ A Prologue, expressynge what is/ meant by certayn signes and tokens that we/ haue set in the Byble. ".'/ the initial F filling the space of five lines, and the last line being "for euer. Amen." with " God saue the Kynge," in large letters 2½ inches below. 6. " ℭ A descripcyon and successe of the kyn-/ges of Juda and Jerusalem," etc. beginning " Dauid raygned ouer Israel the .iij. c. xxix. yere " : On the middle of the reverse begins " ℭ Wyth what iudgement the bokes of the/ Olde Testament are to be red." The text is divided into five parts, each with separate titles except the first : Part I, Genesis to Deuteronomiū, 84 leaves, Fo, j, to Fo, lxxxiiij, Genesis beginning with the initial I nine lines deep, and Deuteronomy ending in the middle of the recto with " ℭ The ende of the fyfth bo-/ke of Moses, called in the Hebrue/ Elle Haddebarim, and in/ the Latin./ Deuteronomium," reverse blank : Title " ❡ The second/ parte of the Byble con-/ tayning these/ bookes." within a border composed of 16 woodcuts, the lower left hand corner one representing three women kneeling before a man sitting, reverse blank ; Text, Josua to Job, 122 leaves, Fo. ij. to Fo. cxxiij. beginning "AFter the death of Mo-"/ and ending on the reverse of folio 123, followed by a blank leaf. Title " ❡ The thirde/ parte of the Byble con-/taynyng these/ bookes."/ in a border of 16 woodcuts, the second one from the top on the right hand side representing an old man kneeling to the king sitting, with a soldier holding a halberd in his left hand standing behind the old man, reverse blank. Text, Psalmes to Malachy, 133 leaves, Fo. ij. to Fo. cxxxiij. ending on the middle of the recto with "synge."./ for the last line, reverse blank. The title of the fourth Part, unlike any of the other editions, is within the same woodcut border as the first title, " ❡ The Volume of/ the bokes called Hagio-grapha."/ having on the reverse, " To the Reader." fifty-four long lines ; Text, The .iij. boke Of Esdras to The seconde boke Of the Machabees, 79 leaves, Fo, ij. to Fo. lxj, so misprinted for Fo. lxxx. ending at the bottom of the reverse with "now make an ende." for the last line. The title of the fifth Part, unlike that of any of the other editions, is within a border composed of six woodcuts. " ❡ The newe Te-/stament in englyshe translated/ after the Greke, cōtaynīg/ these bookes."/ reverse blank ; Text, Mathew to The Revela-cyon, 102 leaves. Fo ii, to Fo. ciij, ending with the fourteenth line in the first column of folio 103 with " Jesu. The grace of oure/ Lorde Jesu Christ/ be with you/ all./ Amen."/ In the centre of the same column begins, " ❡ A Table to fynde/ the Epistles and Gospels vsually red in the/ chyrch, after Salysbury vse," filling that and the three next pages, ending with the colophon given above near the bottom of the reverse of the 104th leaf. This is the first edition of The Great Bible, commonly called Cranmer's Bible, of which, during the years 1539, 1540, and 1541, there were seven distinct editions, reprinted throughout, but so closely resembling each other that of five of them the leaves of each begin and end alike, and are often used, ignorantly or dishonestly, to make up each other. The same similarity exists between the two other editions. There is little difference in the commercial value and bibliographical interest of the seven editions. Any one of them complete, genuine, and in good condition, is an ornament to any library, public or private. Indeed, perfect copies are much rarer than is generally supposed. Mr. Lea Wilson, in our days a most indefatigable collector of Bibles, was so extremely fortunate as to possess the whole seven editions, every one of them perfect, or very nearly so. It was a labour of years to complete them. But his labours were crowned with success, and six of these magnificent volumes (all but this edition of 1539, a perfect copy of which was already in the library) Mr. Panizzi added, after Mr. Wilson's death, to the Library of the British Museum, at the moderate price of £80 each. The other volume of Mr. Wilson's set, 1539, a truly mag-nificent example, was sold by Mr. Pickering to Mr. Gardner, and in July, 1854, was resold in Mr. Gardner's sale by auction for £121. Mr. Henry Huth is now the owner of it. This edition of 1539 differs from all the others in several particulars. 1. Woodcuts are supported by a column or border on each side, which is not the case in any of the other editions. 2. The border of the title to the Apocripha is the same as that of the first title. 3. The New Testament title is surrounded by a border of six woodcuts, while in all the other editions it has the Holbein border. 4. There are pointing hands in the margins and text, all of which have *ruffles* about the wrist, while in the other editions a part of the hands are differently shaped with a *cuff* round the wrist. 5. The *stars* in the text of this edition are all six pointed, while in the other editions part of them are five pointed. There are, however, minute variations on every page. This splendid volume was printed in Paris by François Regnault, for Grafton and Whitchurch, in 1537 and 1538. Coverdale superintended the literary part and saw it through the press as reviser and corrector, while Grafton attended to the business matters. They were interrupted by the Inquisition just before the work was finished, so that they had to escape with what they could, and finish the work in London. The type and plant was apparently got up secretly for this edition (as before in the cases of the Coverdale and the Matthew Bibles at Antwerp), and after the interruption by the Inquisition, found their way to London and were used in producing the six immediately subsequent editions of the *Great Bible*.

814. BIBLE (English). The Great Bible. Another copy. London: R. Grafton, April, 1539. Folio. *Lent by the Rev. Dr. Gott.*

815. BIBLE (English). The Great Bible. Third copy. London: R. E. Whitchurche, April, 1539. Folio. *Lent by Henry White, Esq.*

816. BIBLE (English, Cranmer's, April). ❡ The Byble/ in Englyshe, that is to saye the con-/tēt of al the holy scrypture, both/ of yᵉ olde, and newe testamēt, with/ a prologe therinto, made by/ the reuerende father in/ God, Thomas/ archbysshop/ of Cantor/bury, ❡ This is the Byble apoynted/ to the vse of the churches./ ❡ Prynted by Edward whytchurche/ Cum priuilegio ad imprimendum solum./ M.D. xl./ [*Colophon*] The ende of the newe Testament :/ and of the whole Byble, Fynisshed in Apryll./ Anno M.CCCCC.XL./ + A dño factũ est istud./ Folio. Two copies. *One lent by the Earl of Leicester, the other by Earl Spencer.*

Ten preliminary leaves : 1. within the Holbein border, reverse blank. 2. The Kalender. "January." to "Julye." the fifth line in January reading "xix e,', v' Sign. *ii (Star six points) : 3. The Kalender. "Augustus" to "December," (sixth day of August misprinted xxix,) the last half of the reverse being filled by "❡ Almanacke for, xviii, yeares." all in red except the ❡, which is black : underneath are three lines, one black between two red, the last reading "and syxe houres."; 4. "❡ An exhortacyon to the studye of the holy/ Scripture gathered out of the Byble :'/ the S in Scripture being under n in An, and the signature being *iiii (in 1539 it is * *iiij*, and in December, 1541, there is no signature): on the reverse, "❡ The summe and content " etc. in the sixth line of the fourth paragraph "affeccyon"; 5. "The contentes of the scripture," [continued] beginning, "loue to all men, after the example of Chryst." On the reverse, " ❡ A prologue, expressynge what is/ meant by certayn sygnes and tokens that we/ haue set in the Byble."/ the last line reading "and prayse foreuer. Amen."/ 6. "❡ A descripcyon and successe of the kyn-/ges of Juda and Jerusalem," etc. beginning, "DAuid rayned ouer Israell the. iii. C. xxix. yere" etc. (the last line but one of the recto ending with " ād ") and ending on the middle of the reverse, "into spayne." being the last line, the lower half of the page being blank. 7. "The prologue,/ ❡ A prologue or preface made by the/ moost reuerende father in God, Thomas Archbyshop of Canturbury,"/the initial F filling the space of five lines, and the Latin quotations printed in the same type as the text. 8. The second leaf of Cranmer's Prologue, beginning, "makers shulde be hadd in admiration for theyr hye styles and obscure maner of wrytinge,"/ and the last four lines beginning severally with the words " prestes," " dowes," " estate " and " beleue," catch words " as also ". 9. Third leaf of Cranmer's Prologue, the first line being " Thyrdelye where, and in what audience. There and amonge those that bene studious to le-"/ and the last line of the recto beginning, "God, to ende in matyers of hygh speculatyō," ending in the centre of the reverse, the last being a full line. At the bottom of the page are large flourished capitals, H. R. 2½ inches high, and immediately above them are the same capitals ¾ of an inch square. 10. "☙ The names of all the bookes of the Byble/ and the content of the Chapters of euery booke, with the nombre of the leaffe "/ etc. reverse blank. Text, Genesis to Deuteronomium, 84 leaves, Fo. 1 [not numbered] to Fo, lxxxiiij, the first Chapter of Genesis beginning with the initial I seven lines deep, "I<small>N</small> the begynnynge * God "/ and Deuteronomy ending on the centre of the recto of folio 84 with "☙ The ende of the fyfth boke of Moses, called in the Hebrue Elle/ Hadderbarim, and in the/ Latin./ Deuteronomium."/ reverse blank. Title, "☙ The seconde/ parte of the Byble con-/taynyng these bookes." Josua to Hiob, within a border of 16 wood-cuts, the lower left-hand corner one representing Moses with horns on his head standing before an army, the same as in the edition of December, 1541, but in this edition the twelfth line of the title reads, "The. i. booke of ye chronycles."; Text, Josua to Job, 122 leaves, Fo, ii, to Fo, cxxiij, ending on the reverse with "the fourth generacion./ And so Job dyed,/ beynge old &/ of a perfect age."/+ ☙ Josua, Chapter I. begins with the initial A six lines deep, "After ye death of Moses the"/. Title, "☙ The thirde/ parte of the Byble con-/taynyng these bookes."/ in a border of 16 woodcuts, the second one from the top on the right-hand side representing the Genealogy of Alexander Magnus. Text, Psalmes to Malachy, Fo, ii. to Fo, cxxxii, ending on the recto with "thers, that I come not ād/ smyte the earth with/ cursynge."/ reverse blank. Title, "☙ The Volume of/ the bokes called Hagiographa."/ within a border of 16 woodcuts, the second one from the top on the right-hand side representing a madman astride a hobby-horse. On the reverse, "To the Reader." Text, Esdras to The seconde Booke Of the Machabees, Fo, ij, to Fo. lxxx, ending at the bottom of the reverse with "Je-/wes had the citye in possessiō : And here will/ I now make an ende."/ Title, within Holbein's woodcut border, the same as the first title, "☙ The newe Te-/stamēt in englyshe translated/ after the Greke cōtayning/ these bookes."/ the arms of Cromwell being retained, and the word newe in the first line in red Text, Mathew to The Reuelacion, Fo, ij, to Fo. ciii, (marked Fo. ciiii.) ending with the 14th line on the first column of the recto of folio 103, " The grace of our Lor-/de Jesu Christ be/ ∴ wyth you ∴/ all./ Amen."/ In the middle of the same column begins, "☙ A Table to fynde/ the Epistles and Gospels vsually red in the/ church, after Salysbury vse, wherof ye first/ lyne is the Epistle, & the other the Gospell :"/ filling that and the three next pages, ending on the reverse of folio 104 with the colophon given above, at the bottom of the page.

The second edition of the " Great Bible," and the first containing Cranmer's Preface. The price of this Bible was fixed by Royal Proclamation at ten shillings unbound. Public copies were sometimes attached by a chain to one of the pillars of the church, with the King's injunction that it should be read with "Discretion, Honest Intent, Charity, Reverence, and Quiet behaviour." This is the first edition of the Bible in English with the words on the title-page, "Appoynted to the vse of the churches." The "appointment" may be found expressed in full in the Kalendar. The authorization of the printing, or the licence, is expressed in the words " Cum priuilegio," &c., instead of the words " set forth with the Kynges moost gracious licence " which appeared on Nicholson's first 4to and folio reprints of Coverdale's Bible in 1537. See Nos. 791 and 792.

817. B<small>IBLE</small> (English). Cranmer's. London : Richarde Grafton [or Edward Whitchurch], Fynisshed in Apryll, 1540. Folio.

Lent by Henry J. Atkinson, Esq.

818. BIBLE (English, Cranmer's, May.) ⓒ The Byble in/ Englysh, that is to saye the content/ of all the holy scripture, both of the/ olde and newe Testament with a/ Prologe thereinto, made by/ the reuerende father in/ God, Thomas/ archbyshop/ ,',, of Cantor ,',, / bury. ⓒ This is the Byble appoynted/ to the use of ye churches/ Prynted by Edwarde Whitchurch/ Cum priuilegio ad imprimendum solum./ Finished the xxviii. daye of Maye/ Anno Domini/ M.D. XLI./ [*Colophon*] The ende of the newe Testament :/ and of the whole Byble, Fynysshed in Maye,/ Anno. M. CCCCC. XL i. / + / ⓒ A dño factũ est istud. Folio.

Lent by Mrs. Joliffe.

Six preliminary leaves, viz. 1. Title, within the Holbein border, Crumwell's arms effaced, with "ⓒ The names of all the bookes of the Byble," on the reverse; 2. First leaf of "The Kalender."/ * ii (Star 5 points) ninth line in January reading "v b Joyce ∴ ix"; 3. Second leaf of "The kalender."/ * iii (Star six points) the twenty-ninth line in August, "c Decalla. Jhon bapt. xxix" with "Almanacke for .xviij. yeares."/ occupying the lower half of the verso; 4. "ⓒ A prologue or preface made by the/ moost reuerende father in God Thomas Archbysshop of Cantorburye"/ no signature; 5. Second leaf of Cranmer's Prologue, signature * *; 6. Third leaf of Cranmer's Prologue, signature * * ii. ending in the middle of the reverse with the last line, "the saluacyon of God."/ with the large initials II. R. below. Text, Genesis to Deuteronomium, Fo. i to Fo. lxxxiiij, the first line of Genesis being, "IN the be-"/ and Deuteronomy ending on the middle of folio 84 with, "ⓒ The ende of the fyfth booke, / of Moses, called in the Hebrue. Elle-/haddebarim, and in the Latin :/ Deuteronomium."/ reverse blank; Title, within a border of 16 woodcuts, "ⓒ The seconde/ parte of the Byble con-/taynynge these/ bookes."/ reverse blank; Text, Josua to Job, Fo. ii, to Fol. cxxiii, ending on the reverse, and followed by one blank leaf; Title, within a border of 16 woodcuts, "ⓒ The thyrde/ parte of the Byble con-/taynynge these/ bookes."/ "Zachary. ,',/ reverse blank; Text, Psalmes to Malachy, Fo ij. to 133, falsely printed Fo. cxxxii. ending in the centre of the recto with "chyldren to their fathers, that/ I come not to smyte/ the earth wyth/ cursinge."/ reverse blank; Title, within a border of 16 woodcuts, "ⓒ The volume/ of the bookes called/ Hagiographa."/ with "To the Reader" on the reverse in long lines; Text, Esdras to Machabees. Fo, ij. to Fo. lxxx. ending at the bottom of the reverse with, "And here/ wyll I nowe make an ende."/ Then comes, within the Holbein border, the arms of Cromwell being effaced, "ⓒ The newe Te-/stament in englyshe translated/ after the Greke, cōtaynynge/ these bookes :"/ reverse blank; Text, Mathew to Revelacyon, Fo. ij. to Fo. ciiij. (so marked for ciij.) ending with the fourteenth line in the first column of the recto with, "The grace of our Lord/ Jesu Christ be/ with you/ all/ ,',, Amen./ ,',/" In the centre of the same column begins, "ⓒ A table to fynde the/ Epystles and Gospels vsually red in the/ church, after Salysbury vse, wherof ye fyrst/ lyne is the Epistle, 't the other the Gospell :"/ filling that and the three next pages, ending near the bottom of the verso with the Colophon given above.

819. BIBLE (English), with Cranmer's Prologue. London : Edward Whitchurch, Maye, 1541. Folio. *Lent by the Rev. Dr. Gott.*

820. BIBLE (English, Cranmer's, July). ¶ The Byble in/ Englyshe, that is to saye the con-/tēt of al the holy scrypture, both/ of y^e

olde, and newe testamēt, with/ a prologe therinto, made by/ the reuerende father in/ God, Thomas/ archbyshop/ ∴ of Canter ∴/ bury,/ ¶ This is the Byble apoynted/ to the vse of the churches./ ¶ Prynted by Rychard Grafton./ Cum priuilegio ad imprimendum solum./ M.D. xl./ [*Colophon*] The ende of the newe Testament :/ and of the whole Byble, Fynisshed in July,/ Anno. M. CCCCC. XL./ A domino factum est istud/ This is the Lordes doynge. Folio. *Lent by Francis Fry, Esq.*

Seven preliminary leaves, viz. 1. Title, within Holbein's border, reverse blank : 2. The first leaf of "The Kalender" with signature *ii (star five points) the first line in January reading, 'iii A Circumcisyon ',' i " 3. Second leaf of "The Kalender," signature *iii (Star five points) the seventeenth line in August containing ' Rufe martyr. ,', xxvii "; On the reverse in the middle of the page, "Almanacke for .xviii. yeares "/ 4. First leaf of " ¶ A prologue or preface made by the/ moost reuerende father in God, Thomas Archbyshop of Canterbury "/ the initial F being twelve lines deep, the twelfth line reading, "se to reade, or to heare redde yͤ scripture in theyr vulgar tō-"/ signature +; 5. Second leaf of Cranmer's Prologue, + ii, the last line but one beginning, "estate or cōdicyon soeuer they be, maye ī thys booke learne all "; 6. The third leaf of Cranmer's Prologue, + iii, the thirtieth line beginning "God at all auentures "; ending on the middle of the reverse, the last line reading, "ryght : wyll I shewe the saluation of God." Underneath are the large flourished capitals H. R. 7. " ¶ The names of all the bookes of the Byble,/ and the content of all the Chapters of euery booke, wyth the nombre of the leafe/ where the bookes begynne."/ 1 page, reverse blank ; Text, Genesis to Deuteronomium, 84 leaves, Fo. i. to Fo, lxxxiiii, the last line of the first chapter of Genesis reading "mornyng : was made the sixte daye." and Deuteronomy ending in the centre of the recto of folio 84. " ¶ The ende of the fyfth booke/ of Moses, called in the Hebrue : Elle-/haddebarim, and in the Latin/ Deuteronomium."/ reverse blank ; Title, within a border of 16 wood-cuts, " ¶ The seconde/ parte of the Byble con-/taynyng these/ bookes.'/ the first line being black (except the ¶, which is red) and the second line being all in red, reverse blank. Text, Josua to Job, Fo. ii to Fo, cxxiij, ending on the reverse, followed by a blank leaf ; Title, within a border of sixteen woodcuts, " ☾ The thyrde/ parte of the Byble con-/taynynge these/ bookes."/ the word " thyrde " being in black, reverse blank. Text, Psalmes to Malachy, Fo. ii to Fo. cxxxij, ending on the recto with "and/ smyte the earth with/ cursynge."/ reverse blank. Title, within a border of 16 woodcuts, " ☾ The volume of/ the bokes called Hagiographa "/ the three words in the first line being in red, and the second woodcut from the top, on the left-hand side, representing Daniel in the lion's den ; on the reverse, "To the Reader." in long lines. Text, Esdras to Machabees, Fo. ii, to Fo, lxxx, ending at the bottom of the reverse ; Title, within the Holbein border, Cromwell's arms still retained, " ☾ The newe Te-/stament in Englyshe translated/ after the Greke cōtaynynge/ these bookes."/ the first line of the title being all in black, except the ☾, which is red ; reverse blank. Text, Mathew to Revelacyon, Fo, ij. to Fo. ciij [not numbered] ending with the fourteenth line in the first column of the recto with "The grace of our Lord/ Jesu Christ be/ wyth you all./ ,', Amen. ,',/" In the middle of the same column begins, " ☾ A Table to fynde the/ Epistles and Gospels vsually red in the/ church, after Salysbury vse," filling that page and the three next, and ending with the colophon given above at the bottom of the verso of the last leaf.

821. BIBLE (English, Cranmer's, December). ¶ The Byble in Englyshe, that is to saye the con-/tent of all the holy scrypture, both/ of the olde & newe testament with/ a prologe therinto, made by/ the reuerende father in/ God, Thomas/ archebysshop/ of Can-tor-/bury,/ ¶ This is the Byble appoynted/ to the vse of the churches/ ¶ Printed by Edward Whitchurch/ Cum priuilegio ad imprimendum solum./ An. do. M.D. xl./ [*Colophon*] The ende of the newe Testament,/ and of the whole Bible, Finysshed in December/ Anno. M.CCCCC. XLi./ †/ A domino factum est istud/ This is the Lordes doynge./ Folio.

Lent by Francis Fry, Esq.

Ten preliminary leaves, viz. 1. The Title within Holbein's border, with the arms of Cromwell effaced, reverse blank ; 2. First leaf of "The Kalender." the fifteenth line in January reading, " A Maure Abbot. *iii* xv," sign. * ii (star 5 points). 3. Second leaf of " The Kalender." Signature *iii (star 6 points) with an " Almanacke for .xviij, yeares." occupying the last half of the reverse M.d. xlix, being misprinted "M. xlix." 4. "An exhortacyon to the studye of the holye/ Scripture gathered out of the Byble :/" no signature (April 1539 has *iiij, and April 1540 has *iiii ;) on the reverse, "☾ The summe and content of all the holy/ Scripture, both of the olde and newe Testament."/ sixth line of the fourth paragraph has, "affection ;" 5. "The Contentes of the Scripture,"/ having on the reverse, "☾ A prologue/ expressynge what is/ meant by certayne sygnes and tokens, that we/ haue set in the Byble."/ Twelve lines with large initial F, the last line reading "lefte them oute."/ 6. "☾ A description and successe of the kyn-/ges of Juda and Jerusalem," etc. the initial D, seven lines deep, beginning, "Dauid raygned ouer Israel the .C. xxix. yere of theyr entrynge into the lande,"/ ending a little above the middle of the re-verse with, "into Spayne." for the last line, the rest of the page blank ; 7. The first leaf of Cranmer's Prologue, signature +, "☾ A prologue or preface made by the/ moost reuerende father in God, Thomas Archbysshop of Cantorburye"/ the third line beginning "entrye of this booke,"; 8. Second leaf of Cranmer's Prologue, signature + ii, recto beginning "makers shoulde be had in admira-tion for theyr hye stiles and obscure maner and wrytynge,"/ and the verso end-ing "se, and discerne what is truth."/ 9. The third leaf of Cranmer's Prologue, * iij, the first line reading, "Thyrdely where and in what audience. There and amonge those that ben studyous to"/ ending in the middle of the verso with, "wyll I/ shewe the saluation of God."/ with the large flourished capitals H. R. beneath ; 10. "☾ The names of all the bookes of the Byble,/ and the content of all the Chapiters of euery boke, with the nombre of the leafe/ where the bookes begyn."/ reverse blank. Text, Genesis to Deuterono-mium. Fo. i, to Fol. lxxxiiij, Genesis beginning with initial I fourteen lines deep, "IN ye begyn-/nyng * god/ created hea-/uen & earth./ The erth/," and Deuteronomy ending near the centre of the recto of folio 84. "☾ The ende of the fifth booke/ of Moses, called in the Hebrewe Elle-/haddebarim : and in the latyn/ Deuteronomium."/ reverse blank ; Title, within a border of 16 woodcuts, "☾ The seconde/ parte of the Byble con-/taynge these/ bookes./" reverse blank ; Text, Josua to Job, Fo. ii, to Fol. cxxiii, Josua beginning with the initial A seven lines deep, "AFter ye death of Moses ye seruaut of ye Lord,"/ and Job ending on the reverse of folio 123 with "the fourth generacio./ And so Job dyed,/ beinge olde, & /of a perfecte/ age./[¶]/ followed by a blank leaf ; Title, within a border of 16 woodcuts, "☾ The thyrde/ parte

of the Byble con-/taynynge these/ bookes."/ reverse blank ; Text, Psalmes to
Malachy, Fo. ii to Fo. cxxxii. ending near the middle of the recto with
"fathers, that I come/ not 't smyte the/earth wyth/ cursinge."/ reverse blank ;
Title, within a border of 16 woodcuts, "☾ The volume/ of the bookes called,/
Hagiographia/" with, " To the Reader " on the reverse ; Text, Esdras to
Machabees, Fo. ii. to Fo. lxxx. ending at the bottom of the reverse with, "Je-/wes
had ye cytie in possessyō : And there wyll/ I nowe make an ende."/ Title,
within Holbein's border, Crumwell's arms effaced, "☾ The newe Te-/stamēt
in englyshe, translated/ after the Greke, cōtayning/ these bookes."/ reverse
blank : Text, Mathew to Revelations, Fo. ii. to Fo. ciii. ending with the fourteenth line of the first column of the recto with, "The ende of the newe/ Testament."/ Underneath in the same column is, "☾ A table to fynde the/
Epistles and Gospels vsually red in the/ church, after Salysbury/ vse, wherof
ye fyrst/ lyne is the Epistle, 't the other the Gospell": /filling that and the three
following pages, ending near the bottom of the reverse with the colophon
given above.

822. BIBLE (English). The Byble in Englyshe. Cum privilegio, 1541.
Fynyshed in November, 1540. Folio.
Lent by the University Library, Edinburgh.

With Cranmer's Preface. Cromwell having been disgraced by Henry VIII,
in July, 1540, his arms are erased from the title-page. The full collations of
the two November editions of 1540 and 1541, together with the two other
November editions partly reprinted, may be found in Mr. Francis Fry's excellent book on the Great Bible. The present is a fine large and perfect copy,
the paper stained yellow after being printed.

823. BIBLE (English). Cranmer's. London : Whitchurch, November,
1541. Folio. *Lent by the Rev. Dr. Gott.*

824. BIBLE (English). Cranmer's. London : Edwarde Whitchurch,
November, 1541. Folio. *Lent by Mrs. Joliffe.*

825. BIBLE (English), Cranmer's. London : R. Grafton. Finysshed in
November, 1541. Folio. *Lent by the Archbishop of Canterbury.*

826. NEW Testament (German). Freyburg, durch Johannem Fabrum
Juliacensem, 1539. 8vo. *Lent by Henry J. Atkinson, Esq.*

827. BIBLE (Latin). Lyon : Gryphius, 1540. 32mo.
Lent by Henry J. Atkinson, Esq.

828. CONCORDANCE (Latin). Lugduni, apud Iacobvm Givnetam, 1540.
4to. *Lent by Henry J. Atkinson, Esq.*

829. NEW Testament (English). Erasmus'. 1540. 4to.
Lent by the Archbishop of Canterbury.

830. NEW Testament (First Islandic). Prykt uti konongluen stad
Roschyld af mer Hans Barth. xii Dag Aprilis MDxl. Small
8vo. *Lent by the British and Foreign Bible Society.*

Excessively rare. This copy is imperfect, wanting all before signature D.
and the end. Black letter, 33 lines on a page.

831. BIBLE (Dutch). Den Bibel. Gheprint Thantwerpen By mi Henrick Peetersen van Middelborch. 1541. Folio.
Lent by Henry J. Atkinson, Esq.

832. BIBLE (Swedish). Biblia, Thet år, All then Helgha Scrifft, på Swensko. [Translated from the German version of M. Luther by O. Petri and L. Petri.] 6 parts. First edition. Upsala, 1541-40. Folio, with curious woodcuts. *Lent by Henry White, Esq.*
The Old Testament is in five parts, each with a separate numeration, and the four latter with distinct title-pages; the first four parts are dated 1540.

833. NEW Testament (Latin). Paris: Robertus Stephanus, 1541. 8vo. *Lent by Henry J. Atkinson, Esq.*

834. BIBLE (Latin). Lugduni, Gryphius, 1542. 32mo.
Lent by Henry J. Atkinson, Esq.

835. BIBLE (Latin). With woodcuts by Hans Springinklee. Lyon: Roville, 1542. 4to. *Lent by Henry J. Atkinson, Esq.*

840. BIBLE (Latin). Biblia Sacrosancta Testamēti Veteris & noui, e sacra Hebræorum lingua Græcorumque fontibus, consultis simul orthodoxis interpretib. religiosissime translata in sermonem Latinum. [By Leo Juda, T. Bibliander and P. Cholinus. The New Testament revised and corrected from the translation of Erasmus by R. Gaulter. The whole edited by C. Pellican.] (De omnibus sanctę scripturę libris eorumque præstantia... H. Bullingeri expositio—Argumenta in omnia tam Veteris quam Novi Testamenti capita, elegiaco carmine conscripta per R. Gualth.) 3 parts. Tiguri: Ch. Froschover, 1543. Folio.
Lent by Earl Spencer.

841. NEW Testament (Latin). Testamenti/ Novi/ æditio vvlgata./ Lugduni/ Theobald Paganus, 1543. 32mo.
Lent by Henry J. Atkinson, Esq.

842. NEW Testament (Latin). Mogvntiæ in ædibus Iuonis Schœffer, 1543. 8vo. *Lent by Henry J. Atkinson, Esq.*

843. BIBLE (Latin). Venetiis, de Tridino Montisferrati, 1544. 4to.
Lent by Henry J. Atkinson, Esq.

844. BIBLE (Latin). Zurich: C. Froschover, 1544. 8vo.
Lent by Henry J. Atkinson, Esq.

845. BIBLE (German). Die gantze Bibel, das ist alle bücher allts unnd neüws Testaments, den ursprünglichen sepraachen nach, auffs aller treüwlichest verteütschet. Darzů sind yetz und kommen ein... Register... über die gantzen Bibel. Die jarzal und rachnung der zeyten von Adamen biss an Christum, mit sampt gwüssen Concordantzen, Argumenten, Zalen und Figuren. (Von allen bucheren heiliger und Göttlicher gschrifft... an den Chris-

tenlichen Läser ein klarer Bericht. [by H. Bullinger.] With woodcuts.] 2 parts. Zürich: Christoffel Froschouer, 1545. Folio. *Lent by the British and Foreign Bible Society.*
Each part has a distinct title-page, pagination, and register. Printed in double columns; register in eights.

846. BIBLE (Latin). Robert Stephanus. 1546. Folio.
Lent by Henry J. Atkinson, Esq.

847. BIBLE (Italian). La Biblia [da Antonio Bruccioli]. Vineggia: Girolamo Scotto, 1547. 4to. *Lent by Henry J. Atkinson, Esq.*

848. NEW Testament (English). The newe Testament of the last translacion. By Wylliam Tyndall. With Prologes and Annotacions in the mergēt. London: Wylliam Tylle, 1549-1548. 4to.
Lent by Henry J. Atkinson, Esq.
This is Mr. Fry's No. 18, to which the reader is referred for a careful collation.

849. NEW Testament (English and Latin). London: William Powell, 1548-47. 4to. Fry's No. 16. *Lent by the Archbishop of Canterbury.*

850. BIBLE (English). Matthew's version, revised by Becke. London: Day and Seres, 1549. Folio. Sometimes called "the Bug Bible." See Psalm xci, 5. *Lent by Henry J. Atkinson, Esq.*

851. BIBLE (English). Matthew's version revised by Becke. London: Day and Seres, 1549. Folio. *Lent by Henry J. Atkinson, Esq.*

851*. BIBLE (English). Another copy. *Lent by the Earl of Leicester.*

852. BIBLE (English). Matthew's version, revised by Becke. London: Daye and Seres, 1549. Folio. *Lent by the Rev. Dr. Gott.*

853. BIBLE (English). Matthew's. London: Thomas Raynalde and William Hyll, 1549. Folio. *Lent by Henry White, Esq.*
The woodcut border of the title-page of this edition is from the same blocks as that of Petyt and Redman for Berthelet, folio, 1540, and the Coverdales of 1535 and 1537, all differing, however, in the setting of the texts in the several cartouches.

853*. BIBLE (English). Another copy. *Lent by Henry J. Atkinson, Esq.*

860. BIBLE (English). Cranmer's. London: Edward Whitchurch, 1549. Folio. *Lent by James Watkins, Esq.*

861. NEW Testament (English, and Latin of Erasmus). Lond.: W. Powell, 1549. 4to. *Lent by the Archbishop of Canterbury.*

861*. BIBLE (1st Danish). Biblia, det er den gantske Hellige Scrifft, udsæt paa Danske. [By P. Palladius, O. Gyldenmund, H. Sinnesen, and J. Machabæus.] First edition. Kobenhaffn, 1550. Folio. *Lent by the Rev. Dr. Ginsburg.*

862. BIBLE (Latin). 3 vols. Lugduni : Gryphius, 1550. Folio.
Lent by Henry J. Atkinson, Esq.

863. BIBLE (English, Coverdale's). ⁋ The whole/ Byble,/ that is the holy scripture/ of the Olde and Newe testament/ faythfully translated into/ Englyshe by Myles Couerdale, and/ newly ouer/sene and correcte./ M. D. L./ Pray for vs that the worde of God maye/ haue free passage 't be glorified. ii. Tes. iii./ Prynted for Andrewe Hester, dwellynge/ in Paules Churchyard at the sygne/ of the whyte horse, and are/ there to be solde./ Set forth with the Kynges/ mooste gracious licence. [Christopher Froschover, Zurich, printed] London, A. Hester, 1550. 4to.
Lent by Francis Fry, Esq.

8 prel. leaves, viz. Title in red and black, within an architectural woodcut border, reverse blank ; " ⁋ The bokes of the hole Byble/ how they are named in Englyshe and / Latyn, and how longe they are/ wrytten in the allegations," I p.; on the reverse, "☞ Vnto the moost victorious Prince & our moost/ gracious soueraigne lorde, kynge Edwarde the syxte," 4 pp. signed "Your graces moost humble/ and faithful subiect, Myles/ Couerdale ; " on the reverse begins, " Myles Couerdale, to the Christen Reader." 5 pp.; The Kalender, beginning with "An Almanacke for xliii. yeares;" (from 1550) 4 pp. The Text begins with a woodcut representing the Creation of Eve on Signature A, folio 1. and ends with the Second Book of Machabees, with the tenth line on the recto of Q Q iv. folio ccccxciiii. the remainder of that page and the reverse being blank ; then follows the Text of the New Testament, without separate title, on Signature a a. folio 1. and ends on the reverse of folio cxxi. qq. i. Next comes The Table of the Epistles and Gospels. 5 pp. ending with " To the honoure and prayse of God, was this Byble prynted and fynished in the yeare of oure Sauoure Jesu Christ M. D. L. the xvj. daye of the moneth of August." the reverse blank. This second foreign edition of the Coverdale Bible is printed in double columns, in an angular German type, similar to that of the first Edition, 1535, but smaller, and is now believed to have come from the press of Christopher Froschover, of Zurich. The preliminary leaves, however, must have been printed in England, as they are in an entirely different type, being in small Old English letter. It was again reissued in 1553, before the death of Edward VI. in July, by Richard Jugge, with a new title and new preliminary leaves.

863*. NEW Testament (English, Tyndale's). London : Daye and Seres, 1550. 8vo. *Lent by Francis Fry, Esq.*

This is Mr. Fry's No. 26.

864. NEW Testament (English and Latin). ⁋ The new/ Testament in Englishe after/ the greeke translation anne-/xed wyth the translation of/ Erasmus in Latin./ Whereunto is added a Kalendar, and/ an exhortation to the readying of the/ holy scriptures made by the same/ Erasmus wyth the Epistles taken/ out of the olde testamēt both in Latin/ and Englyshe. wherūto is added a ta-/ble necessary to finde the Epistles and/ Gospels for euery sonday 't holyday/ throughout the yere after the vse of/ the churche of England nowe./ ⁋ Excusum *Londini* in officina Thomæ

Gaultier. pro. I. C./ Pridie Kalendas Decembris anno/ Domini. M.D.L./ London, 1550. 8vo. *Lent by Henry J. Atkinson, Esq.*

    14 prel. leaves, viz. Title in red and black within a broad border, with the cypher of Edward Whitechurch at the bottom ; on the reverse ☧ An almanacke for .xxii. yeares. "J. C. vnto the Christen reder." 1 page, reverse blank ; "☧ An exhortacion to the diligent studye of scri-/pture, made by Erasmus Roterodamus." 9 pages ; "☧ The summe and content of all the holye scri-/pture," etc. 2 pages followed by one blank page ; Kalendar 6 leaves ; Text, in double columns, the English in black letter, occupying the outer, and the Latin in small roman type, the inner column, A to IIh. v. in eights ; then comes "☧ The Epistles of the old testament." 5 pp. reverse blank ; followed by "☧ A table to fynde the Epi-/stles and Gospels vsually reade in the/ Church, accordynge vnto the booke of/ Common prayer :" 3 pp. the reverse of the last leaf being blank, This is Tyndale's Translation, edited, as is generally, but erroneously, supposed, by Sir John Cheke, though I know not upon what authority. All Tyndale's Prologues are omitted, and there are no notes. The running titles and the contents of the chapters are in the same type as the English text. The references, which are only on the outer margin, are in small roman type, like that of the Latin text. There are 54 lines on a full page. The paper, ink, and press work are good. There are no woodcuts or ornamental capitals, except at the beginning of Mathew.

865. CONCORDANCE (First in English). Marbeck's. London : Richard Grafton, 1550. Folio.   *Lent by Henry J. Atkinson, Esq.*

866. NEW Testament (English). Coverdale's (really Tyndale's). Zurich : Ch. Froschover, 1550. 16mo.
Lent by the Archbishop of Canterbury

867. BIBLE (German). Wittemberg : Hans Lufft, 1551. Folio.
Lent by Henry J. Atkinson, Esq.

867*. BIBLE (English). Matthew's [nicknamed the Bug Bible]. London : Nicolas Hyll, for Robert Toy [and others], 1551. [*Colophon*] Imprinted at the coste and charges of certayne honest men of the occupacyon, whose names be upon their bokes. Folio.
Lent by the Archbishop of Canterbury.

    See Psalm XCI, 5. "So that thou shalt not nede to be afraid for any Bugges by nighte, nor for the arrow that flyeth by day." Our present version reads "Thou shalt not be afraid for the terror by night," *etc.* This reading, *Bugges*, is common to Coverdale's, Matthew's, and Taverner's versions, all of which might as fairly be called "Bug-Bibles." The Great Bible of 1539, Cranmer's, the Genevan, and the Bishops' have *terrour.*

868. BIBLE (English). Taverner's, revised by Becke, with third book of Maccabees. London : John Daye, 1551. Folio.
Lent by Henry White, Esq.

869. BIBLE (English). Taverner's, by Becke, with third book of the Macabees. London : John Daye, 1551. Folio.
Lent by the Rev. Dr. Gott.

870. BIBLE (English). London, 1551. Folio.
Lent by Edward Poulson, Esq.

871. NEW Testament (Greek and Latin). Απαντα τα της Καινης διαθηκης. Nouum Iesv Christi D. N. Testamentum cum duplici interpretatione D. Erasmi et veteris Interpretis; Harmonia item Evangelica [by A. Osiander. Edited by R. Estienne]. 2 parts. [Geneva]: ex Officina R. Stephani, 1551. 8vo.
    Part 2 has a distinct title-page and pagination, and the harmony is separately paged. This is the first edition of the New Testament divided into verses according to our present use.

872. NEW Testament (English). Tyndale's. Woodcuts. London: Richard Jugge, 1552. 4to.   *Lent by F. Fry, Esq.*
    A woodcut in the 13th chapter of Matthew represents the Devil with a tail and a wooden leg, sowing tares.

873. NEW Testament (Italian). Il Nuovo Testamento. 2 vols in 1. Curious engravings. Lyone: Gulielmo Rouillio, 1552. 32mo.
    Lent by Henry J. Atkinson, Esq.

874. BIBLE (English). The Byble in English—accordyng to the translaciō that is appointed to be read in Churches. London: Edwarde Whytchurche, 1553. Cum privilegio, &c. Folio.
    Lent by the Rev. Dr. Gott.
    This and the small quarto edition of 1553 by Grafton are the last two editions of the Cranmer version issued in Edward VI.'s reign. This edition has marginal references but no notes. It must have appeared before the 6th July, when Mary mounted the throne, for at the end are three pages containing "a table to find the Epistles and Gospels usually read in the Church, accordinge unto the boke of Common-Prayer." The 4to edition has a "Table to fynd the Epistles and Gospels &c. after Salysbury use."

875. BIBLE (English). Another copy. London: Edwarde Whytchurche, 1553. Folio.   *Lent by Henry White, Esq.*

876. BIBLE (Italian). La Bibbia. 1553.
    Lent by the British and Foreign Bible Society.

877. BIBLE (Spanish). Biblia en Lengua Española traduzida palabra por palabra de la verdad Hebrayca por muy excelentes letrados vista y examinada por el officio de la Inquisicion. Con priuillegio del yllustrissimo Señor Duque de Ferrara. Con yndustria y deligencia de Duarte Pinel Portugues: estampada en Ferrara a costa y despesa de Jeronimo de Vargas Español: en primero de Março de 1553. Black letter. Folio.   *Lent by Earl Spencer.*
    First edition of the Bible in Spanish for the use of Christians. The only difference known between this and the version for the Jews is found in Is. vii., 14. The Jewish having "la moça" instead of "la virgen."

878. BIBLE (Old Testament). Biblia en lengua Española, traduzida palabra por palabra dela verdad Hebrayca por muy excelentes letrados, vista y examinada por el officio de la Inquisicion. [Edited by D. Pinel and A. Usque.] Gothic letter. Large paper. Ferrara, 1553. Folio.   *Lent by Earl Spencer.*

On the verso of the title-page occurs the dedication "All yllustrissimo. . . . Señor . . . Don Hercole da Este el segundo : quarto Duque de Ferrara." Subscribed "Jeronimo de Vargas y Duarte Pinel." The Colophon ends as follows : "estampada en Ferrara a costa . . . . de Jeronimo de Vargas Españól : en primero de Março de 1553." This edition does not contain the Apocrypha.

First impression of the Bible in Spanish. This version was for the use of the Spanish Jews.

885. BIBLE (Spanish). Biblia en Lengua Española. Ferrara, 1553. Folio. Large paper. *Lent by the British and Foreign Bible Society.*

886. NEW TESTAMENT (Dutch). Antwerp : Hans van Ramundt, 1553. 8vo. *Lent by Henry J. Atkinson, Esq.*

887. NEW TESTAMENT (English). Tyndale's. London : Richarde Jugge, 1553. 4to. *Lent by the Archbishop of Canterbury.*

888. NEW Testament (German). Curious cuts. Cöln : Van der Mülen, 1553. 8vo. *Lent by Henry J. Atkinson, Esq.*

889. BIBLE (Latin). Petit Bernard's cuts. Lugduni : Johan. Tornaesius, 1554. 8vo. *Lent by Henry J. Atkinson, Esq.*

890. NEW Testament (Italian). Plates by Petit Bernard. Lione : Giovanni de Tornes e Guillelmo Gazeio, 1556. 32mo. *Lent by Henry J. Atkinson, Esq.*

891. BIBLE Picture Book. Figuren, &c. Engravings by Petit Bernard. Lyons : J. van Tournes, 1557. 8vo. *Lent by Henry J. Atkinson, Esq.*

892. NEW Testament (English, Geneva). The/ Newe Testa-/ment of ovr Lord Ie-/sus Christ./ Conferred diligently with the Greke, and best ap-/proued translations./ VVith the arguments, aswel before the chapters, as for euery Boke/ & Epistle, also diuersities of readings, and moste proffitable/ annotations of all harde places : wherunto is added a copi-/ous Table./ At *Geneva*/ Printed By Conrad Badius./ M. D. LVII./ 16mo. *Lent by the Rev. Dr. Gott.*

On the title page is a woodcut about 1¾ inches square, representing Time restoring Truth ; On the reverse in small italic letters is " The ordre of the Bookes of the/ Newe testament," Then follows on *. ii. " The Epistle declaring that/ Christ is the end of the Lawe, by Iohn Caluin."/ 8 leaves ; " To the Reader " **. ii. 4 pages and eight lines of the next ; then comes ' The Argvment " filling the remainder of that page and the next. The text, The Holy/ Gospel of Iesvs/ Christe, vvrit/ by S. Matthew./ (a. i.) 430 folioed leaves : " The Table of the Newe/ Testament." folios 431 to 455, " The Ende " being on the recto, over the colophon. " Printed by Conrad Ba-.divs M. D. LVII./ This/ x. of Ivne."/ On the reverse in 23 lines, italic type, are " Fautes committed in the Printing." Although this is the first New Testament in English printed at Geneva, it is not, as some suppose, that which is usually called the *Genevan Version*. That was published three years later. This edition was the work of William Whittingham, afterwards Dean of Durham, but at the time of its publication residing in exile at Geneva. It is beautifully printed in small, clear, roman type, and is remarkable for two characteristics for the first time here introduced into the English translations, viz. the division of the text into verses, and the use of *italics* to indicate those explanatory words not to be found in the original tongues. This is not a new translation, but a revision of various others, as the editor informs us in his epistle to the reader. " First as touchig the perusing of the text, it was diligently reuised by the moste approued Greke examples, and conference of translations in other tonges as the learned may easely iudge, both by the faithful rendering of the sentence, and also by the proprietie of the wordes, and perspicuitie of the phrase. Forthermore that the Reader might be by all meanes proffited, I haue deuided the text into verses and sectiõs, according to the best editions in other langages, and also, as to this day the anciët Greke copies mencion, it was wont to be vsed. And because the Hebrewe and Greke phrases, which are strange to rendre in other tongues, and also short, shulde not be to harde I haue sometyme interpreted them without any whit diminishing the grace of the sense, as our lãgage doth vse them, and sometyme haue put to that worde, which lacking made the sentence obscure, but haue set it in such letters as may easely be discerned from the cõmun text."

893. NEW Testament (English) translated by Whittingham. Geneva: Conrad Badius, 1557. 16mo. *Lent by the Archbishop of Canterbury.*

894. BIBLE (German, Weissenham). Ingolstatt: Ecken, 1558. Folio.
Lent by Henry J. Atkinson, Esq.

895. BIBLE (Italian). Bibbia volgare. [Nicolao de Malermi.] Curious engravings. Venegia, 1558. Folio. *Lent by Henry J. Atkinson, Esq.*

896. BIBLE (Latin). Paris: C. Guillard, 1558. Folio.
Lent by Henry J. Atkinson, Esq.

897. BIBLE (French). La Sainte Bible. A Lyon par Ian de Tovrnes, 1559. Folio. *Lent by Henry J. Atkinson, Esq.*

898. BIBLE (Dutch). Antwerpen by die weduwe van Jacob van Liesueldt, 1553, 1560 [1553 at end O. T.] *Lent by Henry J. Atkinson, Esq.*

899. BIBLE (Dutch). Den Bibel. Antwerp: Hans de Last, 1560 [date at end O. T. 1553.] Folio. *Lent by Henry J. Atkinson, Esq.*

909. BIBLE (English, first Genevan). The Bible/ and/ Holy Scriptvres/ Conteyned in/ the Olde and Newe/ Testament./ Translated Accor-/ding to the Ebrue and Greeke, and conferred With/ the best translations in diuers langages./ With moste profitable Annota-/tions vpon all the hard places, and other things of great/ importance as may appeare in the Epistle to the Reader./ At *Geneva*./ Printed by Rovland Hall./ M. D. LX./ 4to. *Lent by Earl Spencer.*

Four prel. leaves. Text, Genesis to II Maccabees, 474 folioed leaves ; New Testament, 122 leaves ; "A Briefe Table" llll.b. iii. to LLl. iii. 13 leaves, followed by one page, "The order of the yeres from Pauls conuersion" etc. reverse blank.

This Bible, the result of the labours of English exiles at Geneva during Queen Mary's reign, was dedicated to Queen Elizabeth—and though never sanctioned by royal authority, or by Parliament, or even by Convocation, for public use in churches, yet it was not only extensively read in churches, but was esteemed the favourite version by many of the clergy, as well as theological writers, insomuch that it continued to be the household English Bible for three quarters of a century. It is commonly known as the "Breeches" Bible from that word occurring in Gen. iii. 7. From 1560 to 1630 it was the most popular Bible in England, and by far the most approved version in Scotland, exceeding in its number of editions all the other translations united. Probably as many as two hundred distinct editions of the Genevan Bible and New Testament were called for during this period. The version of 1611 was slow in breaking its popularity. Both versions, as well as the Bishops', were all printed by the same royal printers.

910. BIBLE (English). First Genevan version. Another copy. Geneva : Rouland Hall, 1560. 4to.   *Lent by Henry J. Atkinson, Esq.*
Another copy, lent by Dr. Gott.

911. BIBLE (English). First Genevan version. Another copy. Geneva : Rouland Hall, 1560. 4to.   *Lent by Henry White, Esq.*
This is one of the very few copies known on large and thick paper, though somewhat cut down.

912. NEW Testament (English), by Whittingham and others [the second issue]. Unique? Geneva, 1560. 16mo.
Lent by the Archbishop of Canterbury.

913. NEW Testament (Latin). Lyon, 1560. 32mo.
Lent by Henry J. Atkinson, Esq.

913*. PSALMS (English). The whole Psalter translated into English Metre [by Archbishop Parker]. London : John Daye, [1560?] 4to.   *Lent by the Earl of Leicester.*

914. BIBLE (English, Cranmer's). The Bi/ble in Englishe ac-/cording to the tran-/slation of the great/ Byble/ 1561./ [*Colophon*] Imprinted at/ *London* in Powles/ Churcheyarde, by Ihon Cawoode./ Prynter to the Quenes Maiestie./ Anno. M. D. LXI. Cum priuilegio Regiæ /Maiestatis./ 4to. *Lent by Henry J. Atkinson, Esq.*

915. BIBLE (1st Polish). Biblia To iest. Kxicigi Stharego y Nowego Zakonu, na Polski iexzyk, z pilnosciax bedlug Lácińskiey Bibliey od Kościoła Krześciańskiego powsschnego prziyiethey, nowo wyłozona [by J. Leopolita-Niez. With marginal references and woodcuts]. Gothic letter. W. Krákowie, 1561. Folio.
Lent by Francis Fry, Esq.

916. NEW Testament (Latin). Many woodcuts. Parisiis, apud Jacobum Keruer, 1562. 8vo.   *Lent by Henry J. Atkinson, Esq.*

917. BIBLE (English, 2nd Genevan). The Bible translated according to the Ebrue and Greke, with most profitable annotations upon the hard places, etc. Geneva [no printer's name], 1562-61. Folio.
Lent by Francis Fry, Esq.
A remarkable typographical error occurs in Matthew v. 9, "Blessed are the *place-makers :* for they shall be called the children of God."

918. BIBLE (2nd Polish). Biblia S'wieta, Tho iest, Ksi̢gi Stárego y Nowego Zakonu, własnie z Zydowskiego, Greckiego, y Lacynskiego, nowo na Polski ięzyk z pilnościa y wiernie wytożone [by S. Zaciusz, P. Statoryusz, G. Orsacius, J. Trzecieski, J. Lubelczyk, and others; edited by M. Radziwił.] W. Brzesciu Litewskim, 1563. Folio. *Lent by Earl Spencer.*
The second published version of the Polish Bible, made by Prince Radziwil and the Protestant Reformers of Pinczow. The first Polish Bible was published in 1561 by the Catholics.

919. BIBLE (Polish). Another copy. 1563. Folio.
Lent by the British and Foreign Bible Society.

920. BIBLE (Dutch). Nicolaes Biestkeno, 1564. 8vo.
Lent by Henry J. Atkinson, Esq.

921. BIBLE (Latin). Antverpiæ : Christ. Plantin, 1564. 32mo.
Lent by Henry J. Atkinson, Esq.

922. BIBLE (Greek). Basiliæ : J. Hervagius, 1565. Folio.
Lent by Henry J. Atkinson, Esq.

923. NEW Testament (Latin). With full-page cuts in Revelation. Dilingæ : Sebaldvs Mayer, 1565. 8vo.
Lent by Henry J. Atkinson, Esq.

924. PSALMS (English). The Form of Prayers etc. used in the English Church at Geneva, with the Psalms of David, in metre. Edinburgh : by Robert Lekprevik, 1565. 8vo.
Lent from the Advocates' Library.
The earliest edition of the Sternhold and Hopkins prepared for the Church of Scotland. There are many subsequent republications.

925. BIBLE (English). Cranmer's version. Rouen : C. Hamillon, at the cost and charges of Richard Carmarden, 1566. Folio.
Lent by Henry J. Atkinson, Esq.

926. BIBLE (French). Geneve : Perrin, 1566. 8vo.
Lent by Henry J. Atkinson, Esq.

927. BIBLE (Italian). Bibbia Volgare. 2 vols. Venetia : Andrea Muschio, 1566. 4to. Curious engravings.
Lent by Henry J. Atkinson, Esq.

928. PSALMS (Latin). Psalmorvm Da-/vidis Paraphrasis Poetica,/ nunc primùm edita,/ Authore Georgio Buchanano/ Scoto, poetarum nostri sæculi facilè/ principe./ Psalmi Aliqvot in ver-/sus item Græcos nuper à dieursis/ translati./ Anno M. D. LXVI./ [*Colophon*] *Argentorati*/ Excudebat Iosias Rihelius./ M.D.LXVI./ 12mo.
Lent by David Laing, Esq.

Sixteen prel. leaves and 352 pp. This is generally believed to be the first edition of this celebrated version of the Psalms, though Brunet thinks that the Paris edition, without date, by Henry Stephens, is anterior, notwithstanding the words " nunc primum edita " on this title-page. On this book rests in a great measure the high reputation of George Buchanan as a poet and scholar. He was born in 1506, and died in 1582. While imprisoned in a monastery in Portugal, by order of the Inquisition, about 1550, he beguiled the tedium of his confinement by translating the whole of the Psalms into Latin verse. There are no less than twenty-nine varieties of metre. On the reverse of the title is, "Index Festorum xxiiii." In the Kalendar, which occupies nine leaves, there are twelve rude but exceedingly curious woodcuts representing the signs of the Zodiac, and the habits and occupations of the good people about Strasbourg. On the recto of B B iiij is the famous epigram of Buchanan to Mary, Queen of Scots, beginning:—

"Nympha, Caledoniæ quæ nunc feliciter oræ
Missa per innumeros sceptra tueris auos."

929. NEW Testament (the first Welsh). Testament Newydd ein Arglwydd Jesu Christ. Gwedy ei dynnu, yd y gadei yr ancyfiaith, au yn ei gylydd or Groec a'r Llatin, gan newidio ffurf llythyreu y gariaedodi. Eb law hyny ymae pop gair a dibiwyt y vot yn andeallus, ai o ran llediaith y'wlat, ai o ancynefinder y devnydd, wedy ei noti ai eglurhau ar'ledemyl y tu dalen gydrychiol. [Preceded by an "Almanach dros xxv. o vlynydden," &c. Translated by W. Salesbury and R. Davies, Bishop of St. Davids; edited by the former, with an Epistle by the latter, "i bop map eneid dyn o vewn ey escopawt." First edition.] Black letter. [London]: H. Denham, 1567. 4to. *Lent by the British and Foreign Bible Society.*

In long lines, thirty-one to the full page. The text is not divided into verses.

930. BIBLE (English). The Holie Bible. Richard Jugge, 1568. 2 vols. Folio. *Lent by Earl Spencer.*

The "Bishops'" Bible, a revision of the "Great Bible" undertaken by Archbishop Parker, with the assistance of eight bishops. It appeared "cum privilegio regiæ majestatis," and its use was sanctioned by Convocation in 1571. It is sometimes called the *treacle* Bible, from Jeremiah viii, 22: "Is there no *tryacle* in Gilead?" rendered *rosin* in the Douai version, and *balm* in that of 1611. It is also sometimes called the "*Leda* Bible," from the use of one of a series of capital letters, designed after Ovid, used by Jugge in his other and previous books.

931. BIBLE (English, first Bishops'). Another copy. London: Richarde Jugge, 1568. Folio. *Lent by Henry J. Atkinson, Esq.*

932. BIBLE (French and Latin). 3 vols. Paris: Sebastien Nyvelle, 1568. 4to.
Lent by Henry J. Atkinson, Esq.

933. BIBLE (Latin). Lugduni: Ioannes Frellon, 1568. 8vo.
Lent by Henry J. Atkinson, Esq.

934. NEW Testament (Greek). 2 vols. Lvtitiæ: Robertus Stephanus, 1568-9. 32mo.
Lent by Henry J. Atkinson, Esq.

935. BIBLE (English). Genevan. Geneva: John Crespin, 1568-70. 4to.
Lent by Henry White, Esq.

936. PSALMS (Dutch). De C.L. Psalmen Dauids. Tot Noorwitz Gheprint by Anthonium de Solemne, 1568. 8vo.
Lent by W. Amhurst Tyssen-Amhurst, Esq.
A work from the same press, entitled "Geneu Kalendaer Historiaal 1570," is bound up with this. These two books, with Nos. 281, 282, 283, together form a unique collection of productions from the Norwich Press. No. 281 is dated 1568.

937. BIBLE (English). The Bishops' version, the first edition in 4to. London: Richard Jugge, 1569. 4to.
Lent by the Archbishop of Canterbury.

938. BIBLE (English). Bishops' version. First edition in 4to. Another copy. London: Richard Jugge, 1569. 4to.
Lent by the British and Foreign Bible Society.

939. BIBLE (Polyglot). Biblia Polyglotta. Antwerp: Plantinus, 1569-73. 8 vols. Folio.
Lent by Earl Spencer.
Edited at the command of Philip II by Arias Montanus, of the University of Alcala. Only 500 copies were printed, of which the greater part were lost at sea.

940. BIBLE (Spanish). La Biblia. (C. de Reyna.) [Basle?], 1569. 4to.
Lent by the British and Foreign Bible Society.

941. BIBLE (Spanish). Another copy, with new title dated 1622, date at end 1569. 4to.
Lent by Henry White, Esq.

942. NEW Testament (Dutch). 1569. 16mo.
Lent by Henry J. Atkinson, Esq.

943. NEW Testament (Latin). Novvm Iesv Christi Testamentvm. Antverpiæ: apud hæredes Arnoldi Birckmanni, 1570. 16mo.
Lent by Henry Stevens, Esq.
This copy belonged to Prince Henry, and has his monogram on the sides.

944. GOSPELS (Anglo-Saxon). The Gospels, &c. London: John Daye, 1571. 4to.
Lent by the Rev. Dr. Gott.

944*. NEW Testament (English). The/ Newe Te-/stament of/ ovr Lord Iesvs/ Christ./ Conferred with the Greke,/ and best approued/ translations./ VVith the arguments, as vvel before the/ chapters, as for euery Boke and Epistle,/ Also diuersities of readings, and/ most profitable annotations of all harde places : vvhere-/unto is added a co-/pious Table./ Imprinted at/ *London* by T. V. for/ Christopher Barker./ 1575./ Cum priuilegio./ [*Colophon* on page 813] Imprinted at *London* by Tho. Vautroullier/ for Christopher Barker./ 8vo. *Lent by Francis Fry, Esq.*

The title is within an elaborate woodcut border having the royal arms at the top, and "Cum priuilegio" in a compartment at the bottom ; on the reverse "The ordre of the Bookes "/ in small italics ; the next leaf begins on * ij. "The Epistle de-/claring that Christ/ is the end of the Law./ By Iohn Caluin."/ 16 pp. Then comes on ℭ ij. "To the Reader mercy/ and peace through/ Christ ovr Saviovr."/ 5 pp. ; on the reverse, in small italics, "The argvment of/ the Gospell, vvrit by the foure Euangelists." 1 p. Text in roman type, paged 1 to 813, ending with a tail-piece over the colophon. On page 814 begins "A declaration/ of the Table to the/ Nevv Testament," 1 p. ; "A table of the principall things" etc. 815 to 850 in double columns. Then follows "A perfect Supputation" etc. 3 pp. the next page blank. It is very seldom that the last two leaves are to be found. The version, with some very slight alterations, is the Genevan, first printed with the Old Testament in 1560 ; but Calvin's Epistle and Whittingham's Preface are taken from the Geneva edition of 1557, as also are the Declaration and the Table at the end. The translation and the notes differ very materially from Whittingham's edition.

945. NEW Testament (Basque). Iesvs Christ/ Gvre Iavnaren/ Testamentv/ Berria./ Rochellan, Pierre Hautin, Imprimicale./ 1571. 8vo. *Lent by the British and Foreign Bible Society.*

946. BIBLE (Latin). Heuteni. Venetiis, apud Ivntas, 1572. Folio. *Lent by Henry J. Atkinson, Esq.*

947. BIBLE (Latin). Antwerpiæ : Apud Viduam & Heredes Ioannis Stelsii, 1572. 8vo. *Lent by Henry J. Atkinson, Esq.*

948. BIBLE (English). Bishops' version. London : R. Jugge, 1573. 4to. *Lent by Henry J. Atkinson, Esq.*

949. BIBLE (English). The second folio, Bishops' version. London : Richard Jugge, 1572. Folio. *Lent by F. Fry, Esq.*

950. BIBLE (Latin). Venetia : Bevilaqua, 1574. 4to. *Lent by Henry J. Atkinson, Esq.*

951. BIBLE (Latin). Biblia advertissima exemplaria nunc recens castigata. Heutenus. Venetiis, apud Haeredes Nicolai Bevilaquæ, 1576. 4to. *Lent by Henry J. Atkinson, Esq.*

951*. NEW Testament (English) Genevan. Notes Englished by L. Tomson. London : C. Barkar, 1576. 8vo. *Lent by George Tawse, Esq.*

960. BIBLE (English). Genevan. London : C. Parker, 1578. Folio. *Lent by the Archbishop of Canterbury.*

961. BIBLE (English and Scotch). The Bible/ and Holy Scriptvres/ conteined in the/ Olde and Newe/ Testament./ Translated according to the/ Ebrue & Greke, & conferred with the beste translations/ in diuers languages./ (∴)/ With moste profitable Annota-

tions/ vpon all the hard places of the Holy Scriptvre,/ and other things of great importance, mete for/ the Godly Reader./ Printed in *Edinbrvgh*/ Be Alexander Arbuthnot, Printer to the Kingis Maiestie, dwelling/ at ye Kirk of feild. 1579./ Cvm gratia et Privilegio Regiae/ Maiestatis./ Folio. *Lent by Earl Spencer.*

Nine prel. leaves. On the title-page, above the imprint, is a woodcut representing the arms of Scotland, 3¼ by 4¾ inches ; on the reverse, "The names and order of all the Bookes/ of the olde & New Testament," 1 p. ; the second leaf begins on (. '.) ij. "To the Richt Excellent Richt/ heich and Michtie Prince Iames the Sixt/ King of Scottis," etc. 3½ pp. dated at the end, "From Edinburgh in our ge-/neral assemblie the tent day of/ Iulie. 1579." the rest of the page blank. Then comes "An dovble Calendare,/ to wit, the Romane and the Hebrew-/ Calendare," etc. "Ane Almanake," etc. 7 pp. On the reverse of the seventh leaf is " ⓒ A table to find out in what signe the Moone is at any tyme for euer" ½ page, under which is "Rvles for vnderstanding/ of this double Calendare," occupying that and half the next page, and signed "R. Pont:" the remainder of this page is filled with verses, " ※ Of the incomparable treasure of the holy Scriptures." On the reverse of the next, or eighth leaf, begins, " ※ A Description and svccesse/ of the Kinges of Ivda and Ierusalem,"/ etc. 1½ pp. ; then comes on the rest of the page " An exhortation to the studie of the holie Scripture ;" on the reverse, " Howe to take profite in reading of the holie Scripture " signed by T. Grashop, 1 p. at the bottom of which is Arbuthnot's device copied from Richard Jugg's, substituting his own arms at the bottom between the initials A. A. The Text, Genesis to Second Maccabees, 503 folioed leaves, ending with "The Third Boke of/ the Maccabees newlie translated out/ of the original Greke." This third book however is not added, but next comes the title of " The/ Newe Testament/ of ovr Lord Ie-/svs Christ./ Conferred diligently with the Greke, and best approved/ translations in diuers languages./ [The arms of Scotland the same as on the first title.] At Edinbvrgh/ ※ Printed by Thomas/ Bassandyne./ M. D. LXXVI./ Cvm Privilegio./" Reverse blank ; the text, A. ij. folioed 2 [misprinted 1] to 125, ending on the middle of the reverse. Then comes " A briefe Table of the Pro-/per names which are chiefly founde in the olde Te-/stament," in double columns not paged or folioed, but beginning on the recto of X. vj. and ending at the middle of the verso of Y. iij. Then follows on "A Table of the principal/ things that are conteined in the Bible," etc. in treble columns, ending on the middle of the reverse of Z. vj. The rest of that page, and the next are filled with " ※ A Perfite svppvtation of the yeres/ and times from Adam vnto Christ" brought down "vnto this present yere of/ our Lord God 1576." On the reverse is "The Order of the yeres from Pauls conuersion " etc. 1 p. The next leaf of this gathering is probably blank, as no copy is known to contain more. This is the first edition of the Bible printed in Scotland. It is the Genevan version, in roman type, in double columns, with the marginal notes in smaller type than the text. There are the usual woodcuts in Exodus, to be found in most of the early Genevan versions. At the thirty-third chapter of Numbers is a detached map, another at the fifteenth chapter of Josua, and at the end of Ezekiel is a plan of the Temple. The present copy is large, clean, pure, and perfect. Before the printing was completed Bassandyne died ; but in all the copies the title of the New Testament bears his name, with date 1576. In 1579 the complete volume was issued under sanction of the General Assembly of the Church of Scotland, with a dedication to James the Sixth, and other preliminary leaves, printed by Alex. Arbuthnot.

962. BIBLE (English). London: Christopher Barker, 1579? 4to.
Lent by Henry J. Atkinson, Esq.

963. BIBLE (Latin). First edition of Tremelius and Junius. London: Middleton, 1580. 4to. *Lent by Henry J. Atkinson, Esq.*

964. BIBLIA Sclavonica. H. Typis Joannis Theodori Jum-ex magnâ Russiâ. Ostrobia, 1581. Folio. *Lent by Earl Spencer.*

965. BIBLE (English). Genevan. London: C. Barker, 1582. 4to.
Lent by Henry J. Atkinson, Esq.

966. NEW Testament (English). The New Testament of JESUS CHRIST, translated faithfully into English, out of the authentical Latin. Cum privilegio. Rhemes: John Fogny, 1582. 4to. Two copies. One lent by *Henry J. Atkinson, Esq.*, and the other by *Earl Spencer.*
The Rhemes New Testament, the result of the labours of Roman Catholic priests, exiles from England in 1568. It is a secondary translation from the Vulgate.

967. BIBLE Picture Book (Dutch). Figuren, etc. Van Borcht, 1582. Obl. 4to. *Lent by Henry J. Atkinson, Esq.*

968. BIBLE (Latin). Antwerp: Plantin, 1582. 8vo.
Lent by Henry J. Atkinson, Esq.

969. BIBLE (English). Genevan. London: C. Barker, 1583. Folio.
Lent by the Archbishop of Canterbury.

970. BIBLE (Latin). Biblia Sacra. Quid in hac editione a theologis Lovaniensibvs præstitvm sit, eorum præfatio indicat. Antwerp: Plantin, 1583. Folio. *Lent by Henry J. Atkinson, Esq.*

971. BIBLE (Wendish). Biblia, tu ie Vse Svetv Pismv, Stariga inu Noviga Testamenta, Slovenski, tolmazhena, skusi Jvria Dalmatina. Bibel, das ist, die gantze Heilige Schrifft, Windisch. Wittemberg, durch Hans Kraffts Erben, 1584. Many woodcuts. Folio.
Lent by the British and Foreign Bible Society.

972. BIBLE (Icelandic). Biblia, þad er, öll Heilög Ritning vtlögd a Norrœnu. [being the previous translations of various parts by O. Gottskalksson, G. Einarsson, and G. Jonsson, revised and corrected by G. Thorlaksson, and the remainder newly translated by him]. Med formalum M. Lutheri. First edition. Holum, 1584. Folio.
Lent by Henry White, Esq.
With woodcuts, for the most part designed and engraved by Bishop G. Thorláksson. Another copy lent by Henry J. Atkinson, Esq.

973. BIBLE (English). The Bishops' version. Authorized and appointed to be read in Churches. London: Ch. Barker, 1585. Folio. *Lent by Henry J. Atkinson, Esq.*

974. BIBLE (Latin). Francofurt: P. Fabricius impensis Sigis. Feirabendi. 1585. 4to. *Lent by Henry J. Atkinson, Esq.*

975. BIBLE (English, Genevan version). London : Christopher Barker, 1585. 4to. Black letter. *Lent by Henry J. Atkinson, Esq.*

976. BIBLE. Old Testament. Η παλαια Διαθηκη κατα τους Εβδομηκοντα. . . . Vetus Testamentum juxta Septuaginta, ex auctoritate Sixti V. Pont. Max. editum. [By A. Carafa, P. Morinus, G. Sirletus, L. Latinius, M. Victorius, P. Dominicanus, E. Sa, P. Parra, A. Agellius, Lælius, F. Turrianus, P. Ciaconius, J. Maldonatus, P. Comitolus, F. Ursinus, J. Livineius, B. Valverda, R. Bellarminus, and F. Toletus.] L. P. Romæ, F. Zanetti, 1586. Folio. *Lent by Earl Spencer.*
    First printed edition of the Codex Vaticanus. It has formed the model for every succeeding edition of the "Septuagint."

977. NEW Testament (English). Beza's. Englished by L. Tomson. London : C. Barker, 1587. 32mo. *Lent by the Rev. Dr. Gott.*

978. BIBLE (English). 2 vols. London : Christopher Barker, 1587. 4to. *Lent by Henry J. Atkinson, Esq.*

979. BIBLE (Bohemian). Vol. IV. Isaiah to Malachi. 1587. 4to. *Lent by Pastor L. B. Kaspar.*
    This Bible was printed for the ancient Bohemian Brethren Church at the private printing establishment of Count Zerotin in Kralice, near Brunn, Moravia, in the year 1587. The original binding was made in 1588.

980. BIBLE (French). Geneve, 1588. 8vo. *Lent by Henry J. Atkinson, Esq.*

981. BIBLE (French). First edition. 8 parts. Geneve, 1588. Folio. *Lent by Henry J. Atkinson, Esq.*

982. BIBLE (Hebrew). 2 vols. Hamburg : J. Wolfius, 1588. Folio. *Lent by Henry J. Atkinson, Esq.*

983. BIBLE (Latin). 2 vols. Lugduni, apud Gvlielmvm Rovillivm. 1588. 4to. *Lent by Henry J. Atkinson, Esq.*

984. BIBLE (the first Welsh). Y Beibl Cyssegr-Lan, Sef yr hen Destament a'r Newydd. London : Deputies of C. Barker, 1588. Folio. *Lent by the British and Foreign Bible Society.*

984*. BIBLE (Second Danish). Biblia,/ det er,/ Deñ gantske Hel-/lige Schrifft, paa Danske *etc.* [after Luther's]. Kiobeñhaffn, Aff Matz Vingaardt, 1589. Folio. *Lent by Henry J. Atkinson, Esq.*

985. BIBLE (English, Genevan version). London : Deputies of Ch. Barker, 1589. 4to. *Lent by Henry J. Atkinson, Esq.*

986. NEW Testament (English). L. Tomson's. London : Deputies of Ch. Barker, 1589. 8vo. *Lent by the Archbishop of Canterbury.*

990. NEW Testament (English). Genevan version. London : Christopher Barker, 1589. 4to. *Lent by Henry J. Atkinson, Esq.*

991. BIBLE (Latin). Biblia Sacra Vulgatæ Editionis tribvs tomis distincta (ad concilii Tridentini præscriptum emendata, et à Sixto V. P. M. recognita et approbata). [Edited by A. Carafa, F. Nobilius, A. Agellius, P. Morinus, A. Rocca, and Lælius.] 3 tom. Romæ: ex Typographiâ Apostolicâ Vaticanâ, 1590. Folio.
Lent by Earl Spencer.
There are two title-pages, the first printed, and the second engraved. Commonly known as the Sixtine Bible. The first complete Latin edition published by Papal authority.

992. BIBLE (Latin). Biblia sacra Vulgatæ editionis, Sixti quinti ... jussu recognita atque edita [by M. A. Columna, W. Allen, B. de Miranda, R. Bellarminus, A. Agellius, P. Morinus, F. Nobilius, Lælius, B. Valverda, F. Toletus, A. Valerius, and F. Borromæus.] Oratio Manassæ, necnon libri duo qui sub libri tertij et quarti Esdræ nomine circumferuntur ... sepositi sunt, ne prorsus interirent, etc. Clementis VIII. auctoritate recognitâ. Romæ: ex typogr. vaticanâ, 1592. Folio. *Lent by Earl Spencer.*
There are two title-pages, one printed and the other engraved: the "Oratio Manassæ" and the third and fourth books of Esdras have a separate pagination. The Clementine Bible. The authentic text of the "Vulgate." This edition is said to considerably differ from the Sixtine edition, but infallibility in the church does not compass printer's stops and errors, or countenance them.

992*. GOSPELS (in Arabic and Latin) with numerous woodcuts by Ant. Tempesta. Rome, 1590. Folio. *Lent by A. Aspland, Esq.*

993. BIBLE (Latin). Londini, Impensis Gulielmi N., 1593-92. Folio.
Lent by Henry J. Atkinson, Esq.

993*. BIBLE (Latin). Biblia Sacra Vulgatæ editionis Sixti Qvinti iussu recognita atque edita. Romæ, 1593. 4to.
Lent by Henry J. Atkinson, Esq.

994. BIBLE (Latin). Tubingæ: G. Gruppenbach, 1593. Folio.
Lent by Henry J. Atkinson, Esq.

995. BIBLE (Latin). Romæ: Typ. Apost. vat., 1593. 4to.
Lent by Henry J. Atkinson, Esq.

996. BIBLE (Latin). Tubingæ, Georgius Gruppenbachius, 1593. 4to.
Lent by Henry J. Atkinson, Esq.

997. BIBLE (English). London: Deputies of Christopher Barker, 1594. 4to. *Lent by Henry J. Atkinson, Esq.*

998. BIBLE (English). London: Deputies of Ch. Barker, 1594. 4to.
Lent by Henry J. Atkinson, Esq.

999. BIBLE (Greek, Latin, and German). Biblia Sacra. Opera Davidis Walderi. 2 vols. Hamburgi: Jacobus Lucius Juni. excudebat, 1596. Folio. *Lent by Henry J. Atkinson, Esq.*

1000. BIBLE (Hebrew). 4 vols. 1595. 16mo.
Lent by Henry J. Atkinson, Esq.

1001. BIBLE (Saxon). Hamborch, dörch Jacobum Lucium den Jungen. 1596. Folio. *Lent by Henry J. Atkinson, Esq.*
On the title of the New Testament is a representation of the Elector and Luther witnessing the baptism of Christ by John.

1002. NEW Testament (Latin). 2 vols. in 1. Morgiis (Switzerland): Excudebat Ioannes le Preux, 1596. Folio.
Lent by Henry J. Atkinson, Esq.

1003. BIBLE (English). The Bible./ That is, the Holy/ Scriptvres Con-/teined in the/ Olde and New/ Testament./ Translated accor-/ding to the Ebrew and Greeke, and/ conferred with the best transla-/ons in diuers languages./ With most Profitable Anno-/tations vpon all the hard places, and other things/ of great importance, as may appear in the/ Epistle to the Reader./ ¶ Imprinted at *London* by the De-/puties of Christopher Barker,/ Printer to the Qveenes most excel-/lent Maiestie./ Anno 1597. Cum priuilegio./ Folio. *Lent by Francis Fry, Esq.*
6 prel. leaves, viz. Title, reverse blank; "To the most ver-/tvovs and noble Qveene/ Elizabith," 3 pp.; "To ovr Beloved in the Lord," 1 p.; "A Table conteining the Cycle/ of the Sunne," etc. 2 pp.; Kalendar, 3 pp.; "☞ The Names and order of all the bookes," 1 p. Text, A. j., in double columns, in roman type, Genesis to Malachi 360 folioed leaves; Apocrypha Aaaa. j. 77 leaves; New Testament, Title and 129 leaves; "¶ A breife Table," Yyyyy. iiij. 9 unnumbered leaves. This is the Genevan version of the text of both the Old and the New Testament, but the New Testament is what is generally known as L. Tomson's translation, or revision. This is, however, a popular error. The text is the Genevan version of 1560, which Tomson has not meddled with. He has only added a translation of Beza's and Camerarius' Notes, Summaries, Expositions, and marginal references. The Arguments preceding the Gospels, the Acts, etc., are omitted, though expressly mentioned in the title.

1004. NEW Testament (English). The/ Newe Testa-/ment of Ovr/ Lord Iesvs/ Christ./ ¶ Faithfully traslated out/ of Greeke./ Imprinted at *London*/ by the Deputies of Christopher Barker,/ Printer to the Queenes most/ excellent Maiestie./ Anno 1598./ 48mo. *Lent by Francis Fry, Esq.*
A to Xx in eights. In clear pearl type. Size of page $2\frac{3}{8} \times 1\frac{3}{4}$ inches. The reverse of the title is blank. Text begins on A 2, and ends on the reverse of Xx 8. This beautiful little volume is in the Geneva version. There are thirty-one lines on a full page. The headings of the chapters and the marginal references are in italic.

1005. NEW Testament (Latin and Greek). Geneva, 1598. Folio.
Lent by Henry J. Atkinson, Esq.

1006. BIBLE (Dutch). Antwerp: Jan Newrentorf and Jan van Keubergen, 1599. Folio. *Lent by Henry J. Atkinson, Esq.*

1007. BIBLE (English, Genevan). The/ Bible,/ that is,/ The Holy Scriptvres/ conteined in the Old and New/ Testament./ Translated according to the Ebrew and Greeke, and/ conferred with the best Translations in/ diuers Languages./ With most profitable Annotations vpon all hard places,/ and other things of great importance./ ⁌ Imprinted at *London*/ by the Deputies of Christopher Barker,/ Printer to the Queenes most/ Excellent Maiestie./ 1599./ 4to. *Lent by Henry White, Esq.*

> 4 prel. leaves, including the woodcut and printed titles; Text, Genesis to Job, 190 folioed leaves; Psalms to Malachi, 127 leaves, one blank leaf; New Testament, 121 folioed leaves; A briefe Table, 11 leaves. Date of Colophon, 1599. There were no less than six or eight editions of the Bible with the date 1599, all purporting to be from the same printer, and so closely resembling each other that it is difficult to distinguish them without having them before you. This edition is described in Lea Wilson's admirable catalogue, under No. 84 of Bibles, and may be distinguished from the other by the third line of the first verse of the first chapter of Esther, reading :—
>> India euen vnto Ethiopa, ouer
>
> The version is the Genevan, with Tomson's revision of the notes of the New Testament. It is in small roman type, in double columns, with the notes in smaller type on both the inner and outer margins.

1008. BIBLE (Latin). Venetia: Apud Damianum Zenarum, 1599. 4to. *Lent by Henry J. Atkinson, Esq.*

1009. NEW Testament (English). The/ Nevv Testament/ of Iesus Christ faith-/fvlly translated into English,/ out of the authentical Latin, diligently conferred with the/ Greeke, and other Editions in diuers languages: VVith Ar/gvments of bookes and chapters: Annotations,/ and other helpes, for the better vnderstanding of the text,/ and specially for the discouerie of Corrvptions in di-/uers late translations and for cleering Controver-/sies in Religion of these dayes: By the English/ College then Resident in Rhemes. Set Forth the second time, by the same College novv/ returned to Dovvay./ VVith addition to one nevv Table of Heretical Cor/rvptions, the other Tables and Annotations somevvhat/ augmented. Printed at *Antwerp*/ by Daniel Vervliet./ 1600. VVith Privilege./ 4to. *Lent by Henry J. Atkinson, Esq.*

> The title within a type-metal border, having on the reverse, the Approbations of the first edition of 1582, and of the present edition. The next leaf a ij begins with "The Preface to/ the Reader," 11 leaves ; "A Table of cer-/taine Places of the Nevv/ Testament corrvptly translated," 6 pp. in double columns ; "The Explication of Certain/ vvordes in this Translation," 2 pp.; "The Bookes of the Nevv/ Testament" 3 pp.; on the reverse, "The Signification or mea-/ning of the nvmbers and markes/ vsed in the Nevv Testament," 1 p.; "The Svmme of the /Nevv Testament," etc. 2 pp.; Text, Mathew to the end of Revelations, pp. 3 to 745. On the middle of page 745 begins "A Table of the/ Epistles and Gospels," Signature B bbbb, 4½ pp.; on the reverse of

B bbbb iij "An ample and/ particvlar Table" of Controversies, 23 pp. in double columns. The book is throughout in roman type, except the headings of the chapters, which are in italics. The text is in large pica type in long lines of three inches and three quarters, and the notes and marginal summaries are in a smaller type. The annotations, which are very numerous and controversial, are at the end of each chapter or book. The marginal summaries or catch-clauses are only on the outer margins, while the inner margins are occupied by references to other places, and by a column indicating the division into verses. The matter is run on into paragraphs, but the beginning of each verse is indicated by this mark. † The Preface to the Reader is historical and critical, and of considerable interest on the important subject of translations into the vulgar tongues. This translation is from the old Latin Vulgate. At the end of the third chapter of Matthew is a slip pasted down containing the words, "Iurie, and from beyond Iordan." the first three words having been omitted in the text. This volume should go with No. 1024 of this catalogue, so as to form a set of the complete Bible.

1010. NEW Testament (English). London: R. Barker, 1600. 4to.
Lent by Henry J. Atkinson, Esq.

1011. NEW Testament (English). Bishop's and Rhemish version. Notes by Wm. Fulke. London: R. Barker, 1601. Folio.
Lent by Henry J. Atkinson, Esq.

1012. NEW Testament (Greek). Franckfurt: Typis Wechelianis, 1601. Folio.
Lent by Henry J. Atkinson, Esq.

1013. BIBLE (English). The Bishops'. Authorised and appointed to be read in Churches. London: Robert Barker, 1602. Folio.
Lent by Henry Stevens, Esq.

There appear to have been two different first titles issued with this last folio edition of the Bishops' version; one like that of the woodcut border of the New Testament title, and the other like that used in the first edition of the 1611 version. A recent writer says that the latter "had often done duty before, notably in the Bishops' Bible of 1602." This is probably a mistake, for we find this folio woodcut border of the 1611 version used in no other previous edition except this 1602 Bishops', and in only a part of this. This handsome volume was manifestly the model for the first issue of the 1611 version, and the revisions and corrections were probably posted on to a copy of this and then deposited as *copy* with Barker. This last folio Bishops' differs almost as much from the first Bishops' of 1568 as it does from the first 1611 itself, it had undergone so many changes and silent revisions.

1014. BIBLE (Spanish). La Biblia, segunda edicion, por C. de Valera. Amsterdam, En casa de Lorenço Iacobi, 1602. Folio. Two copies.
One lent by H. White, Esq., the other by the B. and F. Bible Society.

1015. NEW Testament (English). L. Tomson. Dort: Isaac Canin, 1603. 8vo.
Lent by the Rev. Dr. Gott.

1016. BIBLE (English), Genevan version. London: R. Barker, 1606. 4to.
Lent by Henry J. Atkinson, Esq.

1017. BIBLE (English). Genevan version. London: R. Barker, 1607. Folio. First title wanting.
    Lent by the British and Foreign Bible Society.
This copy belonged to Prince Henry, and bears his monogram on the sides.

1018. BIBLE (English). Genevan. London: Robert Barker, 1606. 8vo.
    Lent by Sir Charles Reed.

1019. BIBLE (Italian). La Bibbia. Nuouamente traslatati da Giovanni Diodati, di nation Lucchese. Geneva, 1607. 4to.
    Lent by the British and Foreign Bible Society.

1020. BIBLE (Latin). Venetia, 1607. 4to.
    Lent by Henry J. Atkinson, Esq.

1021. BIBLE (Dutch). Leyden: Jacobszoon & Jan Bouwensszoon, 1608. 8vo.
    Lent by Henry J. Atkinson, Esq.

1022. NEW Testament (Italian). Il Nuovo Testamento. Geneva: Diodati, 1608. 16mo.
    Lent by Henry J. Atkinson, Esq.

1023. BIBLE (English). Genevan version. London: R. Barker, 1609. 4to.
    Lent by Henry J. Atkinson, Esq.

1024. BIBLE (English, Doway). The/ Holie Bible/ Faithfvlly Trans/-lated into English,/ ovt of the avthentical/ Latine./ Diligently conferred with the Hebrew, Greeke,/ and other Editions in diuers languages./ With Argvments of the Bookes, and Chapters :/ Annotations. Tables : and other helpes,/ for better vnderstanding of the text :/ for discouerie of Corrvptions/ in some late transla-tions : and/ for clearing Controversies in Religion./ By the English College at Doway./ Printed at Doway by Lavrence Kel-lam,/ at the signe of the holie Lambe./ M. DC. IX. 4to.
    Lent by Henry J. Atkinson, Esq.

Two volumes. Vol. I. The title within a type-metal border, having on the reverse, in Latin, "Approbatio." dated "Duaci. 8. Nouembris. 1609." Then comes on †2, "To the right/ vvelbeloved English/ Reader," 12 pp.; "The Svmme and Parti-/tion of the Holie Bible," 4 pp.; "The Argvment of the Booke/ of Genesis." 2 pp.; The text, Genesis to Job, 1114 pp., followed by "To the Cvrteovs Reader," 1 p., promising two Tables for this volume in the next. Vol. II. Title, dated M. DC. X. having the approbation on the reverse as to the first volume : "Proemial Annotations/ vpon the Booke of Psalms." pp. 3 to 14 ; Text, Psalms to the Fovrth Book of Esdras, pp. 15 to 1071. "A Table of the Epistles," page 1072 ; "An Historical Table of the Times," etc. pp. 1073 to 1096 ; "A particular Table of the/ most principal Things," pp. 1097 to 1123 ; "Censura," page 1124 ; Errata of the two volumes, 1 p. These two volumes are printed in a style nearly uniform with the New Testament, 4to, 1600, No. 1009. These three volumes should go together to make the complete Bible. This is the first edition of the Roman Catholic version of the Scriptures in English. It was translated about the year 1580, by some English exiles at Douai, to combat the various English protestant versions. It is a remarkable circumstance that though these volumes bear the dates of 1609 and 1610, they had not reached the hands of the translators of the 1611 version when their long Preface was written. There is distinct allusion to this work, as if to disclaim any knowledge of it. Or perhaps the Preface may have been written before Nov. 1609, the date of the Approval of Vol. I. This is sometimes called the *rosin* Bible, from the reading of Jeremiah viii, 22, "Is there no *rosin* in Gilead?" The Bishops', and other early translations, had *treacle*.

1025. NEW Testament (Greek and Latin). Aurelia Allob. apud Iacobum Stoer, 1609. 32mo. *Lent by Henry J. Atkinson, Esq.*

1026. NEW Testament (Icelandic). Pad Nijca Testamentum. Holum, 1609. 8vo. *Lent by David Laing, Esq.*

1027. BIBLE (English, Genevan). The/ Bible :/ that is,/ The Holy Scriptvres/ conteined in the Old and New/ Testament./ Translated according to the Ebrew and Greeke, and/ conferred with the best Translations in/ diuers Languages./ ⁋ With most profitable Annotations vpon all hard places,/ and other things of great importance./ ⁋ Imprinted at/ *London* by Robert Barker,/ Printer to the Kings most/ Excellent Maiestie./ 1610. 4to.
Lent by Henry J. Atkinson, Esq.

3 prel. leaves ; Text, Genesis to Malachi, A to Qq 7, in eights ; New Testament, Aaa to Qqq 1 ; Table, Qqq 2 to Rrr, 4. date of Colophon, 1611. This is the Genevan version, with Tomson's revision of the notes of the New Testament, and with Junius's Annotations on the Revelations. It is in small roman type, closely resembling the six quarto editions of 1599.

1028. BIBLE (English, Genevan). The/ Bible,/ That Is,/ The holy Scriptures con-/tained in the Old and/ New Testament./ ⁋ Translated according to the Ebrew and Greeke,/ and conferred with the best Translations/ in diuers Languages./ ⁋ With most profitable Annotations vpon all the/ hard places, and other things of great/ importance./ Imprinted at/ *London* by Robert Barker,/ Printer to the Kings most Excel-/lent Maiestie./ 1610./ Folio.
Lent by Francis Fry, Esq.

4 prel. leaves in roman type, viz. Title within a broad woodcut border, with the royal arms at the top, and Cum priuilegio in a compartment at the bottom, reverse blank ; " ⁋ To the Christian Reader." 2 pp. ; within a type-metal border. "⁋ Of the incomparable treasure," etc. 1 p. ; "How to profite in reading," etc. 1 p. ; "⁋ The names and order of all the Books," 1 p. ; on the reverse is a large woodcut, filling the whole page, of Adam and Eve in Paradise. Text in black letter. A to Mmmm 2, in sixes. "⁋ A briefe Table " 8 leaves in roman letter. This is the Genevan version with Tomson's revision of the notes of the New Testament. The text is in double columns, in large black letter. The arguments of the books are in small roman type. The summaries of the chapters are in italics, and the marginal notes are in small black, and the references in small roman letter. The woodcut borders of the titles of the Old and New Testaments are alike. At the beginning of the Psalms there is a title, "This Second Part of the Bible," within a broad woodcut border, with erect female figures on either side, reverse blank.

1028*. BIBLE (English, Genevan). The Bible, that is, the Holy Scriptures. London: Barker, 1610. 8vo. *Lent by Francis Fry, Esq.*
   This is, we believe, the last edition of the Bible of the Genevan version printed in England in octavo.

1029. BIBLE (English, Genevan version). The Bible, that is, The Holy Scriptures contained in the Olde and New Testament, Translated according to the Hebrew and Greeke, &c. At Edinburgh Printed by Andro Hart, and are to be sold at his Buith, on the North-side of the gate. Anno Dom. 1610. Folio. Two copies. *One lent by H. J. Atkinson, Esq., the other by David Laing, Esq.*
   This was long the standard and favourite edition of the Genevan Bible, because it was a handsome, well-printed book, remarkably free from typographical errors.

1030. BIBLE (English), Genevan and Tomson's. London: R. Barker, 1611. Folio. *Lent by the Archbishop of Canterbury.*

1031. BIBLE (English). Genevan version. London: R. Barker, 1611. 4to. *Lent by Henry J. Atkinson, Esq.*

1032. PSALMS (English). The Psalmes of David in Prose and Meeter. With Godly Prayers, &c. Printed at Edinburgh by Andro Hart. 1611. 8vo. *Lent by David Laing, Esq.*

1033. PSALMS (Latin). Paraphrasis Psalmorum Davidis Poetica auctore Georgio Buchanano. Edinburgi, exct. Andreas Hart, 1611. 18mo. *Lent by David Laing, Esq.*

1034. PSALMS (English). Psalms in Prose and Metre with the Tunes. Edinb.: Andro Hart, 1611. 24mo. *Lent by David Laing, Esq.*

1035. BIBLE (English). The Holy Bible, newly translated out of the originall Tongues and with former Translations diligently compared and revised, by his Maiesties speciall commandment. Appointed to be read in Churches. London: Robert Barker, 1611. With the first title engraved on copper by C. Boel of Richmont. Folio. *Lent by Henry Stevens, Esq.*
   This is the first or standard issue of the 1611 version of the English Bible. There was another separate issue of it the same year distinct throughout every leaf. This pair, the parents of millions of our Bibles, we shall distinguish by calling the first the GREAT HE BIBLE, and the other the GREAT SHE BIBLE, from their respective readings of Ruth iii. 15, the one reading "he measured six *measures* of barley, and laid *it* on her: and HE went into the city." The other has "and SHE went into the city." These two editions, both standard but varying in many places, were manifestly deposited in two different printing houses as standard *copy*, because the subsequent editions in quarto and octavo, in roman and black letter, run in pairs, *he* and *she*, and as a general rule the faults of the one follow those of its own office-copy or parent. It is not difficult for a practical printer to point out the true original He Bible, and when that is ascertained many other arguments fall in peacefully. This *he* and *she* distinction is only one of a thousand. The first three or four editions were issued, some copies with an engraved copper-plate title, and others with a woodcut

bordered title, but never with both. We have found the engraved title attached to its follower in both of the 1611 issues, as well as that of 1613. These titles, therefore, do not mark the edition; nor do Speed's genealogies, with which the king saddled and most unjustly burdened the version, as a private sop to a favourite subject. Of the two distinct issues of 1611, some copies of each having the engraved and others the woodcut title, it is of great consequence to establish the priority of one or the other. Mr. Francis Fry after long and patient investigation has, in his exceedingly important work on the subject, pronounced decidedly in favour of the He Bible's being the original; while Mr. Scrivener, in the introduction to his Paragraph Bible, reverses Mr. Fry's decision, and sets up the She Bible as the standard by priority. Our own researches, both before and since Mr. Fry's opinion, have led us unequivocally to the same conclusion as Mr. Fry. We do not find any authority for calling it the *Authorized Version*, the words "Appointed to be read in Churches," meaning not *authorized*, but, as explained in the preliminary matter, simply how the Scriptures were pointed out or "appointed" for public reading. This "Appointment" was afterwards shunted into the Prayer-Book and left out of the Bibles; but why the word *appointed* was left on some of the early title-pages and omitted in others, and how it got gradually to mean *authorized*, we leave to philologists, simply remarking that the 1602 Bishops' Bible, on which our present version was modelled, had both the words "authorized" and "appointed." The Puritans and Presbyterians did not require this "appointment," and hence in many editions it was omitted. We have no objection to the modern suppression or omission by the University and Queen's Printers of the long Preface, the Genealogies, and the "Appointment" of Scripture Readings in Churches. We could spare also the Dedication. But with all these omissions it is difficult to understand why the title is not also purified by leaving out the words "Appointed to be read in Churches." It being the Bible of all churches, denominations, and congregations in Great Britain and English-speaking America, Australia, and India (except the Roman Catholics) as much as of the Church of England, why by this misused word, *appointed*, should our common Bible any longer be even nominally limited to the Church of England, since there never was any exclusive right in the claim. It never was any more the Bible of the Church than of the Puritans. See Dr. Smith's Introduction on this point. Again, it was not a new translation, but about the twelfth revision of a work that belonged to the public, viz., (1, of Tyndale, 2, of Coverdale, 3, of Matthew, 4, of Taverner, 5, of the Great Bible of 1539, 6, of Cranmer, 7, of Becke, 8, of the Geneva New Testament, 9, of the Genevan Bible, 10, of the Bishops' version, 11, of the Bishops' version revised in the edition of 1602, 12, this of 1611,) at once the public repository of the English language and the birthright of Englishmen and the English-speaking people, of America, India, and Australia. This 1611 Bible has thus become indeed a marvel of perfection in the simplicity and beauty of its language, considering that at the time of the last revision there was neither an English grammar nor an English dictionary in the English language. It was never, we believe, formally *authorized* by Parliament, King, Privy-Council, or Convocation, but it by slow degrees grew into use by a higher authority than any of these, viz., the universal law of superiority and the people's own choice.

1036. BIBLE (English). The Holy Bible. London: Robert Barker, 1611. Fine copy of the He Bible, with the woodcut title. Folio. *Lent by Earl Spencer.*

1037. BIBLE (English). The Holy Bible, etc. Appointed to be read in Churches. London: Robert Barker, 1611. Folio.
Lent by Edward G. Allen, Esq.

This is the GREAT SHE BIBLE of 1611, differing in every leaf from the GREAT HE BIBLE. Like No. 1035 and 1036 it was issued, some copies with the engraved and others with the woodcut title. This is certain, because we have found both title-leaves attached to their followers. Neither title marks definitely the edition, but there are many reasons to demonstrate that this is the second or subsequent issue. It may have some better readings and some inferior, but the editions are totally distinct and unquestionably one is the parent of the other. It was probably necessary, in order to multiply copies fast enough, to have two *standard* copies in separate printing offices. The variations are generally not of much importance, and are such as usually occur in copying one book from another, with occasionally a slight correction, but oftener a slight blunder.

1038. BIBLE (English). The 1611 version. London: Robert Barker, 1613-11. Folio. *Lent by Francis Fry, Esq.*
This is generally a mixture of the sheets of the He and the She Bible, issued with a new first title, but the New Testament title remaining unchanged.

1039. BIBLE (English). The/ Holy/ Bible,/ Conteyning the Old Testament/ and the New :/ Newly Translated out of the Originall/ tongues : & with the former Translations/ diligently compared and reuised, by his/ Maiesties special Comandement./ Appointed to be read in Churches./ Jmprinted at London by Robert/ Barker Printer to the Kings/ most Excellent Maiestie./ Anno Dom. 1612./ 4to. *Lent by Henry J. Atkinson, Esq.*
The title is beautifully engraved on copper by Jasper Isac, reverse blank. Dedication to King James, A 2, 3 pp. in italics; on the reverse of A 3, "The Translators To/ The Reader," 9 pp. in small roman type; "☞ The names and order of all the Bookes," 1 p., reverse blank; "The Genealogies," by J. Speed, 18 leaves: "A Description of Canaan, and the bordering Countries," on the back of a woodcut map of the Holy Land, 2 leaves; the text is in double columns, in roman type, Genesis to Revelations, A to Z, Aa to Zz, Aaa to Zzz, [A] to [M], all in eights. This is the first edition of the 1611 Version of the Bible printed in quarto. It is a He Bible.

1040. BIBLE (English). The second edition of the 1611 version in 4to, roman type. She went. London: R. Barker, 1612. 4to.
Lent by Henry J. Atkinson, Esq.

1041. BIBLE (English). The first edition of the 1611 version in octavo. The He edition. London: R. Barker, 1612. 8vo.
Lent by Francis Fry, Esq.

1042. BIBLE (English). The second edition of the 1611 version in octavo. The She edition. London: R. Barker, 1611. 8vo.
Lent by Francis Fry, Esq.

1043. BIBLE (English). 1611 version. London: Robert Barker, 1613. Folio. *Lent by Henry J. Atkinson, Esq.*
This edition in smaller type cannot be confounded with either of the larger folios. Some copies appeared with the 1611 engraved title, but most of them have the woodcut title bearing the date of 1613. We have not observed in this edition the distinction of *he* and *she* in Ruth iii. 15, but it may exist.

1044. BIBLE (English). The 1611 version, black letter, the He edition. London: R. Barker, 1613. 4to. *Lent by Francis Fry, Esq.*

1045. BIBLE (English). The 1611 version, black letter, the She edition. London: R. Barker, 1613. 4to.
Lent by Henry J. Atkinson, Esq.

1046. BIBLE (English). 1611 version, roman type. London: R. Barker, 1613. 4to. *Lent by Henry J. Atkinson, Esq.*

1047. PROVERBS, Job, &c. (Hebrew and Latin). Ex officina Plantiniana. Raphelengi, 1614-15. *Lent by Henry J. Atkinson, Esq.*

1048. BIBLE (English). The/ Bible :/ Translated according to the Hebrew/ and Greeke, and conferred with the best Translati-/ons in diuers languages : With most profitable Annota-/tions vpon all the hard places, and other things of great/ importance, as may appeare in the Epi-/stle to the Reader./ And also a most profitable Concordance for the rea-/dy finding out of any thing in the same conteined./ ¶ Imprinted at/ *London* by Robert Barker,/ Printer to the Kings most/ Excellent Maiestie./ 1615./ 4to.
Lent by Francis Fry, Esq.

Title with verses on the back; "¶ To the Christian Reader," ¶ 3, 1 page; "How to take profit" etc. 1 page. Text in black letter, double columns, Genesis to Malachi, 358 folioed leaves; New Testament, 4 prel. leaves and Text folioed 441 to 554. This is the last edition in quarto of the Genevan Version printed in England. The Arguments, the notes and the running titles are in small roman type. The contents of the chapters are in small italics.

1049. BIBLE (English). Genevan version. London: R. Barker, 1616. Folio. *Lent by Henry J. Atkinson, Esq.*

This is the last folio edition of the Genevan version printed in England.

1050. BIBLE (English). London: R. Barker, 1616-15. 4to.
Lent by Henry J. Atkinson, Esq.

1051. BIBLE (English). Doctrine of the Bible. London: T. Snodham, 1616. 16mo. *Lent by Henry J. Atkinson, Esq.*

1052. BIBLE (English), 1611 version. London: Robert Barker, 1617. Folio. *Lent by Henry J. Atkinson, Esq.*

1053. BIBLE (Latin). Tremellius and Junius. Genevæ: Matthei Berjon, 1617. Folio. *Lent by Henry J. Atkinson, Esq.*

1054. EPISTLES and Gospels (German and Bohemian). 1617. 8vo.
Lent by Henry J. Atkinson, Esq.

1055. BIBLE (Hebrew). 4 vols. Genoa: Cepha. Elon, 1618. 16mo.
Lent by Henry J. Atkinson, Esq.

1056. BIBLE (Latin). Per Andream Osiandervm. Francofurti, Sumptibus Godefridii Tampachii, 1618. Folio.
Lent by Henry J. Atkinson, Esq.

1057. BIBLE (English). Black letter. London: Norton and Bill, 1619. 4to. *Lent by H. Cleaver, Esq.*

1058. BIBLE (German). 3 vols. Lübec, Bey Samuel Jauchen, 1620. 32mo. *Lent by Henry J. Atkinson, Esq.*

1059. BIBLE (English). London: Bonham Norton and John Bill, 1620. 4to. *Lent by Henry J. Atkinson, Esq.*

1060. BIBLE (the second Welch). Y Bibl Cyssegr-Lan, etc. Bishop Morgan's version, revised by R. Parry and J. Davies. Llundain, Bonham Norton a Iohn Bill. 1620. Folio.
Lent by the British and Foreign Bible Society.

1061. BIBLE (Latin). Romæ: A. Brugiotti, 1624. 32mo.
Lent by Henry J. Atkinson, Esq.

1062. BIBLE (English). London: Bonham Norton and John Bill, 1625. 4to. *Lent by Henry J. Atkinson, Esq.*

1063. NEW Testament (Greek). Cambridge: T. Buck, 1625. 8vo.
Lent by Henry J. Atkinson, Esq.

1064. BIBLE (Latin). Biblia Sacra Vulgatæ Editionis Sixti V. Venetiis, apud Juntas, 1627. 8vo. *Lent by Henry J. Atkinson, Esq.*

1065. BIBLE (English). London, 1628. 8vo.
Lent by James J. Parsloe, Esq.

1066. NEW Testament (English). Printers to the University of Cambridge, 1628. 32mo. *Lent by Henry J. Atkinson, Esq.*

1067. NEW Testament (Greek). Sedani ex typog. Ioannis Iannoni, 1628. 32mo. (Smallest.) *Lent by Henry J. Atkinson, Esq.*

1068. NEW Testament (Latin). Antverpiæ: Plantin, 1629. 32mo.
Lent by Henry J. Atkinson, Esq.

1069. BIBLE (English). Microbiblion/ or/ The Bibles/ Epitome :/ In Verse./ Digested according to the/ Alphabet, that the Scriptures/ we reade may more happily/ be remembred, and things/ forgotten more ea-/sily recalled./ By Simon Wastell sometimes of/ Queenes Colledge in Oxford./ *London,*/ Printed for Robert Mylbourne,/ and are to be sold at his shop/ at the signe of the Greyhound/ in Paules Churchyard./ 1629./ 8vo.
Lent by Henry J. Atkinson, Esq.

6 prel. leaves, viz. Title, within a light border, reverse blank; Dedication to Sir William Spencer, 2 leaves; "To the Christian/ Reader," 2 leaves; Lines by George Wither, 1 page; "The names of the Bookes," 1 p. Text, B 506 pages, followed by four leaves.

1070. PSALMS (English), "with the Common Tunes in foure parts, by the most expert Musicians in Aberdene." Aberdene: E. Raban, 1629. 24mo. *Lent by David Laing, Esq.*

1071. BIBLE (English). The 1611 version. Cambridge: T. & J. Buck, 1629. Small folio. *Lent by Francis Fry, Esq.*
   The text of this fine edition appears to have undergone a thorough revision, but by whom or upon what authority is not known. The pains taken in the printing, proof-reading, punctuation, italics, etc. are manifest throughout. But a little typographical error crept in here, we believe for the first time, which, though corrected a hundred times, constantly reappeared for many years, viz., Tim. iv., 16. Take heed unto thyself, and unto *thy* doctrine, for *the* doctrine.

1072. BIBLE (English), 1611 version, roman type. London: Bonham Norton and John Bill, 1629. 4to. *Lent by Francis Fry, Esq.*

1073. BIBLE (English), 1611 version, roman type. London: R. Barker, and assigns of John Bill, 1630. 4to. *Lent by F. Fry, Esq.*
   A recent writer, though he finds some slight variations, pronounces this and the 1629 quarto practically the same edition, and that this one is without the Apocrypha. He is mistaken; the two editions are totally distinct, and vary more than ordinary editions. His copy merely wanted the Apocrypha, as is apparent by the first four leaves of the Apocrypha being the counterfoils of Ccc 1-4, the last half-sheet of the Prophets. Besides, in the 1629 edition (No. 1072) there is a small * at the end of almost every sheet, a printer's mark which we have observed in no other Bible.

1074. BIBLE (Hebrew). Amstelodami, Sumptibus Henrici Laurentii, 1630. 8vo. *Lent by Henry J. Atkinson, Esq.*

1075. BIBLE (English). The/ Holy Bible/ Containing the/ Old Testa-/ment/ and the New./ Newly Translated out of the Ori/ginal¹ Tongues, and with the former/ Translations diligently compared/ and reuised: by his Maiesties/ speciall Commandement./ Ap-pointed to be read in Churches./ Printed at *London* by Robert Barker,/ Printer to the Kings most Ex-/cellent/ Maiestie: and by the/ Assignes of John Bill./ Anno 1631./ 8vo.
   Lent by the Bodleian Library.
   The WICKED BIBLE. Title, within the woodcut border of 24 small and 4 larger oval medallions, with the royal arms on the reverse. Dedication to King James, 1 p.; "¶ The Names and order of all the/ Bookes," in a border, 1 p.; Text in small roman type, double columns, Genesis to Revelations, A 3 to K kk in eights. In 1855 Mr. Henry Stevens exhibited at the Royal Society of Antiquaries a fine and perfect copy of this long-lost, but much bescribbled-about Bible, and at that time nick-named it "The Wicked Bible," from the fact that the negative had been left out of the Seventh Commandment by a typographical error. Selden and Collier, of our old writers, and many others since have failed to name correctly the year of its publication, 1631. Four copies are now known, one in the Lenox Library, New York, one in the British Museum, this one from the Bodleian, and one in Glasgow. There were four octavo, roman type, distinct editions the same year, 1631. This was suppressed, and Laud inflicted a fine of £300, with which it is said he bought a fount of Greek type for Oxford. Mr. Scrivener in his Paragraph Bible, Introduction, page xviii gives the date 1632, and says that a single copy is said to survive in the Library at

Wolfenbüttel. On inquiry we are informed that no such book exists there, or as far as known ever has, but on looking into the matter, the librarian found a German edition of just a century later with the same extraordinary omission, which makes Germany also to boast of its "Wicked Bible." We have not been informed that a like authority exists in France. This is no doubt a purely typographical error, and there are some ten or twelve others in the same sheet. It is probably the wickedest error of the kind that ever occurred; but we have always had great sympathy for David in his agony over proof sheets, ever since we learned from Cotton Mather that a blundering typographer made him exclaim in a Bible printed before 1702, "*Printers* have persecuted me without a cause." Psalm CXIX. 161.

1076. BIBLE (English). London: R. Barker and Assigns of John Bill, 1631. 8vo. *Lent by Henry J. Atkinson, Esq.*

1077. NEW Testament (Greek). Cambridge: T. Buck, 1632. 8vo. *Lent by Henry J. Atkinson, Esq.*

1078. BIBLE (English). The Holy Bible. With engraved title and frontispiece. Edinburgh: Printed by the Printers to the King's Majestie. Anno Dom. 1633. 8vo. *Lent by David Laing, Esq.*
    The 1611 version and the earliest edition of it printed in Scotland. This copy has at the end "The Psalmes of David in Meeter as they are sung in the churches of Scotland. Edinburgh, 1633. But the tunes are not given.

1079. BIBLE (English). Cambridge: Printers to the University, 1633. 4to. *Lent by Henry J. Atkinson, Esq.*

1080. NEW Testament (English). Fourth edition, Rhemish version. [Rouen]: John Cousturier, 1633. 4to.
    Lent by Henry J. Atkinson, Esq.

1081. NEW Testament (English). London: R. Barker, 1633. 32mo. *Lent by Miss Cole.*
    Bound back to front with Sternhold and Hopkins' Psalms of same date.

1082. NEW Testament (Greek). Amsterdami, apud Guil. Blaeu, 1633. 32mo. *Lent by Henry J. Atkinson, Esq.*

1083. NEW Testament (Greek). Londini, apud Richardvm Whittakervm, 1633. 8vo. *Lent by Henry J. Atkinson, Esq.*

1084. BIBLE (English). London: Robert Barker, 1634. Folio. *Lent by Henry J. Atkinson, Esq.*

1085. BIBLE (English). The 1611 version. London: R. Barker and Assigns of John Bill, 1634. 8vo. *Lent by Henry J. Atkinson, Esq.*

1086. PSALMS (English). The Psalms in Prose and Metre. Edinburgh, 1634; with the title, 1640. 18mo. *Lent by David Laing, Esq.*

1087. PSALMS (English). Another edition, with the tunes in foure parts or mo. Edinburgh: Heires of Andro Hart, 1635. 8vo.
Lent from the Signet Library.

1088. PSALMS (English). Both prose and Metre. London: by T. C., 1635. 16mo. *Lent by W. H. Sheehy, Esq.*

1089. NEW Testament (Greek). London: R. Whittaker, [1635?] 4to.
Lent by Henry J. Atkinson, Esq.

1090. BIBLE (English). London: Robert Barker, 1635. 4to.
Lent by Thomas Stapleton, Esq.

1091. BIBLE (English). Douay Old and Rhemes New Testament, 3 vols. Rouen: John Cousturier, 1635. 4to. *Lent by Henry White, Esq.*
For the New Testament see above, No. 1080.

1092. BIBLE (French). Amsterdam: Laurents, 1635. 8vo.
Lent by Henry J. Atkinson, Esq.

1093. BIBLE (English). Cambridge: T. Buck and Roger Daniel, 1637. 4to. *Lent by Henry J. Atkinson, Esq.*

1094. BIBLE (English). Edinburgh, 1637. 8vo.
Jeremiah, iv. 17. "Because she hath been *religious* against me, saith the Lord," for *rebellious*.

1095. BIBLE (Latin, Vulgate). Lugduni, Ex typog. Claudii Devilliers, 1637. 8vo. *Lent by Henry J. Atkinson, Esq.*

1096. BIBLE (Dutch). Leiden: Paulus Aertsz van Ravestyn, 1638. 8vo. *Lent by Henry J. Atkinson, Esq.*

1097. BIBLE (English). London: R. Barker and Assigns of J. Bill, 1638. Folio. With Psalms. *Lent by Henry J. Atkinson, Esq.*

1098. BIBLE (English). The Holy Bible [revised]. Cambridge: Tho. Buck and Roger Daniel, 1638. Folio.
Lent by the University Press, Cambridge.
This, perhaps the finest Bible ever printed at Cambridge, being revised at the time and carefully printed, has served as standard for many subsequent editions. There are, however, some extraordinary errors in it which have led smaller sheep astray. The famous typographical error that is said to have cost Cromwell a £1,000 as a bribe in the Roundhead times, is found here in Acts VI. 3, "whom *ye* may appoint," instead of *we*, which, of course, clears Cromwell.

1099. BIBLE (English). London: R. Barker and J. Bill, 1638. 8vo.
Lent by Henry J. Atkinson, Esq.

1110. PSALMS (American). The/ VVhole/ Booke of Psalmes/ Faithfully/ Translated into English/ Metre./ Whereunto is prefixed a discourse de-/claring not only the lawfullnes, but also/ the necessity of the Heavenly Ordinance/ of singing Scripture Psalmes in/ the Churches of/ God./ Coll. III./ Let the word of God dwell plenteously in/ you, in all wisdome, teaching and exhort-/ing one another in Psalmes, Himnes, and/ spirituall Songs, singing to the Lord with/ grace in your hearts./ Iames v./ If any be afflicted, let him pray, and if/ any be merry let him sing psalmes./ Imprinted/ 1640./ 4to. *Lent from the Bodleian Library.*

Eight preliminary leaves (Signatures, *, **, in fours) viz. The title, within a light type-metal border, reverse blank; "The Preface," 12 pp., and 7 lines on the next, the remainder of the twelfth page and the reverse being blank; Text, "The Psalmes/ In Metre"/ A to Z, and A a to L l 3, in fours, ending with the fourth line on the reverse of L l 3. The rest of that page (L l 3 verso) is occupied with "An admonition to the Reader." On the recto of the last leaf, L l 4, is "Faults escaped in printing," reverse blank. In all there are 148 leaves. Signatures * ** A B C D E F G H I K L M N O P Q R S T V W X Y Z Aa Bb Cc Dd Ee Ff Gg Hh Ii Kk Ll, in all 37 sheets, or 148 leaves.

This first book in the English language printed in America is usually called THE BAY-PSALM-BOOK, from Massachusetts Bay. It was translated by John Eliot, Thomas Welde and others, in Boston and Roxbury, and was printed by Stephen Daye at Cambridge in New England. It is very rare even in America, and this fine clean and perfect copy is believed to be the only one known in Europe. Here is a sample:—

O Blessed man, that in th' advice
  of wicked doeth not walk :
nor stand in sinners way, nor sit
  in chayre of scornfull folk.
2 But in the law of Iehovah,
  is his longing delight :
and in his law doth meditate,
  by day and eke by night.
3 And he shall be like a tree
  planted by water-rivers :
that in his season yeilds his fruit,
  and his leafe never withers.

4 And all he doth, shall prosper well,
  the wicked are not so :
but they are like vnto the chaffe,
  which winde drives to and fro.
5 Therefore shall not ungodly men,
  rise to stand in the doome,
nor shall the sinners with the just,
  in their assemblie *come*.
6 For of the righteous men, the Lord
  acknowledgeth the way :
but the way of vngodly men,
  shall vtterly decay.
        Psalm I.

1111. BIBLE (English). London: R. Barker and Assigns of John Bill, 1640. 4to. Black letter. *Lent by Henry J. Atkinson, Esq.*

1112. BIBLE (English). London: R. Barker and J. Bill. 1640. 8vo. *Lent by Henry J. Atkinson, Esq.*

1113. BIBLE (English). London: R. Barker and Assigns of John Bill, 1640. 4to. *Lent by Henry J. Atkinson, Esq.*

1114. BIBLE (Italian). Diodati's second edition. La Sacra Bibbia. Geneva, per Pietro Chovét, 1641. Folio. *Lent by Henry J. Atkinson, Esq.*

1115. NEW Testament (Greek). Paris: Typ. Regis, 1642. Folio.
Lent by Henry J. Atkinson, Esq.

1116. BIBLE (second Icelandic). With extraordinary woodcuts. Hoolum, 1644. Folio. *Lent by Henry White, Esq.*

1117. BIBLE (Polyglot). Biblia Polyglotta. Lutetiæ Parisiorum. Exc. Antonius Vitré. 1645. Large Paper. 9 vols. Folio.
Lent by Earl Spencer.
The Paris Polyglot, published under the patronage of Guy Michael Le Jay, who rejected Cardinal Richelieu's offer to re-imburse him for the sums spent in the undertaking on condition that the Cardinal's name should be affixed to the Bible instead of that of Le Jay. The first printed edition of the Samaritan appeared in this Polyglot.

1118. BIBLE (Latin, Vulgate). Antverpiæ, ex officina Plantiniana, 1645. 4to. *Lent by Henry J. Atkinson, Esq.*

1118*. BIBLE Picture Book (French). Figures, &c. Paris: Guillavme Le Bé, 1646. Folio. *Lent by Henry J. Atkinson, Esq.*

1119. BIBLE (English). London: Robert Barker, 1647. 8vo.
Lent by the Bodleian Library.
With a fine view of London on the title-page.

1120. NEW TESTAMENT (French). Le Nouveau Testament (with the metrical Psalms). Charenton, Par Pierre des Hayes, 1647. 24mo.
Lent by the Rev. Dr. Gott.

1121. BIBLE (French). Geneve: J. & P. Chouet, 1647. 8vo.
Lent by Henry J. Atkinson, Esq.

1122. NEW TESTAMENT (Latin, Vulgate). Colo. Agr. Gualterr, 1647. 32mo. *Lent by Henry J. Atkinson, Esq.*

1123. BIBLE (English). Annotations (with text) by Diodati. Second edition. London: Miles Flesher, 1648. 4to.
Lent by Henry J. Atkinson, Esq.

1124. BIBLE (Latin). Amstelodami, apud Ioannem Janssonum, 1648. 8vo. *Lent by Henry J. Atkinson, Esq.*

1125. BIBLE (Latin). Biblia Sacra Vulgatæ editionis. Venetiis, apud Iuntas et Baba, 1648. 8vo. Woodcuts. *Lent by Henry J. Atkinson, Esq.*

1126. BIBLE (English). The Holy/ Bible/ Containing the/ Old and New/ Testaments/ Newly Translated/ out of yᵉ Originall/ Tongues, and/ with the former/ Translations dili/gently compared,/ and revised/ *London*/ Printed/ by/ Iohn Field/ Printer to the/ Parliament. 1653./ 32mo. *Lent by Henry Stevens, Esq.*
Title engraved by W. V., reverse blank. Text in double columns, pearl type; Genesis to Malachi, A 2 to Q q 2 in twelves; New Testament title is Q q 3; Text Q q 4 to D dd 11; ending with the colophon on the recto.

Kilburne informs us that 20,000 copies of this Bible were dispersed. It is full of errors of the press, both by omitting words and sentences, and by change of readings. Many of these errors were corrected, as they were discovered, by cancelling the leaves. This copy possesses about half of the cancels. This edition may be distinguished from the following by the whole of the first four Psalms being upon the recto of folio A a 8, and by the running titles being in capital letters. A very pretty little pearl Bible, measuring 4¼ by 2½ inches. Among the typographical errors in some of the copies are such as these: "Know ye not that the unrighteous shall inherit the kingdom of God."— 1 Cor. vi. 9. "Ye cannot serve and Mammon" (*God* left out).—Matt. vi. 24.

1127. BIBLE (English). The Holy/ Bible/ Containing y^e/ Old and New/ Testaments/ Newly Translated/ out of ye Original/ Tongues, and/ with the former/ Translations/ diligently com-/pared and/ revised./ *London,*/ Printed by/ Iohn Field, Printer to the/ Parliament,/ 1653./ 32mo. *Lent by Henry Stevens, Esq.*

Title engraved by L. Lucas, with the names of the Books on the reverse. This is probably a Dutch counterfeit of the preceding. The running titles are in lower case letters, and only the first two verses of the first Psalm are on the recto of A a 4.

1128. BIBLE (English). London: J. Field, 1653. 32mo.
Lent by Henry J. Atkinson, Esq.
The edition with the first four Psalms all on one page.

1129. BIBLE (English). London: John Field, 1653. 32mo.
Lent by the Rev. Dr. Gott.
It is difficult to find two copies to correspond throughout, there were so many cancels. Very many copies of some of the editions were seized and destroyed, so the story goes; but others say only faulty sheets were cancelled and destroyed.

1130. BIBLE (English). London: Giles Calvert, 1653. 8vo.
Lent by Henry J. Atkinson, Esq.

1131. NEW Testament (English). London: Giles Calvert, 1653. 8vo. In same book, Concordance, R. Barker, 1579. 8vo.
Lent by Henry J. Atkinson, Esq.

1132. BIBLE (Greek, Septuagint). Londini: Roger Daniel, 1653. 8vo.
Lent by Henry J. Atkinson, Esq.

1133. BIBLE (English). E. T. [Evan Tyler] for a society of Stationers. London, 1655. 8vo. *Lent by Henry J. Atkinson, Esq.*

1134. BIBLE (Latin). Londini: E. T. and A. M., 1656. 8vo.
Lent by Henry J. Atkinson, Esq.

1135. BIBLE (Polyglot). Biblia Sacra Polyglotta. Edidit Brianus Waltonus. Londini: imprimebat Thomas Roycroft, 1657. 6 vols. Large folio. *Lent by Earl Spencer.*

One of the 12 copies struck off on large paper. By Cromwell's permission the paper for this work was allowed to be imported free of duty, and honourable mention is made of him in the Preface. On the Restoration this courtesy was dishonourably withdrawn, and the usual Bible dedication sycophancy transferred to Charles II at the expense of several cancels; and in this, the "Loyal" copy, so called in contradistinction to the "Republican," Cromwell is spoken of as "maximus ille Draco." This is said to have been the first work printed by subscription in England.

1136. BIBLE (Dutch). Eerst t' Antwerpen by Jan van Mœrentorf en nu by Pieter Iacopsz Paets, 1657. Folio.
Lent by Henry J. Atkinson, Esq.
Curious engravings by C. van Sichem.

1137. BIBLE (English). The Holy Bible. London: John Field, 1658. With Psalms by Sternhold, Hopkins, and others. London: John Field, 1658. 32mo. *Lent by Henry Stevens, Esq.*
The first page of the Psalms in the Bible ends with the second line of the 6th verse of chapter iv. With a fine view of London on the title-page.

1138. BIBLE (English). The Holy/ Bible/ Containing the/ Old Testament/ and the New/ Newly translated/ out of the originall Tongues/ and with the former/ Translations diligently/ compared and revised/ by his Majesties speciall/ Command./ Appointed to be read in Churches/ *London,/* Printed by John Field, one of His/ Highness's Printers, 1658./ 32mo. *Lent by Henry J. Atkinson, Esq.*
Engraved title (Moses on the left, Aaron on the right, and a view of London at the bottom), with the order of the books on the reverse; Text in pearl type, double columns, A 2 to D dd in twelves.

1139. BIBLE (English). The Holy/ Bible/ Containing the/ Old Testament/ and the New./ Newly translated/ out of the originall tongues/ and with the former/ Translations diligently/ compared and revised/ by his Maiesties speciall/ Command./ Appointed to be read in Churches./ *London,/* Printed by John Field one of His Highness's Printers 1658. 32mo. *Lent by Henry J. Atkinson, Esq.*
What has been written above about Field's pearl Bibles of 1653 applies equally well to these of 1658. They abound in typographical errors, but owing to repeated cancels, some copies are far less faulty than others. They are collected now chiefly for their errors; the more numerous and gross they are, the higher the price.

1140. NEW Testament (French). With Psalms, 1666. Charenton: Lucas, 1658. 8vo. *Lent by Henry J. Atkinson, Esq.*

1141. NEW Testament (Greek). Editio nova. Studio S. Curcellæi. Amsterdam: Elzevir, 1658. 16mo.
Lent by Henry J. Atkinson, Esq.

1142. PSALMS (Gaelic). The first 50 Psalms and Shorter Catechisme; translated into Gaelic by the Synod of Argyle. Glasgow: Aindra Anderson, 1659. 18mo. *Lent by David Laing, Esq.*

1143. BIBLE (English). Cambridge, 1660. Folio.
Lent by Henry White, Esq.

1144. NEW Testament in Shorthand, by Rich. London, 1660? 32mo.
Lent by the British and Foreign Bible Society.

1145. BIBLE (English). London: H. Hills and John Field, 1660. 4to.
Lent by Henry J. Atkinson, Esq.

1146. BIBLE (Spanish). Amsterdam: J. Atkins, 1660. 8vo.
Lent by Henry J. Atkinson, Esq.

1147. PSALMS (English). David's Harp strung and tuned. London: William Leake, 1662. Folio. *Lent by Henry J. Atkinson, Esq.*

1148. BIBLE (English). Good plates. Cambridge: John Field, 1663. 4to. *Lent by Henry J. Atkinson, Esq.*

1149. NEW Testament (Syriac). Hamburg, 1663. 8vo.
Lent by Henry J. Atkinson, Esq.

1149*. BIBLE Picture Book (Latin). Theatrum Biblicum. Piscator, 1674. Obl. 4to. *Lent by Henry J. Atkinson, Esq.*

1150. BIBLE (English). London: Bill and Barker, 1665. 4to.
Lent by Henry J. Atkinson, Esq.

1151. BIBLE (French). Leyde: Philippe de Croy, 1665. 8vo.
Lent by Henry J. Atkinson, Esq.

1152. BIBLE (French). J. A. and S. de Tournes, 1665. 8vo.
Lent by Henry J. Atkinson, Esq.

1153. BIBLE (German, Churfurst version). Die Propheten, *etc.* Wittemberg: Balthasar-Christoph Wustens, 1665. Folio.
Lent by Henry J. Atkinson, Esq.

1154. NEW Testament (Italian). Haerlem, Jacob Albertz, 1665. 8vo.
Lent by Henry J. Atkinson, Esq.

1155. NEW Testament (Italian). Il Nuovo Testamento (Diodati's). Haerlem, 1665. 16mo. *Lent by Henry J. Atkinson, Esq.*

1156. BIBLE (English). "The Preacher's Bible." Cambridge: J. Field, 1666. 4to. *Lent by Henry J. Atkinson, Esq.*

1157. NEW Testament (French). Beautiful plates. Paris: Francois Muguet, 1666. 8vo. *Lent by Henry J. Atkinson, Esq.*

1158. PSALMS (English). A separate edition of the Common Psalm Tunes. Printed at Aberdeen, 1666. Oblong 4to.
Lent by David Laing, Esq.

This probably never had a title-page.

1159. PSALMS (Greek and Latin). Cambridge: J. Field, 1666. 4to.
Lent by Henry J. Atkinson, Esq.

1160. BIBLE (English). Cambridge: John Field, 1668. 4to.
Lent by Sir Charles Reed.

1161. BIBLE (French). La Saincte Bible. Amsterdam: Louis et Daniel Elzevier, 1669. Folio. 2 vols. *Lent by Earl Spencer.*
A magnificent copy on large paper.

1161*. BIBLE (French). Another copy. Small paper.
Lent by Henry J. Atkinson, Esq.

1162. BIBLE (Latin). Col. Agrip. Balth. Egmond, 1670. 32mo.
Lent by Henry J. Atkinson, Esq.

1163. BIBLE (English). [First title] The Bible. [Second title] Verbum Sempiternum. Aberdene: John Forbes, 1670. 64to.
Lent by A. Gardyner, Esq.
A good specimen of the "Thumb Bible," measuring about one inch square and nearly half-an-inch thick; probably the smallest book in the exhibition.

1164. NEW Testament (German). Nuremberg: Christoph Endters, 1670. 8vo. *Lent by Henry J. Atkinson, Esq.*

1165. BIBLE (English). London: John Bill and C. Barker, 1671. 4to.
Lent by Henry J. Atkinson, Esq.

1166. NEW Testament (English). J. Bill and R. Barker, 1673. 8vo.
Lent by Henry J. Atkinson, Esq.

1167. BIBLE (English). The Holy, etc. Oxford, 1675. 4to.
Lent by the Bodleian Library.
The first edition of the Bible printed in Oxford. A very neat and tidy edition, but will not stand criticism. It is full of typographical errors and changes in spelling, punctuation, and the use of italics.

1168. NEW Testament (English). London: J. Bill and C. Barker, 1675. 4to. *Lent by Henry J. Atkinson, Esq.*

1169. NEW Testament (French). Amsterdam, chez la Veuve de Schippers, 1677. 16mo. *Lent by Henry J. Atkinson, Esq.*

1170. BIBLE (French abridgment). Paris: Jean Couterot, 1678.
Lent by Henry J. Atkinson, Esq.

1171. BIBLE (English). The Holy, etc. By his Majesty's Command. Oxford, 1679. 4to. *Lent by the Bodleian Library.*
The second edition of the Bible printed at Oxford; a very difficult book to find quite perfect.

1172. BIBLE (Latin). Cologniæ: apud J. Naulæum, 1679. 32mo.
Lent by Henry J. Atkinson, Esq.

1173. BIBLE (Latin). Biblia Sacra. Lugduni, Sumpt. Pet. Guillimin, & Ant. Beaujollin, 1680. Folio. *Lent by Henry J. Atkinson, Esq.*

1174. BIBLE (Latin). Londini, exc. R. Norton, prostant Nath. Ponder, 1680. 8vo. *Lent by Henry J. Atkinson, Esq.*

1175. BIBLE Picture Book (Latin). Icones, etc. Genevæ: S. de Tournes, 1680. 8vo. *Lent by Henry J. Atkinson, Esq.*

1176. BIBLE Picture Book (German). Figuren, etc. Augsburg: Kysel, 1680. 4to. *Lent by Henry J. Atkinson, Esq.*

1177. NEW Testament (French). London: R. Bentley, 1681. 8vo. With Psalms, 1686. *Lent by Henry J. Atkinson, Esq.*

1178. BIBLE (English). Oxford, 1682. With Prayer and Psalms. Folio. *Lent by Henry J. Atkinson, Esq.*

1179. BIBLE (Latin). Coloniæ: Balth. ab Egmond, 1682. 8vo. *Lent by Henry J. Atkinson, Esq.*

1180. BIBLE (English). Cambridge: John Hayes, 1683. 4to. *Lent by Henry J. Atkinson, Esq.*

1181. NEW Testament (Dutch, French, and English). Amsterdam: S. S. Jacobus's widow, 1684. 8vo. *Lent by Henry J. Atkinson, Esq.*

1181*. BIBLE (Irish). Le a Bhuir, *etc.* The Books of the Old Testament translated into Irish by Dr. William Bedel, late Bishop of Kilmore. London, 1685. 4to. *Lent by the British and Foreign Bible Society.*

1182. BIBLE (German). Ulm, Bey Matthæo Wagnern, 1688. Folio. *Lent by Henry J. Atkinson, Esq.*

1183. PSALMS (Gaelic). The Psalms, translated into Gaelic by Robert Kirk. Edinburgh, 1684. 12mo. *Lent by David Laing, Esq.*

1184. BIBLE (Latin). Biblia Sacra Vulgatæ Editionis. Venetiis, apud Nicolaum Pezzana, 1688. Folio. *Lent by Henry J. Atkinson, Esq.*

1185. NEW Testament (Swedish). Stockholm: Nicolas Waukife, 1688. 8vo. *Lent by Henry J. Atkinson, Esq.*

1186. NEW Testament (French). Amsterdam: P. & I. Blaeu, 1690. 8vo. *Lent by Henry J. Atkinson, Esq.*

1187. BIBLE (Irish). W. Bedel's and W. O'Donnell's Irish Bible, revised and printed at London by R. Ebheringtham in 1690. *Lent by David Laing, Esq.*

A small volume for the use of the Highlanders, by the Rev. Robert Kirk, M.A. at the expense of the Honourable Robert Boyle.

1187*. BIBLE (English). The History of the Old and New Testament, with sculptures. London: Richard Blome, 1691. 8vo.
Lent by Henry J. Atkinson, Esq.

1188. BIBLE (German). Zürich, by David Gessner, 1691. Folio.
Lent by Henry J. Atkinson, Esq.

1189. BIBLE Picture Book (English). London: Richard Blome, 1691. 8vo.
Lent by Henry J. Atkinson, Esq.

1190. BIBLE (English). London: C. Bill and T. Newcomb, 1693. 8vo.
Lent by Henry J. Atkinson, Esq.

1191. BIBLE, New Testament, and Psalms in Shorthand, by Abdy. London, 1695. 16mo.
Lent by George Unwin, Esq.

1192. BIBLE (Latin). A Sebastiano Schmidt. Argentorati, J. F. Spoor, 1697. 4to.
Lent by Henry J. Atkinson, Esq.

1193. NEW Testament (French). Charenton: Collier, 1697. 16mo.
Lent by Henry J. Atkinson, Esq.

1194. NEW Testament (French). Amsterdam: P. & I. Blaev, 1697. 16mo.
Lent by Henry J. Atkinson, Esq.

1195. BIBLE (English). With Canne's preface and notes. London: C. Bill and T. Newcomb, 1698. 8vo.
Lent by Henry J. Atkinson, Esq.

1196. NEW Testament (Greek). Amsterdam: Wetsten, 1698. 16mo.
Lent by Henry J. Atkinson, Esq.
With Hebrew Bible, 1701, &c.

1197. BIBLE (English). With John Canne's notes. London: Charles Bill and Executrix of Thomas Newcomb, 1700. 4to.
Lent by Henry J. Atkinson, Esq.

1198. GOSPELS (Greek and Latin). Harmonica Evangelica (J. Clarier). Amsterdam: Huguetanorum, 1700. Folio.
Lent by Henry J. Atkinson, Esq.

1199. NEW Testament (English and Dutch). Amsterdam, By de Widuwe van Steven Swart, 1700. 8vo. *Lent by Henry J. Atkinson, Esq.*

1200. BIBLE (English). Bishop Lloyd's, with additional marginal references. London: C. Bill and the Executrix of T. Newcomb, 1701. Folio. *Lent by the Archbishop of Canterbury.*

1201. BIBLE (German). Nurnberg: Luther, 1702. 4to.
Lent by Henry J. Atkinson, Esq.

1202. BIBLE (Latin, Vulgate). Venetiis: Jacob Bertani, 1702. 8vo.
Lent by Henry J. Atkinson, Esq.

1203. BIBLE (English). London: C. Bill and T. Newcomb, 1703. 4to.
Lent by Henry J. Atkinson, Esq.

1204. BIBLE (English). Oxford: Printers to the University of Oxford, 1704. 16mo. *Lent by Henry J. Atkinson, Esq.*

1205. BIBLE (German). Stuttgart: Augustus Metzler, 1704. 8vo.
Lent by Henry J. Atkinson, Esq.

1206. NEW Testament (English). University Printers, Oxford, 1704. 32mo. *Lent by Henry J. Atkinson, Esq.*

1207. BIBLE (German). Historischer Bilder Bibel. Augsburg: Kraussen, 1705. Folio. *Lent by Henry J. Atkinson, Esq.*

1208. NEW Testament (English). University Press, Oxford, 1705. 8vo.
Lent by Henry J. Atkinson, Esq.

1209. BIBLE (English). London: C. Bill and T. Newcomb, 1707. 8vo.
Lent by Henry J. Atkinson, Esq.

1210. BIBLE (English). London: C. Bill and T. Newcomb, 1708. 4to.
Lent by Henry J. Atkinson, Esq.

1211. BIBLE (English). The 1611 version with Genevan notes. London: [Holland printed?] 1708. Folio.
Lent by Henry J. Atkinson, Esq.

1212. BIBLE (Latin, Vulgate). Venetiis, N. Pezzana, 1709. Folio.
Lent by Henry J. Atkinson, Esq.

1213. NEW Testament (French). Paris: Jean de Nully, 1709-10. 8vo.
Lent by Henry J. Atkinson, Esq.

1214. NEW Testament (Greek). Amsterdam: Wetsten, 1711. 8vo.
Lent by Henry J. Atkinson, Esq.

1215. BIBLE (Italian). La Sacro Santa Bibbia. Norimbergo: Mattia d'Erberg, 1712. Folio. *Lent by Henry J. Atkinson, Esq.*

1216. BIBLE (Dutch). Antwerp: Jan Moerentorf, 1713. Folio.
Lent by Henry J. Atkinson, Esq.

1216*. BIBLE (English). The Holy Bible [the first edition of the 1611 version printed in Ireland]. Dublin: A. Rhames, for William Binauld, 1714. Folio. *Lent by Francis Fry, Esq.*

1217. BIBLE (English). The Holy Bible. Edinburgh: James Watson, 1716. 24mo. *Lent by David Laing, Esq.*

1218. NEW Testament (Greek). Lyon: Sacy, 1716. 32mo.
Lent by Henry J. Atkinson, Esq.

1219. PSALMS (English). London: Heptinstall, 1716. 8vo.
Lent by Henry J. Atkinson, Esq.

1220. BIBLE (English). The 1611 version. Oxford: J. Baskett, 1717-16. Imperial folio. 2 vols. *Lent by Henry J. Atkinson, Esq.*

    Nicknamed the "Vinegar Bible," because the headline of Luke, chapter 20 reads, "the parable of the *Vinegar*," instead of the *Vineyard*. Of this most sumptuous of all the Oxford Bibles three copies at least were printed on vellum, but as it was soon after its appearance styled "a *Baskett*-full of printer's errors," its beautiful typography could not save it. Indeed it is now mainly sought by collectors for its celebrated faults.

1221. BIBLE (English). The History of the Old and New Testament. In verse. 3 vols. 330 sculptures by J. Sturt. London: John Hooke, 1716. 8vo. *Lent by Henry J. Atkinson, Esq.*

1222. NEW Testament (Latin). Venetiis, apud Nic. Pezzana, 1720. 32mo. *Lent by Henry J. Atkinson, Esq.*

1223. BIBLE (English). The Holy Bible, &c. By his Majesty's special Command. Appointed to be read in churches. Edinburgh: James Watson, 1722. Folio.
Lent by the Signet Library, Edinburgh.

    This is a choice copy, on large paper, of perhaps the finest Book ever printed in Scotland.

1224. BIBLE (English). London: John Baskett, T. Newcomb, and Henry Hills, 1723. Folio. *Lent by Henry J. Atkinson, Esq.*

1225. BIBLE (French). Basle: Jan Hoff, 1724. 8vo.
Lent by Henry J. Atkinson, Esq.

1226. NEW Testament (English). London: J. Baskett and H. Hills, 1725. 8vo. *Lent by Henry J. Atkinson, Esq.*

1227. BIBLE (Latin). Venetiis, apud Nic. Pezzana, 1727. 8vo.
Lent by Henry J. Atkinson, Esq.

1228. BIBLE (Hebrew). With Italian notes and curious plates. 1730. 4to. *Lent by Henry J. Atkinson, Esq.*

1229. BIBLE (German). Kupfer Bible. 4 vols. Augsburg: Scheuchzer, 1731. Folio. *Lent by Henry J. Atkinson, Esq.*

1230. PENTATEUCH (Portuguese). Amsterdam, 1732. 4to.
Lent by Henry J. Atkinson, Esq.

1231. BIBLE (German). 2 vols. Wien: Georg Lehmann, 1733-34. Folio. *Lent by Henry J. Atkinson, Esq.*

1232. BIBLE Picture Book (French). 2 vols. Paris: Royaumont, 1736. 4to. *Lent by Henry J. Atkinson, Esq.*

1233. BIBLE (Latin, Vulgate). Venetiis, apud Christophorum Zane, 1737. 4to. *Lent by Henry J. Atkinson, Esq.*

1234. NEW Testament (English). Fifth edition. Rhemish version. 1738. Folio. *Lent by Henry J. Atkinson, Esq.*

1235. BIBLE (English). Oxford: J. Baskett, 1739. 4to. *Lent by Henry J. Atkinson, Esq.*

1236. BIBLE (French). Cologne, 1739. 8vo. *Lent by Henry J. Atkinson, Esq.*

1237. BIBLE (German). Sandershausen: Bock, 1740. 8vo. *Lent by Henry J. Atkinson, Esq.*

1238. BIBLE (Latin). Venetiis, ex typ. Hertziana, 1740. 3 vols, 8vo. *Lent by Henry J. Atkinson, Esq.*

1239. BIBLE (French). La Sainte Bible, 2 vols in one. Amsterdam: M. C. le Cene, 1741. Folio. *Lent by Henry J. Atkinson, Esq.*

1240. BIBLE (English). London: Thomas and Robert Baskett, 1744. 8vo. *Lent by Henry J. Atkinson, Esq.*

1241. BIBLE (Italian). La Sacra Biblia tradotta da G. Diodati. Lipsia, Giacomo Born, 1744. *Lent by Henry J. Atkinson, Esq.*

1243. CONCORDANCE (English). A Rational Concordance, or an Index to the Bible. By Matthew Pilkington. Nottingham: George Ayscough, 1749. 4to. *Lent by Henry J. Atkinson, Esq.*

1244. BIBLE (Dutch). Utrecht, etc.: J. van Poolsum, etc., 1750. 4to. *Lent by Henry J. Atkinson, Esq.*

1245. BIBLE (Latin). Ex Castellionis interpretatione. Leipzig: B. C. Breitkopf, 1750. 8vo. *Lent by Henry J. Atkinson, Esq.*

1246. PSALMS (English). A New Version of, &c. Translated by John Barnard. Boston: J. Draper, 1752. 8vo. *Lent by the Bodleian Library.*

1247. BIBLE (English). London: T. Baskett, 1756. 8vo. *Lent by Henry J. Atkinson, Esq.*

1248. BIBLE (Portuguese). Old Testament printed at Trangambar, 1757, and New Testament, 1765.
Lent by the British and Foreign Bible Society.

1249. BIBLE (Sclavonic). 1757. Folio.
Lent by the British and Foreign Bible Society.

1250. NEW Testament (Greek). Glasgow: R. et A. Foulis, 1759. 4to.
Lent by Henry J. Atkinson, Esq.

1251. BIBLE (Latin, Vulgate). 2 vols in 1. Venetiis, ex Typog. Remondiniano, 1758. Folio. *Lent by Henry J. Atkinson, Esq.*

1252. BIBLE (English). 2 vols. Oxford: Thomas Baskett, 1760. 32mo.
Lent by Henry J. Atkinson, Esq.

1253. NEW Testament (English). London: A. & C. Corbett, 1761. Folio. *Lent by Henry J. Atkinson, Esq.*

1254. BIBLE (Latin). 6 vols. Vindobonæ: Joh. Tho. Trattner, 1761. 8vo. *Lent by Henry J. Atkinson, Esq.*

1255. NEW Testament (Greek). Typis Joannis Baskerville [Birmingham], Oxonii e Typ. Clarend. 1763. 4to.
Lent by Henry J. Atkinson, Esq.

1256. NEW Testament (Greek). Typis Joannis Baskerville [Birmingham], Oxonii, Typ. Clarend. 1763. 8vo.
Lent by Henry J. Atkinson, Esq.

1257. NEW Testament (Latin). Novum Testamentum. Juxta Exemplar Millianum. Typis Joannis Baskerville. E Typographeo Clarendoniano Sumptibus Academiæ Oxonii, 1763.
Lent by the Oxford University Press.

1258. BIBLE (Latin). 2 vols. Venetiis, N. Pezzana, 1765. Folio.
Lent by Henry J. Atkinson, Esq.

1259. BIBLE Picture Book (French). Les Peintures Sacrées, etc. Paris: De Summaville, 1665. Folio. *Lent by Henry J. Atkinson, Esq.*

1260. BIBLE (Hebrew). Cura J. Simonis, Hallæ, 1767. 8vo.
Lent by Henry J. Atkinson, Esq.

1261. BIBLE (English). The 1611 version [edited and revised by Rev. Dr. Blayney] with new marginal references. Oxford: Wright and Gill, 1769. Folio. *Lent by Francis Fry, Esq.*
This and the quarto edition, commonly called Dr. Blayney's Revisions, were adopted as standards by the University Press, Oxford, in 1769, and are still the Oxford Standard with some slight modifications.

1262. BIBLE (English). The 1611 version [edited by Dr. Blayney]. Oxford: Wright and Gill, 1769. 4to. *Lent by Francis Fry, Esq.*

1263. DANIEL (Greek and Latin). Romæ: Typ. Prop. Fidei, 1772. Folio. *Lent by Henry J. Atkinson, Esq.*

1264. BIBLE (English). Bristol: William Pine, 1774. 16mo.
Lent by Henry J. Atkinson, Esq.
With notes at the bottom to be retained or cut off.

1265. BIBLE (English). London: Pasham, 1776. 32mo.
Lent by Henry J. Atkinson, Esq.
With notes at the bottom of the page to be retained or cut off.

1266. NEW Testament (Greek). 2 vols. in 1. London: J. D. Cornish, 1776. 8vo. *Lent by Henry J. Atkinson, Esq.*

1267. NEW Testament (Latin). A Sebastiano Castalione. Lond.: C. Bathurst, 1776. 8vo. *Lent by Henry J. Atkinson, Esq.*

1268. BIBLE (Dutch). 2 vols. Haarlem: Enschede, 1778. 8vo.
Lent by Henry J. Atkinson, Esq.

1269. GENESIS (English). The 51st chapter of Genesis, "Abraham and the Stranger, or the Parable against Persecution." Written in Scripture style by Dr. Franklin about 1769, while residing in London as agent of some of the Colonies. Privately printed by Franklin, at his private press at Passy, near Paris, about 1780. 8vo. *Lent by Henry Stevens, Esq.*
This is one of the original single leaves which Franklin used to insert in his Bible at the end of Genesis, and read to his friend when they were discussing toleration and persecution. He first gave a copy of it to Lord Kames in 1769, who had asked Franklin for whatever he had published. Though then probably in manuscript, Lord Kames first printed it in his "Sketches" in 1774, greatly to the annoyance of the Doctor, because it spoilt his little joke. This copy is much worn and is slightly imperfect, but it is believed to be the only genuine copy known, it having long been used by Franklin himself. The authorship of the chapter and Franklin's part in it are fully told by Dr. Jared Sparks in his Life of Franklin.

1270. BIBLE (English). 2 vols. Edinburgh: A. Kincaid, 1784. 16mo.
Lent by Henry J. Atkinson, Esq.
With Scotch Psalms.

1271. BIBLE (English). London: Scatcherd, 1790. 32mo.
Lent by Henry J. Atkinson, Esq.
The notes at the bottom cut off in the binding.

1273. BIBLE (English). A curious Hieroglyphick Bible; or select passages in the Old and New Testaments, represented with emblematical Figures, for the Amusement of Youth: the 11th edition. London: T. Hodgson, 1792. 12mo.
Lent by J. F. Thorpe, Esq.

1274. BIBLE (English). History of the Bible by way of Question and Answer. By Dr. Isaac Watts. Hull: Innes and Gray, 1793. 8vo.
Lent by Henry J. Atkinson, Esq.

1275. BIBLE (English). 2 vols. Edinburgh: Mark and Charles Kerr, 1795. 16mo.
Lent by Henry J. Atkinson, Esq.

1276. BIBLE (Dutch). Haarlem: Enschede, 1795-6. 16mo.
Lent by Henry J. Atkinson, Esq.

1277. NEW Testament (Greek). Jo. Jac. Griesbach. 2 vols. Londini et Hallæ, 1796-1806. 8vo. *Lent by Henry J. Atkinson, Esq.*

1278. BIBLE (French). Amsterdam, ches F. G. onder de Linden, 1797-6. 16mo. *Lent by Henry J. Atkinson, Esq.*

1279. BIBLE (English). Cambridge: John Burges, printer to the University, 1798. 4to. *Lent by Henry J. Atkinson, Esq.*
With Wilberforce's autograph.

1280. NEW Testament (English). From the Greek, by Nathaniel Scarlett. London: T. Gillet, 1798. 8vo.
Lent by Henry J. Atkinson, Esq.
See curious table of time for reading each book, &c.

1281. BIBLE (English). University Press, Oxford, 1801. 8vo.
Lent by Henry Stevens, Esq.
Proverbs xxvii. 2, "Let another man praise thee, and *to* thine own mouth," for *not;* Zech. vi. 1, "There came *forth* chariots out from between two mountains," for *four*, and repeated in the 8vo. edition of 1810; Zech. xi. 17, "Woe to the *idle* shepherd that leaveth the flock," for *idol;* John xx. 29, "Blessed are they that *they* have not seen," *they* added; Rom. xvi. 18, "And by good *works* and fair speeches deceive the hearts of the simple," for *words;* Jude 16, "These are *murderers*," for *murmurers*.

1282. BIBLE (English). The King's Printers, London, 1802. 4to.
Lent by Henry Stevens, Esq.
1 Tim. v. 21. "I *discharge* thee before God," for I *charge* thee.

1283. BIBLE (Welsh). Caerfyrddin: Joan Evans, 1802. 8vo.
Lent by Henry J. Atkinson, Esq.

1284. BIBLE (English). Bristol: Farley, 1803. 32mo.
Lent by Henry J. Atkinson, Esq.

1285. BIBLE (English). University Press, Oxford, 1804. 8vo.
Lent by Henry Stevens, Esq.

An Oxford Bible, pre-eminently distinguished for its typographical errors, some few of which are the following:—Numbers xxxv. 18. "The murderer shall surely be put *together*," for *to death*. 1 Kings viii. 19. "Out of thy *lions*," for *loins*. Gal. v. 17. "For the flesh lusteth *after* the Spirit," for *against*.

1286. BIBLE (English). University Press, Cambridge, 1805. 12mo.
Lent by Henry Stevens, Esq.

This is the famous "*to remain* Bible." The reader is said to have had a doubt about a comma, and on sending to the proper authority to inquire, the answer came back that the comma was *to remain*. On this message being sent up, the foreman, finding the two words written in pencil in the margin, took out the comma and put in the words, *to remain*, which fortunately happened neither to make sense or nonsense. The passage was in Gal. iv. 29. "Persecuted him that was born after the Spirit to remain even so it is now," for "Spirit, even so it is now." This same error appeared in an 8vo edition, 1805-6, printed for the Bible Society, as well as in another 12mo edition of 1819.

1287. BIBLE (English). King's Printers, London, 1806. 4to.
Lent by Henry Stevens, Esq.

Ezekiel xlvii. 10. "The *fishes* shall stand upon it" [the river] for *fishers*. Repeated in the 4to edition of 1813 and the 8vo of 1823.

1288. BIBLE (English). University Press, Oxford, 1807. 8vo.
Lent by Henry Stevens, Esq.

Matthew xiii. 43. "Who hath ears to *ear*," for *hear*. Hebrews ix. 14. "How much more shall the blood of Christ . . . . . purge your conscience from *good works* to serve the living God?" for *dead* works.

1289. BIBLE (English). University Press, Oxford, 1810. 8vo.
Lent by Henry Stevens, Esq.

Luke xiv. 26. "If any man come to me, and hate not his father . . . . . yea, and his own *wife* also, he cannot be my disciple," for *life*.

1290. NEW Testament (English). Wycliffe's version by Baber. London: Edwards, 1810. 4to. *Lent by Henry J. Atkinson, Esq.*

1291. BIBLE Picture Book (English). Designs by Thurston and Craig. Engraved by Bewick. London, 1810. 8vo.
Lent by Henry J. Atkinson, Esq.

1292. BIBLE (English). Edinburgh: Blair and Bruce, 1811. 32mo.
Lent by Henry J. Atkinson, Esq.
Said to be the smallest Bible ever printed in Scotland.

1293. NEW Testament (English). London: R. Edwards, 1811. 32mo.
Lent by Henry J. Atkinson, Esq.

1294. NEW Testament (Italian). Shacklewell: T. Rutt, 1813. 8vo.
Lent by Henry J. Atkinson, Esq.

1295. NEW Testament (Greek).   London : S. Bagster, 1813.   32mo.
Lent by Henry J. Atkinson, Esq.

1296. BIBLE (English).   King's Printers, London, 1817.   8vo.
Lent by Henry Stevens, Esq.
John xvii. 25, "Righteous Father, the world hath known thee," *not* omitted.

1297. BIBLE (English).   University Press, Cambridge, 1819.   12mo.
Lent by Henry Stevens, Esq.
Malachi iv. 2, "Shall the *Son* of righteousness arise with healing in his wings; and shall go forth, and grow up as calves of the stall," for *Sun*, and *ye* shall go forth.

1298. BIBLE (English).   University Press, Oxford, 1820.   12mo.
Isaiah lxvi. 9, "Shall I bring to the birth, and not *cease* to bring forth," for *cause*.

1299. BIBLE (English).   London : Porteusian Bible Society, 1820.   8vo.
Lent by Henry J. Atkinson, Esq.

1300. BIBLE (English).   King's Printers, London, 1822.   24mo.
Curious for its typographical errors.   Psalm xviii. 50. "And sheweth mercy to his *appointed*," for *anointed*.

1301. BIBLE (English).   The King's Printers, London, 1823.   8vo.
Lent by Henry Stevens, Esq.
Genesis xxiv. 61. "And Rebekah arose, and her *camels*," for *damsels*.

1302. BIBLE (Italian).   Bibbia Sacra.   Rome, 1823.   8vo.
Lent by Henry J. Atkinson, Esq.

1303. BIBLE (English).   University Press, Cambridge, 1826.   24mo.
Lent by Henry Stevens, Esq.
Psalm xlii. 1. "As the *heart* panteth after the water-brooks," for *hart*. This error repeated in the 24mo and 12mo editions of 1830.

1304. NEW Testament (Welsh and English).   Dolgelley : Jones, 1827.   16mo.
Lent by Henry J. Atkinson, Esq.

1305. NEW Testament (Greek).   London : Pickering, 1828.   32mo.
Lent by Henry J. Atkinson, Esq.

1306. BIBLE Picture Book (French).   Amsterdam : Jan Luiken, 1729.   Folio.
Lent by Henry J. Atkinson, Esq.

1307. BIBLE (Italian).   Bibbia Sacra (Child's Bible).   Naploli, Vedova di Salvati, 1830.   8vo.
Lent by Henry J. Atkinson, Esq.

1308. BIBLE (Irish). (Bedel.) Dublin : Godwin, 1830. 16mo.
Lent by Henry J. Atkinson, Esq.

1309. NEW Testament (Welsh and English). Rhydihain, 1831. 8vo.
Lent by Henry J. Atkinson, Esq.

1310. BIBLE (English). The Holy Bible, an exact reprint, page for page, of the authorized version published in the year 1611. Printed at the University Press by Samuel Collingwood and Co., printers to the University. Oxford, 1833. 4to.
Lent by Henry J. Atkinson, Esq.

1311. BIBLE (English). Another copy in Oxford case. Oxford : University Press, 1833. 4to. *Lent by the University Press, Oxford.*

1312. BIBLE (Dutch). Biblia. dat is, de Gantsche H. Schrifture en Apocryphe Boecken. By der Nedrl : Bybel Compagnie, Amsterdam. Haarlem, 1843. Folio.
Lent from the Guildhall Library.
This beautiful stereotyped folio edition in the old Dutch black letter and orthography, with engravings, is the work of Messrs. Enschede en Zonen, of Haarlem.

1313. BIBLE (Hebrew). Van der Hooght, & Hahn. Leipzig : Tauchnitz, 1833. 8vo. *Lent by Henry J. Atkinson, Esq.*

1314. BIBLE (English). The King's Bible, printed for presentation to King William the Fourth. Cambridge : University Press, 1837. 4to. *Lent by the University Press, Cambridge.*

1315. BIBLE (Hebrew). Van der Hooght, & Hahn. Leipsiæ : Tauchnitz, 1838. 8vo. *Lent by Henry J. Atkinson, Esq.*

1316. BIBLE (English). Douay version. Belfast : Simms & McIntire, 1839. 16mo. *Lent by Henry J. Atkinson, Esq.*

1317. NEW Testament (English). Reprint of the Geneva New Testament of 1557. Large paper. Samuel Bagster, 1842 ? 4to.
Lent by Henry J. Atkinson, Esq.

1318. BIBLE (English). Douay and Rhemes version. Dublin : Coyne, 1846. 8vo. *Lent by Henry J. Atkinson, Esq.*

1319. NEW Testament (English). Wycliffe's version. London : Chiswick Press for W. Pickering, 1848. 4to.
Lent by Henry J. Atkinson, Esq.

1320. GOSPELS (English). The four Gospels, published under the superintendence of C. Heath. London, 1849. 4to.
Lent by Arthur George Hockley, Esq.
    This copy is printed on India paper and mounted on the leaf, to preserve the level tissue paper is pasted round the India paper. Each page is surrounded by a border illustration of the contents of the page. The borders and engravings were designed by French artists. The engravings were made ready and worked by the late Mr. Henry Hockley, of Hammersmith, at the printing office of Mr. Strangeways, Castle Street, Leicester Square. This copy is unique, being the only one worked on India paper.

1321. BIBLE (English). Wycliffe's version. The Holy Bible, containing the Old and New Testaments, with the Apocryphal Books, in the earliest English versions made from the Latin Vulgate by John Wycliffe and his followers; edited by the Rev. Josiah Forshall, F.R.S., etc., late Fellow of Exeter College, and Sir Frederic Madden, K.H., F.R.S., etc., Keeper of the MSS. in the British Museum. Oxford: At the University Press, 1850. In 4 vols. Royal 4to. *Lent by the University Press, Oxford.*

1322. BIBLE (English). The Seven Seals Broke Open: or, the Bible of the Reformation Reformed. By John Finch. London: James Rigby, 1853. 12mo. *Lent by Henry J. Atkinson, Esq.*

1323. NEW Testament (Greek). Ἡ Καινὴ Διαθήκη. Novum Testamentum. Accedunt Parallela S. Scripturæ Loca necnon Vetus Capitulorum notatio et Canones Eusebii. E Typographeo Clarendoniano. Oxonii, 1863. *Lent by the Oxford University Press.*

1324. NEW Testament (German). Leipzig: Brockhaus, 1864. 4to.
Lent by Henry J. Atkinson, Esq.

1325. NEW Testament (English), with Engravings on Wood from designs of Fra Angelo, Pietro Perugino, Francesco Francia, Lorenzo di Credi, Fra Bartolommeo, Titian, Raphael, Gaudenzio Ferrari, Daniel di Volterra, and others. London: Longmans, 1864. Large paper. 4to. *Lent by Thomas Longman, Esq.*
    Only 250 copies of this most exquisite specimen of English printing and high art were taken off for this original impression, all on large paper. The work was partly set up at the Chiswick Press, and wholly printed by Messrs. Clay. The artists concerned are all named in the work, while Henry Shaw, F.S.A., had the general supervision. On the wall adjacent Mr. Longman also exhibits a large frame containing choice proofs of the title and eight of the finest pages of this New Testament illustrated after the old masters.

1326. BIBLE. A description of the Great Bible, 1539. . . . also of the Editions, in large folio, of the Authorized Version of the Holy Scriptures. Printed in the years 1611, 1613, 1617, 1634, 1640. By Francis Fry, F.S.A. London, 1865. Folio.
Lent by Francis Fry, Esq.

1327. NEW Testament (Hungarian). Pesth : Reicharal, 1866. 32mo.
          Lent by Henry J. Atkinson, Esq.

Bibles (English) exhibited in separate glass case on the stairway, by the University Press, Cambridge. Printed 1877.

1328. CAMBRIDGE Bible. Imperial 4to.
  Great Primer type, marked in sections wherever any lesson begins and ends.

1329. CAMBRIDGE Bible. Imperial 4to.
  Great Primer type, printed in red and black.

1330. THE Lectionary Bible. With Apocrypha. Crown 8vo.
  Nonpareil type. Marked in sections wherever any Lesson begins and ends.

1331. BIBLE. 16mo.
  Nonpareil type, with marginal references.

1332. BIBLE. Crown 8vo.
  Minion type, with marginal references.

1333. BIBLE. Fcap. 8vo.
  Pearl type, with marginal references.

1334. CAMBRIDGE Paragraph Bible. Crown 4to.
  Printed in paragraphs, the text revised, references remodelled, with notes. and introduction by the Rev. F. H. Scrivener, M.A., LL.D.

1335. THE Student's Edition of the above. Crown 4to. 2 vols.
  Printed on good writing-paper, with wide margins for MS. notes.

1336. CAMBRIDGE Prayer Book. Imperial 4to.
  Double Pica type, with the rubrics printed in red.

1337. PRAYER-BOOK. Crown 8vo.
  Bourgeois type, with rubrics, &c., in red.

1338. PRAYER-BOOK. Royal 24mo.
  Long Primer type, with rubrics, &c., in red.

1339. PRAYER-BOOK. Imperial 32mo.
  Bourgeois type, with rubrics, &c., in red.

1340. THE Complete Book of Church Services. Crown 8vo.
  Brevier type. Containing the Prayer-Book, Proper Psalms, and Lessons for Sundays and Holy Days, and the Daily Lessons of the Calendar, printed in full.

1341. THE Book of Daily Lessons. Crown 8vo.
  Brevier type. Containing the Daily Lessons of the Calendar printed in full.

1342. OFFICES of the Church. 8vo.
With rubrics, &c., in red.

Oxford University Press Bibles and Prayer Books.

1343. OXFORD Reference Bible. Royal 4to. 1877.
This is the Standard Edition from which all the smaller Bibles are verified.

1344. OXFORD Reference Bible. Medium 4to. 1875.

1345. OXFORD Reference Bible. Post 4to. 1877.

1346. OXFORD Reference Bible. Royal 8vo. 1876.

1347. OXFORD Reference Bible. Demy 8vo. 1876.

1348. OXFORD Reference Bible. Crown 8vo. 1877.

1349. OXFORD Reference Bible, with border lines and headings in red. 8vo.

1350. OXFORD Reference Bible, printed from old stereo plates. 1876.
The only Oxford stereo edition.

1351. OXFORD Reference Bible. 16mo. 1877.

1352. OXFORD Reference Bible. Fcap. 8vo. 1877.

1353. OXFORD Reference Bible. 16mo. 1876.

1354. OXFORD Reference Bible. 16mo. 1875.

1355. OXFORD Bible. Folio. 1867.

1356. OXFORD Bible. Royal 4to. 1873.

1357. OXFORD Bible. Medium 4to. 1872.

1358. OXFORD Bible. Royal 8vo. 1876.

1359. OXFORD Bible. 8vo. 1875.

1360. OXFORD Bible. 8vo. 1877.

1361. OXFORD Bible. 16mo. 1877.

1362. OXFORD Bible. 8vo. 1859.

1363. OXFORD Bible. Paragraph. 1859.

1364. OXFORD Bible. 16mo. Square. 1865.

1365. OXFORD Bible. 16mo. 1877.

1366. OXFORD Bible. 24mo., with border lines. 1876.

1367. OXFORD Bible. 24mo. 1876.

1368. OXFORD Bible. 24mo. 1877.

1369. OXFORD Bible. 16mo. 1866.

1370. OXFORD Bible. 24mo. With border lines. 1877.

1371. OXFORD Bible. 24mo. 1876.

1372. OXFORD Bible. 24mo. Thin. 1877.

1373. OXFORD Bible. 48mo. Printed by hand at the University Press, 1849.

1374. OXFORD New Testament. 8vo. 1872.

1375. OXFORD New Testament. 8vo. 1876.

1376. OXFORD New Testament. 16mo. Square. 1877.

1377. OXFORD New Testament. 24mo., with the marginal readings of 1611. 1829.

1378. OXFORD New Testament. 24mo., in 12 parts. 1876.

1379. OXFORD New Testament. 32mo., in 12 parts. 1876.

1380. OXFORD New Testament. 32mo. 1876.

1381. OXFORD New Testament. 32mo. 1876.

1382. OXFORD New Testament. 32mo. 1876.

1383. OXFORD New Testament. 48mo. 1874.

1383.*a* OXFORD Prayer Book. Red rubrics. Royal folio. 1865.

1383*b*. OXFORD Prayer Book. Red rubrics. Demy folio. 1861.

1383*c*. OXFORD Prayer Book. Red rubrics. Royal 4to. 1875.

1383*d*. OXFORD Prayer Book. Red rubrics. Demy 4to. 1875.

1383*e*. OXFORD Prayer Book. Red rubrics. Royal 8vo. 1874.

1383*f*. OXFORD Prayer Book. Red rubrics. Demy 8vo. 1876.

1283*g*. OXFORD Prayer Book. Red rubrics. 8vo. 1876.

1383*h*. OXFORD Baskerville Prayer Book. 1864.

1383*i*. OXFORD Victoria Prayer Book.   Red rubrics.   1876.
1383*j*. OXFORD Prayer Book.   Red rubrics.   24mo.   1876.
1383*k*. OXFORD Prayer Book.   Red rubrics.   32mo.   1877.
1383*l*. OXFORD Prayer Book.   Red rubrics.   32mo.   1876.
1383*m*. OXFORD Prayer Book.   Red rubrics.   48mo.   1877.
1383*n*. OXFORD Communion Service.   Royal 4to.   1876.
1383*o*. OXFORD Communion Service.   Red rubrics.   Royal 8vo.   1876.
1383*p*. OXFORD Prayer Book.   Not rubricated.   Folio.
1383*q*. OXFORD Prayer Book.   Not rubricated.   4to.
1383*r*. OXFORD Prayer Book.   8vo.
1383*s*. OXFORD Prayer Book.   8vo.
1383*t*. OXFORD Prayer Book.   Small 4to.
1384. OXFORD Prayer Book.   16mo.
1385. OXFORD Prayer Book.   24mo.
1386. OXFORD Prayer Book.   24mo.
1387. OXFORD Prayer Book.   24mo.
1388. OXFORD Prayer Book.   32mo.
1389. OXFORD Prayer Book.   32mo.
1390. OXFORD Prayer Book.   32mo.   Square.
1391. OXFORD Prayer Book.   Royal 32mo.
1392. OXFORD Prayer Book.   32mo.
1393. OXFORD Prayer Book.   48mo.
1394. OXFORD Prayer Book.   48mo.   Thin.
1395. OXFORD Prayer Book.   The smallest Prayer Book in the World.
1396. OXFORD Communion Services.   Not rubricated.   Royal 4to.
1397. OXFORD Communion Services.   Demy 4to.
1398. OXFORD Communion Services.   Imperial 8vo.

1399. THE Book of Offices and Ordination Services.   Crown 8vo.

1400. OXFORD Bible.   Welsh folio.

1401. OXFORD Prayer.   Welsh folio.

1402. OXFORD Altar Service.   Welsh 8vo.

Bibles, &c., lent by Messrs. Bagster and Sons, exhibited in glass case on staircase.

1403. BIBLIA Sacra Polyglotta.

1404. THE Comprehensive Bible.

1405. THE Bible of every Land.

1406. BIBLIA Ecclesiæ Polyglotta.

1407. THE Hexaplar Psalter.

1408. THE English Hexapla.

1409. BIBLE (English).   Coverdale's.

1410. NEW Testament.   Tyndale's.   Published in 1526.

1411. THE Commentary wholly Biblical.

1412. THE Codex Zacynthius.

1413. BIBLE (Hebrew and English).

1414. THE Septuagint, with an English Translation.

1415. THE Vulgate New Testament.   Compared with the Douay version of 1582.

1416. NEW Testament (Greek and English).

1417. NEW Testament (Syriac), with a Literal English Translation.

1418. COMMON Prayer, The Octaglot Book of.

Lent by Messrs. Eyre & Spottiswoode.

1419. CRANMER'S Bible, printed by Whitchurch.   1541.   Folio.
    This book is considered a very fine specimen, not having been washed or cleaned.

1420. BIBLE, printed by Barker, King's printer, with Calendar in red and black, illustrated Genealogy.   1611.   Folio.

1421. BIBLE, printed by Barker, King's printer. 1613. Folio.

1422. PRAYER Book, Bible, and two Concordances by R. F. H., in one vol. Printed by Barker, King's printer. 1614. 4to.

1423. BIBLE, with Calendar in red and black. 1617. Folio.

1424. BIBLE, printed by Bonham Norton and John Bill, King's printers. 1625.

1425. FIELD's Bible.

1426. HOLY Bible, with "Annotations on the hard places." The first Bible with annotations. 1683.

1427. COMMON Prayer, printed from engraved silver plates by permission of Mr. John Baskett. With curious illustrations. 1717.

1428. HOLY Bible, printed by Baskett, King's printer. 1753.

1429. BIBLE, printed by Charles Eyre and William Strahan, successors as King's printers to Baskett, and founders of the present firm of Eyre and Spottiswoode. 1772.

1430. MINIATURE Prayer Book, printed by C. Eyre and W. Strahan, 1774.

1431. MINIATURE Bible, on India paper. (See the thin Bible of 1875.) 1816.

1432. THE whole volume of Statutes at large, which at anie time heretofore haue beene extant *in print, since* Magna Charta, Vntill the xxix yeere of the reigne of our most gratious souereigne ladie Elisabeth xxx. &c. &c. London Christopher Barker Printer to the Queene's most excellent Maiestie 1587.

1433. PRINTED Statutes of Elisabeth. 1589-1593.

1434. THE Lectern Bible, with the Lessons marked with red lines at the side of the text.

1435. THE Bible, with various Renderings and Readings by the best Scholars.

1436. THE Student's Bible. Printed in red and black, on writing paper, with wide margin for notes.

1437. THE Sunday School Teacher's Bible (with Appendix for Teachers). Small 8vo.

1438. THE Sunday School Teacher's Bible (with Appendix for Teachers). Fcap. 8vo.

1439. THE Sunday School Teacher's Bible (with Appendix for Teachers). Pearl 16mo.

1440. THE Sunday School Teacher's Bible (with Appendix for Teachers). Pearl 24mo.

1441. THE School Bible, with the proper names divided and accented for pronunciation.

1442. THE Smallest Complete Bible, on India paper, date 1816.

1443. THE Smallest Complete Bible. (The miniature edition), 1875.

1444. THE Pica 4to. Reference Bible (fine paper).

1445. THE 4to. Bible in Welsh.

1446. ROYAL 4to. Prayer Book (fine paper).

1447. THE Imperial 8vo. Altar Service (red rubricks).

1447.*THE Smallest Prayer Book.

1448. THE Diamond 48mo. Prayer Book (red rubricks).

1448*.THE Bourgeois 32mo. American Prayer Book.

1449. BIBLE (six versions). The Hexaglot Bible, comprising the Septuagint, the Syriac (of the New Testament), the Vulgate, and the authorized English and German, and the most approved French versions. Edited by Edmund Riches de Levante. London: R. D. Dickinson, 1876. 6 vols. 4to.

1450. BIBLE (English). [In Memoriam Gul. Caxton.] The Holy Bible, containing the Old and New Testaments: Translated out of the Original Tongues: and with the former Translations diligently compared and revised, by His Majesty's special Command. Appointed to be read in Churches. Oxford: Printed at the University Press; London: Henry Frowde, Oxford University Press Warehouse, 7, Paternoster Row; New York: 42, Bleecker Street. June 30, 1877. Cum Privilegio. Minion 16mo.

Lent by Henry Stevens, Esq.

Facing the title is "Wholly printed and bound in twelve hours, on the 30th day of June, 1877, for the Caxton Celebration." Only 100 copies were printed. The *last* Bible printed—called the "CAXTON MEMORIAL BIBLE."

Our list opens with the *first* Bible printed with moveable metal types, 1450-1455, and we close it with this *last* Bible printed with moveable metal types on the 30th of June, 1877, the day of the opening of the Caxton Celebration Exhibition. As the circumstances and facts connected with this Memorial Bible have been somewhat misunderstood and not a little misrepresented, I may perhaps as well tell the true story here.

Taking my hint from Caxton himself, who, in 'The Recuyell of the Histories of Troye,' 1471, in Epilogue to Book III, wrote: ."Because I haue promisid to dyuerce gentilmen & to my frendes to addresse to hem as hastely as I myght this sayd book/ Therefore I haue practysed and lerned at my grete charge and dispense to ordeyne this said book in prynte after the maner & forme as ye may here see/ and is not wreton with penne and ynke as other bokes ben/ to thende that euery man may haue them attones/ ffor all the bookes thus empryntid as ye here see were begonne in oon day/ & also fynyshid in oon day/ which boke I haue presentid to" &c. Whatever idea Caxton by these quaint words may have meant to convey, I resolved, if possible, to have a Bible printed in Oxford and bound in London on the 30th of June, 1877, in time for Mr Gladstone's after-déjeuner speech. Accordingly, some four or five days before, I made application to Professor Bartholomew Price and Mr Henry Frowde, representing the University Press, Oxford, and through them the hint was suggested. They both apparently favoured the idea, though at first some doubt was expressed as to the possibility of performing the feat. Professor Price asked if I could give a few hours for consideration. The answer was, "yes, till twelve to-morrow; but you must keep the secret, so that in the event of your declining to undertake the enterprise, it may be offered to the University Press, Cambridge, or to the Queen's Printers, London, or, as a last resort, by cable to the American Bible Society, New York," for, as I told them, I was resolved, if possible, to have a Bible honestly and fairly printed and bound on the morning of the 30th of June. So we separated, Mr Frowde urging the Professor to bring about the accomplishment of the feat if possible. The next morning Professor Price telegraphed from Oxford, "it shall be done."

It was subsequently arranged between Mr Frowde and myself that there should be one hundred copies printed, and no more; that they should all be numbered in print from 1 to 100, and all be exactly alike in binding and ornament; that all the copies should be presented in the name of the University Press to Libraries, Societies, distinguished individuals and others, in all parts of the world, and that no copies on any account should be sold; that the first, or N° 1, should be reserved for Her Majesty the Queen, and the last, or N° 100, should be for Mrs Henry Stevens. A list of one hundred numbers was next made, and it was agreed that the nominations of the presentees should be divided into three parts, that is, Bible N° 1 and every third number thereafter should be allotted by the University Press; N° 2 and every third number thereafter should be in the nomination of Mr Henry Stevens; and N° 3 and every third number thereafter to be at the disposal of the Delegates of the University Press and the Dons of Oxford. And finally, that, before the end of the year, when the majority of the presentations would most likely be made, a list be printed with the numbers and names of presentees as far as then settled.

All these plans having been made and definitely settled, early on Saturday morning, June 30th, the chief particulars were briefly written out by myself, and submitted personally to Mr Gladstone at his house about nine o'clock, with the offer that Mr Gladstone was at liberty to make a point of them in his forthcoming speech in the afternoon if he liked, with a copy of the projected Bible in hand. Mr Gladstone at first expressed great doubts about the possibility of carrying out the project in time; said that he had once dined with a gentleman in the North of England, who presided at the dinner table in the evening in a dress-coat that had been made from cloth made from the wool of a sheep sheared that morning on the lawn before the house in the presence of some of the guests; but, added he, "if our Oxford friends accomplish this feat to-day with their Bible, they will outdo the enterprise of my northern friend." Mr Gladstone entered fully into the spirit of the enterprise, and, well knowing Professor Price, expressed his entire confidence in the honour and squareness of the transaction. He was distinctly told by me that the book was to be printed in Oxford from standing moveable type, and the whole of the one hundred copies to be bound in London, all on that Saturday. The overcoming of the distance of the sixty-three miles between Oxford and London was to be considered as an essential part of the feat. Mr Gladstone was then, I submit, "properly instructed," and I should perhaps here add that he did not in his speech say that this Bible was 'set up' or 'composed' that day, as one of the five or six morning papers which reported him erroneously declared that he did.

A parcel containing ten copies of the Caxton Memorial Bible reached Mr Stevens at the Western Gallery, South Kensington, precisely at 2 o'clock that day, so that when Mr Gladstone, accompanied by Mrs Gladstone and the Emperor of Brazil, came to the table at about half-past two, a paper was placed before him with the words in pencil, "the parcel has arrived all right and just as planned," and then, by way of confirmation, three copies of the Memorial Bible were placed in his hands, inscribed N° 1, to Her Majesty the Queen, N° 2, to Mrs Gladstone, and N° 10, to His Majesty the Emperor of Brazil. So far there had not been a hitch, and the point that Mr Gladstone made of the "Caxton Memorial Bible" in his speech about four o'clock is known to everybody, while he held it up in the presence of the "Six Hundred" as "the climax and consummation of the art of printing." During the short time that Bible N° 1 was on the table before Mr Gladstone, a small drop of wine accidentally fell upon the gilt top edge of the book, and, before I had time to wipe it away, had made a slight but beautifully coloured purple star on the gilding. Not deeming this 'suspicion of Gladstone claret' by any means a blemish, the stain was allowed to remain as an additional and unique souvenir of the day. The Book so marked was therefore, after being displayed under glass during the Caxton Exhibition, sent, enclosed in a morocco case, to Her Majesty.

The volume was printed at Oxford, bound in London, and delivered at the South Kensington Exhibition Buildings literally within twelve consecutive hours. The book was printed, not from stereotype plates, as has been erroneously stated by some of the morning papers, but from moveable type set up a long time ago, and not used for years. To guard against any fraud hereafter, it was thought best to take the forms of an edition that was entirely out of print. The printers commenced to make their preparations soon after midnight, and the printing actually commenced at two A.M.; the sheets were artificially dried, forwarded to London by the nine o'clock express train to the Oxford University Press Binding Establishment, Barbican, where they were folded, rolled, collated, sewn, subjected to hydraulic pressure, gilded, bound, and taken to South Kensington before two P.M. The book consists of 1,052 pages, 16mo, minion type, and is bound in turkey morocco, bevelled boards, flexible back, gilt-lettered on back and inside cover, with the arms of the Oxford University in gold on its obverse side ; and is free from the "set-off" or blemish which its hasty production might well have excused. One hundred and one persons, I have been told, were engaged in the Oxford University Press Binding Establishment, Barbican, London, that day on this Memorial Bible, all of whom received extra wages, besides a holiday the following Monday. The volume contains an explanatory inscription and an extra title : "In memoriam Gul. Caxton," with the occasion and date of the edition printed at the bottom of each of its thirty-three sheets, thus : "The Oxford Caxton Celebration Edition, 1877."

Mr Gladstone concluded his interesting speech with the following words, which are given as reported in "The Times" of July 2nd, with a few slight corrections : —"If you look at the list of works produced by Caxton and compare them at the same time with the works produced in the Continental Press, you will be struck by their great difference of character. The works produced by Caxton appear mainly to belong to a low stage of civilization. He did not print the Bible, because the translated Bible, then popular among the people, was the translation of Wycliffe, and the translation of Wycliffe had been proscribed by the Church ; but he never attempted to print any one of the great standard classical works of antiquity. Are we to condemn him on that account? Not at all. His proceeding was an eminently English proceeding. Caxton conceived in his own mind that idea which we consider to be an eminently English idea—that he would make his great enterprise independent and self-supporting. Caxton seems to have determined to throw himself as far as he could upon the sympathies and intelligence of his countrymen—to do all he could by translations to bring learning near to their comprehension, and having brought them as near as he could, to trust them to do the rest. And the industry of this man was marvellous. We are told that by the time he died he had translated nearly 5,000 folio pages for the benefit and instruction of his countrymen. Printing, too, was not looked upon by him so much as a mere manual art or accomplishment as that it was his business to develope the art as a link between the literary works on the one side which he had printed and the minds of his countrymen on the other side, and thus of bringing them into contact. This is a very remarkable and interesting history, and I venture to say that those who have not had the opportunity of closely examining it will find that the career of Caxton, considered as a biography, had a deep interest for any reader interested in the history of literature, and for most civilized of English readers it is a subject that will well repay any amount of diligence and care bestowed on it.

"Well, ladies and gentlemen, I will not detain you much longer. My wish is gained if those who have not made his character and career a special subject for examination shall happily be induced to look a little into the matter. The relatively backward condition of England at Caxton's time was evinced by the fact that after his death he had no English followers. Here I must say one word to point to the good sense and sagacity of Caxton. As I have said, he determined to make his press self-supporting, and he did so; and I dare say when he died, if he was not a wealthy man, he was a man of substance. And he was not a "high flying" printer. He took a hint from those who preceded him. Those Germans, Sweynheym and Pannartz, who were first established [at Subiaco] in the neighbourhood of Rome printed a great number of magnificent editions of the Greek and Latin Classics, and what was the consequence? They became bankrupts. That was a very melancholy end of a noble enterprise, but it enables us to understand the modesty, good sense, and sagacity of Caxton when we see how he steered clear of those rocks. He saw there would not be demand enough in England for what may be called an ideal press. He limited himself to practical objects, and thus laid a sound foundation of what was a progressive work."

Mr Gladstone here took up a bound volume, and continued,—" I now call attention in a few words to the progress of this art, and I hold up a volume in my hand to which I beg every one to direct his eye, because I think it may be called the climax and consummation of the art of printing. This volume is bound, as you see, and stamped with the arms of the University of Oxford. It is a Bible bound in a manner that commends itself to the reader; I believe in every respect an excellent piece of workmanship, containing more than one thousand pages. Well, you will say, 'That is very commonplace, why bring it before us?' I do so in order to tell you that the materials of this book sixteen hours ago did not exist. The book was not bound, it was not folded, it was not printed. Since the clock struck twelve last night at the University Press in Oxford the people there have printed and sent us this book to be distributed here in the midst of your festival. They have sent several copies, one of which will be presented to the Emperor of Brazil, who has but just left our table. This shows what can be done, and is what has been done, and it shows the state to which this great art is now happily arrived. If I began with a humiliating confession on the part of my countrymen as to the small share we could claim in contributing to the early history of printing, we may leave off, ladies and gentlemen, in a better spirit, because I think that such a performance as this is one that will be admitted to be a credit in any portion of the world. (Applause.) Now I will trouble you no longer, but will ask you to drink with me to the memory of that valued and honoured name,

William Caxton—the first English printer, and for a while the solitary printer in this our beloved country."

The paper was made at the Oxford University Press Paper Mills at Wolvercote, near Oxford, specially for this edition, only a day or two before it was printed. It might have been made (and is perhaps a matter of regret that it was not) on the morning of the 30th of June in time for the printing of this Memorial Bible.

It has been said that scores of houses might have done the same thing. But they didn't, and the possibility of any other house in England doing it depends upon the single fact whether any other printing-house out of Oxford keeps the Bible standing in moveable type. It could not probably have been printed from stereo-plates in the time, and it has been estimated by the compositors of one of the largest printing establishments in London, that it would have taken 2,000 compositors and 200 readers to have 'set up' and properly read the Bible in these same twelve hours, to say nothing of the press-work and binding. Unquestionably the Bible, with all its points, capitals, italics, and small capitals, is the most difficult of all books to print with perfect accuracy. Again no inconsiderable part of the enterprise was in overcoming the sixty-three miles between Oxford and London.

A List of the Oxford Caxton Memorial Bibles allotted up to Christmas,
MDCCCLXXVII.

N.B.—The 33 Numbers printed in the Roman numerals were assigned to Mr Stevens for Allotment.

1 Her Majesty the Queen.
ii Mrs William E. Gladstone.
3 The Marquis of Salisbury, D.C.L. Chancellor of the University of Oxford.
4
v James Lenox, Esq. for the Lenox Library, New York.
6 The Archbishop of Canterbury, for Lambeth Palace Library.
7
viii
9 Mr John Henry Stacey, Oxford University Press.
10 His Majesty the Emperor of Brazil.
xi The Hon. Stephen Salisbury, for the American Antiquarian Society, Worcester, Massachusetts.
12 Mrs Combe.
13 Ex-President General and Mrs Ulysses S. Grant.
xiv Mrs Edwards Pierrepont, Wife of the United States Minister at London.
15 The Reverend J. E. Sewell, D.D. Warden of New College, and Vice-Chancellor of the University of Oxford.
16
xvii The Library of the Massachusetts Historical Society, Boston, N.E.
18 The Reverend Mark Pattison, B.D. Rector of Lincoln College, Oxford.
19
xx The Library of the Parliament of Victoria, Melbourne.
21 The Reverend John Griffiths, D.D. Warden of Wadham College, Oxford.
22 The Right Hon. the Earl of Beaconsfield.
xxiii The Library of the British Museum.
24 Mr H. E. P. Platt, M.A. Fellow of Lincoln College and Junior Proctor, Oxford.
25
xxvi Mr J. S. Hodson, Secretary of the Caxton Celebration, 1877.

List of the Caxton [1877

27 The Reverend Henry Octavus Coxe, M.A. Bodley's Librarian, Oxford.
28
xxix The Library of Parliament, Dominion of Canada.
30
31
xxxii
33 The Reverend Bartholomew Price, M.A. Sedleian Professor of Natural Philosophy, Oxford.
34
xxxv
36 The Bodleian Library, Oxford.
37 The Library of the British and Foreign Bible Society, London.
xxxviii The Library of the American Bible Society, New York.
39 The Reverend William Bright, D.D. Regius Professor of Ecclesiastical History, Oxford.
40
xli Mrs John Carter Brown, Providence, Rhode Island, N.E.
42 Mr Francis Fry, F.S.A. Cotham, Bristol.
43
xliv J. Hammond Trumbull, LL.D. for the Watkinson Library, Hartford, Connecticut, N.E.
45 The Reverend H. G. Woods, M.A. Fellow of Trinity College, Senior Proctor, Oxford.
46
xlvii
48
49
l The Very Reverend H. G. Liddell, D.D. Dean of Christ Church, Oxford.
51 Mr H. J. S. Smith, M.A. Savilian Professor of Geometry, Oxford.
52
liii Henry J. Atkinson, Esq. Gunnersbury House, Acton, Middlesex.
54 The Reverend William Stubbs, M.A. Regius Professor of Modern History, Oxford.
55 The University Library, Cambridge.
lvi The Library of Congress, Washington, United States.
57 The Reverend Edwin Palmer, M.A. Corpus Professor of Latin, Oxford.
58
lix William Blades, Esq. Author of the Life of William Caxton.
60 The Archbishop of York.
61
lxii
63 John Walter, Esq.
64 The Reverend Newman Hall.
lxv The Library Company, Philadelphia.
66 The Right Hon. W. E. Gladstone.
67 The Library of the Hibernian Bible Society, Dublin.
lxviii George Bullen, Esq. British Museum, Chairman of Caxton Committee No. 1.
69
70 His Grace the Duke of Devonshire.
lxxi
72 The Library of the Society for Promoting Christian Knowledge, London.
73 The Reverend G. G. Bradley, M.A. Master of University College, Oxford.
lxxiv Samuel Christie-Miller, Esq. Britwell House, Burnham.
75 Mr Edward Pickard Hall, M.A. Oxford University Press.

```
    76 The Right Hon. the Earl Spencer, K.C.B.
lxxvii Mr Henry Frowde.
    78
    79 The Library of the Académie Française, Paris.
 lxxx Prof. Dr Reinhold Pauli, for the Library of the University of Göttingen.
    81 F. Max Müller, M.A. Professor of Comparative Philology, Oxford.
    82 His Royal Highness Prince Louis Lucien Bonaparte.
lxxxiii The Library of Harvard University, Cambridge, N.E.
    84 Mr William Nelson.
    85
lxxxvi M. de Lisle, for the Bibliothèque National, Paris.
    87
    88
lxxxix Mr Alexander Macmillan.
    90
    91
   xcii Chancellor J. V. L. Pruyn, for the New York State Library, Albany, N.Y.
    93
    94
    xcv The Library of Yale College, New Haven, Connecticut, N.E.
    96 M. Alfred Chaix, Paris.
    97
 xcviii The Newberry Library, Chicago.
    99
   100 Mrs Henry Stevens, Vermont House, 13, Upper Avenue Road, N.W. London.
```

Bibliography   The Tree of Knowledge

APPENDIX.

An Act for prynters & bynders of bokes. 25⁰ *Hen. VIII. c* 15. A.D. 1533-4. *Statutes of the Realm, Vol. ii. p. 456.*

HEREAS by the pvysyon of a statute made in the fyrst yere of the reigne of Kynge Richarde the thride it was pvyded in the same acte, that all strangers reparyng into this Realme myght lawfully bryng into the seid Realme pryntyt and wrytyn bokę to sell at theire libtie and pleasure; by force of which pvysyon there hath cōmen into this Realme sithen the makyn of the same a marveylous nombre of pryntyd bokes and daily doth ; And the cause of the makyng of the same pvysion semeth to be, for that there were but fewe bokes and fewe prynters within this Realme at that tyme which cold well excercise and occupie the seid science and crafte of pryntyng ; Never the lesse sithen the makyng of the seid pvysion many of this Realme being the Kynges naturall subjectes have geven theyme soo dylygently to lerne and excercyse the seid craft of pryntyng that at this day there be within this Realme a greatt nombre cōnyng and expert in the seid science or craft of pryntyng as abyll to exercyse the seid craft in all poyntę as any Stranger in any other Realme or Countre ; And furthermore where there be a great nombre of the Kynges subjectę within this Realme which [leve] by the crafte and mystie of byndyng of bokę and that there be a great multy-

Proviso in Stat. 1 Ric. III c. 9, as to importation of Books.

Increase of Printing in England since that time, &c.

tude well expert in the same; yet all this not withstondyng there are dyv̱se p̱sones that bryng frome [behonde] the See great plentie of pryntyd bokes not only in the latyn tonge but also in our maternall englishe tonge, sõme bounde in bourdẹ sõme in lether and sõme in p̱chement and theym sell by retayle, wherby many of the Kynges Subjectẹ being bynders of bokes and having none other facultie wherwith to gett theire lyvyng be destitute of worke and lyke to be undon, except sõme reformacion here in be hade; Be it therefore enacted by the Kyng our Soveraigne Lorde the Lordes spirituall and temporall and the Comons in this present parliament assembled and by auctoritie of the same, that the seid provyso made the furst yere of the seid Kyng Richard the thride frome the feast of the natyvytie of our Lorde [Good] next comyng shalbe voyde and of none effect.

The said Proviso repealed.

II.

And further be it enacted by the auctoritie aforeseid that noo person or persones recyant or inhabytaunt within this Realme, after the seid feast of Cristemas next cõmyng, shall bye to sell agayn any prynted bokes brought frome any partes out of the Kynges obeysaunce redy bounden in bourdes lether or perchement, uppon payne to lose and forfett for every boke [bounde] out of the seid Kynges obeisaunce and brought into this Realme and bought by any person or persons within the same to sell agayne contrary to this Acte vjs. viijd.

None shall buy foreign bound Books to sell again; Penalty 6s. 8d. per Book.

III.

And be it further enacted by the auctoritie aforeseid that no person or persones inhabytaunte or reciaunt within this Realme, after the seid feast of Cristemas, shall [by] within this Realme of any Stranger borne out of the Kynges obedyence other then of denyzens, any maner of pryntyd bokes brought frome any the parties [behonde] the See, except only by engrose and not by retayle uppon payne of forfayture of vjs. viijd. for every boke soo bought by retayle contrary to the forme and effecte of this estatute : The seid forfaytures to be alwayes levyed of the beyers of any suche bokes cont'ry to this Acte, the one half of all the seid forfaytures to be to the use of our Soveraigne Lord the Kynge, and the other moytie to be to the partie that wyll sease or sue for the same in any of the Kynges Courtes, be it by byll playnt or informacion wherein the defendaunt shall not be admytted to wage hys lawe nor noo proteccion ne essoyne shalbe unto hym allowed.

Like penalty on buying such Books of Aliens by Retale.

Recovery of Penalties.

Appendix. 151

IV.

Provided alway and be enacted by the auctoritie aforeseid, that yf any of the seid prynters or sellers of prynted bokes, inhabyted within this Realme, at any tyme hereafter happen in suche wyse to enhaunce and encrease the prices of any suche prynted bokes in sale or byndyng at to high and unreasonable pryces, in such wyse as complaynt be made thereof unto the Kynges Highnes or unto the Lorde Chaunceler Lord Tresourer or any of the chefe Justices of the one benche or of the other, that then the seid Lord Chaunceler Lorde Tresourer and two chefe Justices or two of any of theym, shall have power and *(Lord Chancellor, &c. may regulate the Price of Books and binding.)* auctoritie to enquyre thereof as well by the othes of twelf honest and discrett psones as otherwyse by due examynacion by theire discreacions; And after the same enhaunsyng and encresyng of the seyd pryces of the seid bokes and byndyng shalbe soo founde by the seid xij men, or other wayes by examynation of the seid Lord Chaunceler Lord Tresourer and Justices or two of theym, that then the same Lorde Chaunceler Lorde Tresourer and Justices or two of theym at the least frome tyme to tyme shall have power and auctoritie to reforme and redresse suche enhaunsyng of the pryces of prynted bokes from tyme to tyme by theire discreacions and to lymytt pryces as well of the bokes as for the byndyng of theym ; and over that the offender or offenders thereof being convicte by the examynacion of the same Lorde Chaunceler Lorde Tresourer and two Justices or two of theym or otherwyse, shall lose and forfett for every boke by theym solde whereof the pryce shalbe enhaunsed, for the boke or byndyng thereof iijs. iiijd. the one half therof shalbe to the Kynges Highness and the other half unto the parties greved that wyll *(Penalty on selling at higher Prices ; 3s. 4d. per Book.)* complayne upon the same in maner and forme before rehersed.

Τέλος, *laus Deo.*

www.ingramcontent.com/pod-product-compliance
Lightning Source LLC
Chambersburg PA
CBHW030312170426
43202CB00009B/976